Lure of the Trade Winds

TWO WOMEN SAILING THE PACIFIC OCEAN

Jeannine Talley

iUNIVERSE, INC.
NEW YORK   BLOOMINGTON

Lure of the Trade Winds
Two Women Sailing the Pacific Ocean

iUniverse books may be ordered through booksellers or by contacting:

iUniverse
1663 Liberty Drive
Bloomington, IN 47403
www.iuniverse.com
1-800-Authors (1-800-288-4677)

*Because of the dynamic nature of the Internet, any Web addresses or links contained in this book
may have changed since publication and may no longer be valid.*

ISBN: 978-1-4502-5173-0 (sc)
ISBN: 978-1-4502-5175-4 (dj)
ISBN: 978-1-4502-5174-7 (ebk)

Library of Congress Control Number: 2010912773

Printed in the United States of America

iUniverse rev. date: 9/20/2010

To Suzanne for your generous help and unbounded support

Contents

Prologue

In 1985, after dissolving two yacht chartering and sailing instruction businesses and resigning from professional employment of many years, Joy Smith and I set sail in our 34-foot yacht *Banshee*. At the end of March we left Los Angeles, sailed down the coast of Mexico where we explored Baja California and the Sea of Cortez before heading southwest, bound for the South Pacific.

Two and a half years later, we had visited a succession of island groups encompassing French Polynesia, Samoa, Tonga and Fiji. For the second time we sailed into New Zealand, this time to spend a year and a half working to put some money in our pockets and to purchase some new equipment for *Banshee*.

While in New Zealand I completed *Women at the Helm* (published by Mother Courage Press, 1990), a book recounting many of our adventures and encounters with Melanesian and Polynesian islanders in the South Pacific. After a lengthy stay in New Zealand, we resumed our nomadic seafaring in June 1989, heading once again in a northwesterly direction across the South Pacific. One year later, five days after leaving Australia, we encountered an unseasonal cyclone (hurricane) five hundred miles off shore. In this lethal storm, we were rolled and dismasted.

Four days later we were picked up by a freighter and then flown by helicopter back to Australia. Our boat was also rescued many days later. Before even beginning repairs on *Banshee*, at the behest of my publisher, Mother Courage Press, I wrote my second book, *Banshee's Women Capsized in the Coral Sea*.

In writing this third book about our voyaging, I have often thought about women and long distance voyaging in small craft. Seafaring and navigating vessels across oceans have been male domains for centuries. With few exceptions, it has only been in this century that women have begun to take an active part in sailing as recreation or as a sport. When Joy first began sailing in the 1960s, a few women from yacht clubs in Los Angeles were crewing in weekend races around the buoys. This kind of participation was reflected elsewhere in the U.S. and in some European countries.

By the 1970s, when I had my first exhilarating experiences on a sailboat, more women were becoming involved, albeit usually as "first mates". More often than not, women on sailboats in these days were "galley slaves" who stayed below preparing food for the "sailors" and washing dishes. There is no worse place to be on a rolling sea than confined below decks trying to cook. Without benefit of fresh air and a distant horizon on which to focus, most novice sailors find themselves prone to seasickness. If these women seemed less than enthusiastic about sailing, their position in the boat may have had more than a little to do with shaping their attitudes.

Significant changes, however, were brewing in the 1970s. Women started coming topside, handling sails, steering and learning how to navigate. A few actually set out on their own, making single-handed ocean passages and competing in long distance races. Englishwoman Clare Francis competed in the Observer Single-handed Transatlantic Race (OSTAR), filming her exploits and publishing a book about them. At the end of September 1979, three women joined the Mini-Transatlantic. They were Amy Boyer (USA) -- who came in first despite losing her headstay and lower shrouds and hitting a whale, which loosened her keel -- Margaret Hicks (Great Britain) and Brigette Aubrey (France).

By June 1980, more women entered the OSTAR competition: two Americans, Joan Connors and Judy Lawson; French woman Florence Authaud, and Naomi James under a British flag. Aside from these major competitions, a few women went to sea as solo sailors. Ingeborg Von Heister (German) was the first woman to make a double transatlantic crossing in *Ultima Ratio*, a 35-foot ketch in 1969-70. New Zealander,

Annette Wilde, was the first woman to single-hand back and forth across the Tasman Sea in *Valya*, a 34-foot sloop, in 1977-78.

A few women were setting records sailing alone around the world. The earliest of these appears to be a Polish woman, Krystyna Chojnowska-Liskiewica. At least that is the record. Australian Ann Gash, also known as the "Sailing Granny" because she undertook her circumnavigation at age 52, personally told me she was the first woman to complete a solo circumnavigation in 1975-77. But from time to time, Ann had crew, a factor that negated her status as a singlehander. In 1978 Naomi James, a New Zealander by birth, broke a speed record in her 272-day solo circumnavigation that took her around notorious Cape Horn. Since then a few other women have made record circumnavigations. American Tanya Aebi, 18 when she started, completed her circumnavigation in 1988 thereby becoming the youngest person to complete a solo rounding of the world under sail.

In her voyage lasting from November 29, 1987, to June 5, 1988, Australian Kay Cottee broke multiple records as a female solo circumnavigator, her most outstanding accomplishment being that her voyage was nonstop around five capes in 189 days, and the quickest circumnavigation.

All of these voyages are notable accomplishments because these women are pioneers in seafaring. I believe we can see a kind of progression in the types of voyages being undertaken by women. Tanya Aebi's voyage differs from most other female voyagers in that she did not enter any kind of race. Instead she was involved in "cruising", taking time to do some sightseeing at various ports and interacting with other cruisers and some of the local people. In this respect, her voyage was not unlike that of Ann Gash who is a cruiser rather than a racer.

As more women begin to cruise their boats in a leisurely fashion, I believe it indicates that women have made a tremendous leap forward in asserting themselves as seafarers. First of all, cruising means not only a commitment to long distance voyaging, but also that the sailor possesses the confidence to repair or replace equipment to keep the vessel seaworthy. Most of these repairs will, of necessity, have to be undertaken by the woman herself --- there are no plumbers at sea --- and because of the prohibitive cost of hiring someone else to do all the maintenance. Unlike racing, which involves a concentrated effort to manage a boat for a specific purpose and a limited period of time, cruising means a change of lifestyle and involves developing a totally different view of oneself and the world.

Women who make blue water passages show that they can handle the rigors of sea voyaging. When I say rigors, I don't mean simply handling the boat in heavy weather. I mean dealing with all circumstances that arise from such things as engine problems, rigging failures, electrical failures, in short, everything from mechanical malfunctions to breakage of equipment. These problems, for the most part, are the incidents that, stacked one on top of the other --- and that's the way they invariably occur --- wear one down. If a sailor knows her stuff and her boat, heavy weather sailing is not significantly more difficult than light weather sailing. It doesn't really take more strength: it takes more endurance.

Above all, it is endurance that solo and shorthanded sailors need in abundance. I can honestly say that knowing the demands made upon two at sea, I have no wish to undertake ocean passages on my own. Nevertheless, I think the desire or the compulsion to write about our voyages has a lot to do with the nature of the experience itself. It is a type of endeavor that transports us to the very limits of who we are, an encounter that propels us to the edge of the world and our own interior selves. Probably mountain climbing, or any other peak (no pun intended) experience that takes one into an isolated area has the same kind of effect, because there in that solitary place one exists outside the world of other human beings. It is an experience of solitude, a place where we are suspended in the midst of hugeness.

As to our voyaging, Joy and I did not break any records, except perhaps for the slowest passages, but breaking records was not why we sailed. Our motivation was to see as much of the world as we could in as much detail as possible. Traveling as we did allowed us much more freedom and flexibility as to where we went, whom we met, and what we could do. As long as we were not infringing on the laws of a country, we were able to go to some of the most remote areas of the world and interact with the inhabitants within their social setting. This mode of travel, of course, is the antithesis to jet set tours. Sailing permitted us to become acquainted with villagers. We visited them in their homes and they visited aboard ours. Often we ate their food and shared ours with them. Indeed, it was a great adventure to unravel some of the world's mysteries, to plunge into the unknown, to seek realities outside those into which we were born and bred. By its very nature, adventure stimulates your mind and sends the blood coursing through your veins.

The world is changing rapidly. Remote villages, entire cultures, languages, traditions and customs are diminishing at a rate as mind-numbing and frightening as the rapid depletion of our rain forests. There is no substitute for walking and living among such people. Such contact imparts something of their essence, a glimmer of values often unlike our own, values with some protean quality that once invigorated the human race, permitting our species to survive for centuries while living in harmony with the natural world. The eighteen years I spent exploring the Pacific region brought a kind of enlightenment that can only be gained through first-hand experience. For the first time in my life, I was the *minority* instead of the majority.

Why write this book? Several years ago a reviewer for *The New York Times Book Review* wrote about cruising sagas that "there is no longer much novelty left in the genre." For the most part, I would agree. For one thing, this genre is represented almost entirely by white male writers, no doubt because they have dominated ocean passage making. But there is another problem with the genre that goes much deeper. Its roots lie in writings of exploratory oceanic voyaging that began about four centuries ago and developed in tandem with colonialism. Building upon this literary tradition, small boat sailors often echoed the racist and misogynist attitudes of their Western predecessors. Such writers have likewise clung to the fantastic image of the South Pacific as a Paradise. In earlier accounts, writers frequently depicted Pacific Islanders as being culturally and mentally inferior. Above all, these Western writers exhibited an extreme fascination with "savage cannibals" and, of course, the presumed sexually promiscuous dark-skinned native women, whom they described as alluring, uninhibited and, like wild fruits, luscious and merely waiting to be plucked.

More recently, literature about the South Pacific has continued to promote these stereotypic views. Such notable authors as Melville, Maugham, Michener and even painter Gauguin's Tahitian images present what is often perceived as the dark side of the natives and the sexual availability and desirability of island women.

In the type of writing I've been describing, two themes dominate the characterization of the Pacific Islands: sin and paradise. Was this an attempt to have one's cake and eat it too? Perhaps. Whatever the reasons, such ideas and notions fermented and flourished in the patriarchal society that began its plunge into colonialism with the fateful voyage of Columbus and succeeded so well that by the 1930s, colonies and excolonies covered 84.6 percent of the globe!

As this astonishing figure indicates, Western colonialism nearly engulfed the entire non-Western world in its domination of societies comprised of people of color. During four centuries of conquest, Western explorers cultivated the racial myth of white supremacy and perpetuated the subordination of women of any color. These twin myths account for untold misery affecting both the world of the colonizers as well as the colonized.

It is time to reassess the peoples and cultures that were routinely and unconscionably misrepresented and abused. Hence, one of the main objectives of this book is to strip the Pacific people of these fantasized and mythologized images as seen through Western writers' distorted gaze.

My awakening and reflection on these matters, concerning the Pacific, started with the first landfall in the Marquesas. Here in these remote and sparsely populated islands, I began to detect some of the effects of colonialism, and as time went by I became more attuned to what white European and American intrusion has meant to Pacific Islanders. I tried to learn as much as I could about all the island groups I visited. I talked with as many inhabitants as possible in an attempt to understand their feelings and ideas about their lives. The longer I stayed in the Pacific, the more I observed the insidious and ongoing effects of colonialism. Even when certain island nations have achieved independence, the impact of colonialism does not suddenly vanish leaving no trace. The extent and depth of colonialism's influence permeates the culture and has irrevocably brought on a kind of identity crisis for indigenous peoples. Colonization succeeded because it struck at two vital areas: religion and economy. Unfortunately, this assault on the very core of a society also inflicts a mental impact, resulting in what some have called "the colonization of the mind," a situation that occurs when the conquered people internalize the negative attitudes held by their conquerors. I believe some day psychologists will recognize that such deep-set psychic damage reverberates even through future generations. For all of these reasons, I find it necessary to describe the Pacific islanders through a cultural and historical prism. To ignore these realities would be a serious injustice to Pacific islanders.

I also began to perceive the similarities between sexism and racism as they played out globally. For several centuries, the Europeans came to the North and South American continents laying claim to the territory; the British came to Australia and New Zealand doing the same. In all instances native peoples already inhabited these places. What right did the newcomers have to plant their flags on the land and then claim it for another nation? And for that matter, what right did European males have to plant their seed in native women, then depart the country, leaving behind the children they had sired? What was the ultimate fate of these women and children? Were they outcasts, were they looked down upon? Such behavior shows that the intruders regarded native women and children as no more than white male property to be used or disposed of.

Another abuse of human beings concerns the importation of slaves to the New World to do the intensive, backbreaking agricultural labor, thereby securing wealth for these European nations and individual Europeans who settled in North America. A similar practice occurred in the Pacific where Pacific islanders were taken as indentured servants or forcefully captured and transported to other areas of the Pacific to do hard labor. Many never returned home to family and children. In fact, during the nineteenth century, the British brought Indians to Fiji as indentured servants, resulting in friction between native Fijians and Indo-Fijians that continues to manifest today in political upheavals and on-going coups.

Voyaging in a small boat brings one face to face with the continuing impact of human abuse. Whereas tourists usually come for a short time and visit only the capital city of these island groups. They stay in a resort comfortably furnished. Naturally, from such limited exposure, they usually gain a skewed view of what the islands are like. One example that comes to mind is Port Vila, Vanuatu. French restaurants and sidewalk cafes lend a very mellow and cultivated atmosphere to the tropical ambience of this capital city. But just a few miles away on other islands, the people often live in their native dwellings, producing their own foods, living a lifestyle totally different from those in urbanized Port Vila and still grappling with continuing multiple effects of colonial rule. But the tourist knows nothing of how these people live.

By contrast, on a sailboat we were able to go to these villages and see firsthand how most of the islanders live. In many instances we spent considerable time—weeks or months—with villagers in various islands groups. With the opportunity afforded me to interact and become acquainted with individuals and families, I was able to gain insight into their attitudes and feelings. While I did not approach them with a specific agenda, as would an anthropologist (or even a systematic investigation), nonetheless the exchange enabled me to gain significant insight into their day-to-day lives, their difficulties, and their aspirations. Many times we were privy to local celebrations. These were not events staged for the entertainment of tourists. Through such experiences I felt that some people learned to trust me and spoke openly of their concerns.

In 1992, we sailed to Guam, a U.S. Territory, sailing back into the northern hemisphere for the first time in about seven years. Our objective was to find work in an effort to recoup money spent repairing *Banshee* after the mid-ocean dismasting almost two years earlier. The sixteen months rebuilding *Banshee* in Australia had greatly depleted our funds. Thus, we found ourselves needing employment. Once in Guam, Joy was hired by the public school system as an administrator, and I became an Assistant Professor of English and Women and Gender Studies at the University of Guam.

What I did not know upon arriving in Guam, was how this sojourn would ultimately further my knowledge and understanding of Pacific peoples and their culture and ultimately redirect my own life.

Chapter 1

A RIGOROUS PASSAGE TO NEW CALEDONIA

Suddenly the sails began flogging. It was just after five a.m. on this wild June night. Joy and I were three days out of New Zealand on a passage to Noumea, New Caledonia. Under stormy skies the horizon gave no hint that sunrise was less than an hour away.

At five, I had poked my head out the hatch, as I had been doing every 20 minutes to look around for other vessels. I didn't expect to see any. At latitude 31° 20'S, longitude 172 ° 50'E, the closest land was New Zealand, about 300 miles south. In every other direction there was just a vast expanse of the Pacific Ocean. After three days of almost continuous gale force winds, the seas had become large and nasty. Seeing nothing but mounds of confused sea, I woke Joy for her watch and wearily crawled into my bunk.

Then the sails started flogging, just when I was on the brink of falling asleep. The furious sound of the whipping sails penetrated my semi-conscious state. I knew I had to get up and put on my foul weather gear and boots. A dismal prospect. After a three and a half hour watch on this miserable night, I was exhausted. I had been fighting seasickness for three days. For the last two, I had eaten hardly anything. Without adequate food and sleep, I was becoming weak and shaky. At the moment I was shaking with chills, not so much from cold as from tiredness.

"Damn," Joy exclaimed, "what has gone wrong now?"

"Mildred (the steering vane) has got some problem," I responded dully. " Until now she's been performing fine."

"Yeah, but something's going on."

It was taking all my energy to hang on and dress, balancing against the boat's pitching.

Jason, our eight-month-old New Zealand cat who had been with us for four months, stretched and then curled up snug on top of the sleeping bag that lay heaped up in my empty bunk. I could just imagine his contented sigh. Lucky old cat, sleeping and eating on schedule no matter what.

Finally, we were zipped up tightly, resembling two white sausages in our wet weather gear. Joy opened the hatch cautiously, allowing just enough room to squeeze through. Occasional seas were smashing over the yacht. Joy was taking precaution lest one of these came tumbling through the hatch. We didn't need any salt water on our electronic gear. She scrambled out nimbly with me right behind her. Cold wind blasted freezing rain into our faces.

Immediately we both saw it: lights from a ship! But, as so often happens at night, it was not possible to tell where it was going. We could only see two white lights, parallel. This configuration was confusing because usually one light is higher than the other. If you see only white - no red or green - then you are seeing the stern of the vessel as she steams away. Occasionally, as we watched, we thought we could see a hint of red. That would mean we were seeing the port side of the ship. Possibly we were on a collision course.

All of these thoughts and comments took place as I was hand steering *Banshee*. One quick glance had revealed why Mildred stopped steering. She has two control lines that run from struts off the stern up through two blocks on deck, which are then tied to a drum on the wheel. The screws holding one block had pulled out. The tremendous strain of three days of heavy weather had taken their toll on the steering mechanism.

The block had pulled loose from the teak combing. Illumination by flashlight revealed that the wood around the screws had rotted. Joy thought she could find some good wood to refasten to. She retreated below to get some tools, screws, a new block and to call the ship on channel 16 on the VHF radio.

Finally she got a response from someone speaking a heavily accented English. It was a Japanese *maru* (ship). Apparently they couldn't see us. While I strained to hear the exchange on the radio, I suddenly felt a jolt of fear. I could see red, green and white lights. The ship was abeam of us, coming right at us! I was trying to hold a course of northwest, but the seas were pushing us around as if we were a mere toothpick. Because of the rough seas, our heading was swinging about 15 degrees to either side of our intended course.

I heard Joy tell them to go on a course of southwest. Alarmed, I shouted down to her, "God no, on that course they could run us down!" By now the ship was really close -- no more than half a mile to a mile off. Joy mistakenly thought we were sailing due north. "Tell them to steer east," I yelled. "That'll get us clear of them quickly."

She told them and shortly I saw the *maru* obligingly change course. Soon they were disappearing into the night over the horizon.

Joy came back on deck and started repairing the block. In no time we had things back together and Mildred was again steering. But we both knew the repair was only temporary. We could only hope the screws would hold until daylight when conditions might settle down a bit.

As soon as the repair was made I was sick. Vomiting gave only temporary relief to my head, which felt like it was squeezed inside a giant vice. I was terribly thirsty, but couldn't keep any fluid down. Being inexperienced with *mal de mer*, I was just learning how demoralizing and debilitating it can be. For one thing I was unable to concentrate or focus on anything. Several times I tried to plot fixes, but I could not read the latitude and longitude correctly. I didn't realize that, of course, but when Joy later examined my plot, she discovered I was way off! In fact, my discomfort was so overwhelming I couldn't think of anything else. In addition to being extremely weak, I felt very depressed.

To recover I needed to stay in my bunk and get some rest as sleep was the only thing that made me feel better. As soon I arose and tried to function, I was once again very sick.

Speaking on the ham radio with Kerikeri Radio in New Zealnad, Joy learned sailors on other yachts going through the same weather system as we were also seasick. The seas were unusually turbulent, even for the Tasman Sea.

Leaving New Zealand had been difficult. All kinds of strings pulled at us. After being tied to land for a year and a half, preparing again for an ocean passage required enormous energy. Thousands of minor jobs had to be done as well as some major ones. For at least a month before leaving New Zealand, I suffered from separation anxiety. Leaving all our friends, Joy and I agreed, was going to be very difficult.

Inevitably, the day of departure came. On June 5, at 9:30 in the morning, we powered *Banshee* over to the Panmure Yacht Club dock for the last time to top up with water. It was a cold winter morning drenched with sun that soon warmed the air. At 10:00 a.m., Bert and Enid arrived with Janet. Then Sue from *Seaward* rowed over. All came to have morning tea with us before saying farewell.

Time passed quickly. Before we knew it we had kissed and hugged everyone good-bye, and *Banshee* was heading down the ruffled water of the Tamaki River, her engine purring. We looked back, full of nostalgia and waved to those behind waving at us. Sea gulls and molly hawks keened and circled overhead as we slipped past the broad grassy shore. Two hours later we were chugging into West Haven Marina where several thousand masts stood, incongruously poised before Auckland's modern skyline of mirrowed glass and towering concrete.

Much to our surprise, our friend Graham Boswell was standing on the dock. The slip we had been assigned was occupied, so Graham motioned us into an empty slip. Since it was the Queen's birthday and the marina office was closed, we eased into the slip, taking a chance that no one would turn up and lay claim to it.

Throughout the afternoon and evening other friends came, bringing gifts and saying good-bye: Libby and Louise with a bottle of wine, Mark and Rob with jokes and best wishes, Joyce and Jim with a year's supply of homemade jellies, jams and chutneys. It was a happy time being with our friends but also a sad one, knowing we might never see them again.

Waking early the next morning at West Haven, we soon climbed on deck and tried to work in the chilly air. Presently the sun shone brilliantly, drying up pools of dew and thawing the air. Our first job was to pull *Nessie*, the hard dinghy, onto the dock so we could scrub off a week's growth of weed and tiny colonies of marine life that had sprung to life from the Tamaki River. Once cleaned, *Nessie* was loaded onto the foredeck, turned upside down and lashed securely.

Joy went off on her bicycle to make some last minute purchases while I stayed aboard topping up the water tank and doing odds and ends, awaiting the delivery of our duty free goods. By noon, our last minute chores completed, we left West Haven Marina and went to nearby Kawau Island to wait for the right weather for our departure. We anchored in Smelting Cove, a secure place to sit out the gales lashing New Zealand. When it wasn't raining we completed many boat projects.

On the second day there, we decided to do engine maintenance. Normally the whole routine takes the two of us three hours at most. Not this time. When we tired to drain the sump oil, the pump was dead. Joy suspected an electrical failure. After cleaning the corrosion off the wires, the pump still refused to work. Cursing and straining, Joy finally removed the pump from its almost inaccessible place in the engine room. Even when hooked up to an extraneous power source the pump refused to function. No wonder, as we soon discovered, it was caked with rust and salt.

We tore the pump apart. After we cleaned the shaft and plugged it in, the motor whirred to life. Now I sanded the faces which we then greased and put the pump back together after inserting a new gasket. After three hours of work the pump was as good as new.

But now we found that the pump switch was also faulty. Rather than take another hour or so to do this repair, we took the shortcut, plugging the pump directly into 12 volts.

June 8 was another day of steady work. We greased the anchor windlass, made and installed two canvas panels to cover the open spaces at the gates. Joy made two mast boots -- one for the mainmast and one for the radar mast. The former, though only a year old, had deteriorated badly. By chance I discovered it was letting in a trickle of water. During our strenuous passage it would surely have given way and let in buckets of water.

The day before our departure, *Tamure*, an American yacht we'd not met before, came in to Bon Accord Bay --- where we had reanchored when the wind shifted --- and anchored beside us. Scott, Kitty and their two sons were heading for Noumea also, and, like us, were merely waiting for appropriate weather.

June 13, a Tuesday, dawned overcast, but the clouds soon burned off. Even the air temperature was mild, almost summery. The weather report indicated the high was upon us. This was our signal to leave New Zealand.

Banshee nosed out of the placid cove. Having left before us, *Tamure* was a quarter of a mile ahead. Leaving behind sun-dappled hills and soft bird calls, we plunged into a murky dank world, pushed along by lumpy seas and a freshening breeze off the quarter.

Who would have guessed that the high giving us desirable southeasterlies would move off before midnight? By late evening, as we approached Poor Knights, the wind dramatically shifted to the East, causing a midnight fire drill shortening sail. In less than 24 hours the high had passed, leaving in its wake a trough and cold, wet weather.

The easterly wind put New Zealand's North Island to our lee. Sailing hard on the wind, we fought to stay clear of the coast. We especially wanted to be well off North Cape as foul ground extends 60 or 70 miles offshore. Gradually the wind shifted from northeast to north, relentlessly threatening to push us further westward towards the very hazards we wished to escape. But amazingly, our satellite navigation fixes (a precursor to GPS, which was a new technology) kept showing our course made good more northward than we could steer by compass. Obviously, we had a current assisting us in staying clear of the rocks and shoals of North Cape.

Incidentally, for purists who shun satnavs (Satelite Navigation System), insisting on using nothing more modern than a sextant, let me point out that for three days we could not possibly have taken a sight with a sextant. A combination of rain, mist and cloud cover obliterated the heavens.

Another invaluable navigational tool, which we had for the first time, was radar. Many people claim that radar is their most prized possession. We began to see just how useful it could be as we approached Poor Knights. Poor Knights, a tall island, has a navigational light, but a very dangerous group of offshore rocks is unlit. With radar we could get our distance off and a bearing.

Our close encounter with the ship and the stormy conditions were a bleak introduction to dawn. By mid-morning, though, the sky had cleared to a deep azure blue. The wind continued to howl, pushing the royal blue sea into breaking waves that sparkled in the sunlight. Because of the boisterous seas we remained below, looking out every twenty minutes. Just after noon the repaired block gave way and the flogging started again. Hastily we pulled on foul weather gear and went topside. The southerly swell was now 15 to 20 feet, not large as seas go, but there was only a short interval between the crests, rendering the seas sharp and steep.

It took a while to make the repair. I steered while Joy reinstalled the block. Then we reset the wind vane and waited to see how Mildred would handle it. For about two minutes everything went fine until an unusually large sea picked *Banshee* up and pushed her bow over. Instead of quartering the seas, she turned dead down wind. I was watching to see Mildred steer us back up. Our speed accelerated alarmingly as we slid down the steep slope right into the cavernous trough. We had barely started riding up the backside of the wave to the crest when a second very large sea lifted our stern and mightily shoved us forward toward the yawning valley below. The knot meter jumped from 7 knots to 11.1! My heart beat wildly and my stomach shot up into my throat. I felt a searing jolt of fear, anticipating that the force of acceleration would drive the bow under the sea and we would pitch pole (go end over end) into the sea. Grabbing the wheel, I immediately disconnected the self-steering. Using my body weight for leverage, I pulled the wheel hard to port. I felt enormous pressure on the rudder. Momentarily, I feared that the rudder might snap in two or that the boat would not respond. Luckily at the last second *Banshee's* bow rode up to the frothing crest. I exhaled and licked my lips. They were dry and caked with salt spray.

Obviously, in these particular seas, Mildred could not steer the boat on a broad reach. We readjusted the steering so that she sailed closer to a beam reach. Now when a sea tried to push the boat down, the wind vane recovered by steering back up to windward.

What a terrible passage this had been so far. For three days we had sailed through an occluded front and a cold front. On the third night the front trampled us. Just at dusk heavy winds and rain began thrashing us. For the thousandth time --- it seemed --- we put on our weather gear as quickly as possible. The danger in not reducing sail soon enough could be a knockdown. If *Banshee* were pushed down with her spreaders in the water, we could lose part of our rigging or otherwise seriously damage the boat.

Out on deck all hell had broken loose. Rain fell in heavy sheets. *Banshee* was heeled over at least 25 degrees. Periodically an extra heavy gust knocked her lee rail under and tons of white foaming seas washed over the decks and cabin top. Raging seas also smashed into the high side, sending blinding cascades of water everywhere. Some of these torrents filled the cockpit. The maelstrom pushed and pulled at our bodies as if to pry us from our refuge. But our safety harnesses were our insurance, our umbilical cord, securing us to *Banshee*. The wind shrieked in a high-pitched angry moan. The cacophony of wind and sea blended in a deafening din, crescendoing to a percussive explosion.

As quickly as possible, we cast off the jib halyard and winched the sail down with the downhaul in the cockpit. As the sail came down, the wind ripped at the expanse of dacron, whipping it so hard it sounded like cannon volleys, until we could secure it on the deck and tie it securely to the lifeline. Momentarily rendered unstable as the sail was dropping, *Banshee* wobbled back and forth on her beams' end.

While I went below to fix us a substantial meal, Joy stayed on deck to see how things were holding. Because of the bad weather we had eaten very little since leaving and in my case almost nothing. I knew that because of our fatigue level and extreme energy output we needed to eat a good, hot meal. I was washing some potatoes and carrots in the galley sink when I suddenly realized the sink was filling faster than it could drain. That meant we were heeled over at a considerable degree, which put the drain lower than the waterline. The motion of the boat pounding on her beam was pushing seawater up into the sink.

I grabbed the trashcan from under the sink and started bailing water into it. No matter how fast I bailed I just couldn't keep up. The water was sloshing out over the back of the sink onto the counter and then onto the floor. I knew the thruhull had to be turned off, but that meant taking all kinds of things out of the cupboard so I could reach the valve.

Just then Joy pushed open the hatch and stuck her head down. "We've got to take down more sail," she shouted. "I need you on deck right now so we can put another reef in the main."

"Look what's happening here," I screamed. "Help me first. You shut off the valve and I'll keep bailing."

Finally she had the valve shut off and the water stopped pouring in. Joy hurried back on deck while I crammed myself back into my foul weather suit, shouting a few obscenities each time the sea threw me around.

On deck I couldn't believe how much worse the situation had become. *Banshee* was heeled over with her lee rail under, barreling along at 7 to 8 knots under only a double-reefed main! Tons of white water smashed over us as we slammed down into the raging sea. Everywhere, from every direction mountains of boiling seas blasted us, sweeping over the cabin top, over the rails, hissing like swollen rivers into the scuppers.

To help Joy put in the third reef in the main, I eased the mainsheet. The sail thrashed and popped, flogging wildly until at last the reef was secured.

Back below I found cunning Jason had found the chicken sitting in a pot on the stove. He was gobbling it up. This was on top of his dinner. He had consumed almost all of our meat! My stew was light on chicken, heavy on vegetables. I kept thinking I must write a book called "Ten Ways to Wok Your Cat!"

Finally, by the fifth day, fair weather. With light winds and calm seas our appetites returned. Joy busied herself in the galley and fixed an Amazonian sized breakfast of pancakes, bacon, eggs, fresh oranges and a full pot of coffee made from freshly ground beans. Everything tasted wonderful, especially when contrasted with what the weather had been.

As it turned out, life on this passage was either feast or famine. After all the stormy weather, the wind became so light we had to turn on the engine. Unhappily, I soon discovered that the contents of my hanging net, mostly my underwear, were soaking wet because the port dog had not been tightened completely. We sacrificed some fresh water for rinsing and soon the sides of the boat were festooned with drying clothes.

Toward afternoon, tired of the droning engine, we hoisted the drifter and sailed along in blissful silence. All day the fishing line had trailed behind without any bites. Around five, just as we were dropping the drifter, something hit the hook. It was a mahi mahi. As soon as it was landed in the cockpit, its brilliant blues and greens began rapidly fading. It was a small female, weighing only about 35 pounds. Jason's eyes almost popped out. He'd never seen a live fish and this one took up almost half of the cockpit floor! When Joy sliced off a couple of pieces of fish for him, Jason was unsure what to do with it until she wiped his nose with a piece of fish. For days afterwards he approached the cockpit with apprehension, slinking around cautiously as he searched for the fish. We jokingly came to refer to this behavior as Jason's fear of the fish spirit.

The reprieve of calm weather was short-lived. Just after sunset the wind increased and continued to rise through the night. By midnight we had to reduce sail. Once we passed through this disturbance, we were approaching the tropics where we entered the convergence zone. Here in this no man's land, squalls ominously circled the horizon, but they contained little wind and only light rain.

Then, once again, the wind died. We turned on the diesel. After some hours we noticed it was sputtering and running erratically and then, without further notice the engine shut down. We suspected that the fuel filters had become clogged, even though we had changed all filters just prior to leaving New Zealand. Undoubtedly all the bashing had stirred up gunk in the fuel tank. Fortunately it was a flat calm when Joy had to pull off the engine cover and check. She found tons of sludge lodged in the filters and lots of water as well. Sitting for the better part of a year in the Tamaki was certainly a contributing factor, allowing condensation and gunk to accumulate in our tank. Now we were paying the price. It took Joy all morning to change the filters and get the engine going again.

The calm did not continue. Late in the afternoon a northeasterly breeze rippled the water and soon we were gliding along smoothly on a broad reach. After sunset, the wind began to blow and increased to a piercing whistle. Within a couple of hours rain fell steadily, ushering in a gray, sodden dawn. Around 4 a.m., we reefed the main. The wind continued to rise, and by 7:30 we dropped the jenny and hoisted the much smaller staysail. Only minutes later when a nasty squall laid us over, we scrambled on deck to drop the main, which left us reaching under only a reefed staysail. Conditions deteriorated so much that we could not cook that day.

Gale force winds persisted through the next day, only gradually moderating. Two days later, around noon, the wind shifted to northwest and lightened. We shook out the reefs, sailing to weather under full main and jenny. Slowly and laboriously *Banshee* crawled up leftover seas. With 100 percent cloud cover the horizon and sea blended into a somber grayness that felt empty and lifeless. The dying wind left the seas in formless masses that toppled over on themselves.

The last two days of the passage, we had no wind. The engine droned on monotonously, day and night. Now we were running parallel to the reefs, which extend south and west of New Caledonia. It is a treacherous approach because the reef extends for miles off the landmass and few navigational lights mark the reefs. To be safe, we stayed ten to fifteen miles west of the reef.

On the final day of the passage the rising sun sailed over the dark, jagged edges of New Caledonia's peaks. A kind of mist hugged the mountains and barren hillside, blending into a hazy spray that shimmered over distant reefs. Without warning, the engine coughed, and now, being attuned to its every nuance in tone and pitch, we shut it down immediately, knowing the filter was clogged again.

By the time we had cleaned the filter and drained off the sludge, we had reached the point of turning toward the island. The sun flamed over the peaks, painting a dazzling golden swath on the water that was absolutely blinding. We needed to see Amedée Light, our landmark for finding our course through the pass. I could see nothing but the brilliant sun.

The radar saved the day. It picked up a wreck on the reef to the north of the pass. With this information, Joy was able to keep track of our position. Gradually, as we came closer, the sun moved enough that I could begin to make out the lighthouse atop the island. I had the terrible feeling that as we steered for the lighthouse we were headed straight for a reef! Suddenly I saw and heard the splash and hiss of the surf. We were already in the pass! No wonder so many boats go up on the reef here because it's almost impossible to see the reef until it is too late.

Ahead was a four-hour power through the lagoon to Noumea. Our destination was the city wharf at Baie de la Moselle. It was Sunday and it seemed all the inhabitants of Noumea were out boating and fishing in the huge lagoon. Because the wind was light, we continued to power, wanting to get in as quickly as possible. Already we were anticipating a fresh warm shower, a big hot meal followed by a long sleep in a bed that stayed flat.

After sailing a total distance of 1,232 nautical miles, we finally made Noumea, a charted distance of 950 miles from New Zealand. We had expected a nine or ten day pleasant passage, but it had taken 12 days and was by far the most demanding transit we had ever had.

Chapter 2

NOUMEA, PARIS OF THE SOUTH PACIFIC

People who have never made an open water passage in a small boat probably cannot imagine the kind of impact an extended ocean crossing exerts on humans. After a lengthy passage nothing has more appeal than a port with people, trees, vegetation, and all the varied facets of human enterprise. Upon making landfall, one's senses enliven. For me, colors vibrate and smells almost knock me over. Does the exaggerated sensory response come as a result of certain sensual deprivations? For the most part the color spectrum at sea tends to be limited to blues, grays, greens and whatever warmer hues present themselves in the sky --- the most vivid being the warm colors at sunrise and sunset. Most often, though, the sky presents the cooler part of the spectrum. If a passage is marked by bad weather, usually the predominant color is gray. Surprisingly, even fair weather may offer a very limited palette, one restricted to a deep marine blue and a medium blue sky verging on turquoise with white froth and foam providing limited variation.

At sea, odors are limited to the immediate environment, which can be body odors or cooking smells from the galley. The salt air appears to have a cleansing, very salutary effect on humans' sense of smell. Probably in urban areas our olfactory sense becomes stultified or greatly impeded by the sheer number of pollutants that assail us. Perhaps this cleansing effect of sea air accounts for the heightened sense of smell sailors experience when approaching land after a passage of a week or two. As usual, after so many days at sea, we were eager to set foot on land.

Baie de la Moselle, the port of Noumea, New Caledonia, is enclosed on one side by a large wharf crowded with tugs, supply ships and fishing vessels. A concrete seawall frames the remainder of the small bay, squeezing it into a lopsided rectangle. The city, positioned at the head of the bay, is dominated by the twin spires of a Roman Catholic cathedral. Nestled into the surrounding hillside are an assortment of European style buildings and corrugated iron structures such as one finds on any South Pacific island. Clumps of greenery, palms and indigenous straggly pines soften the angular shapes.

Noumea, known as "Paris of the South Pacific", blends European and island flavors not only in its architectural forms but also in cuisine, clothing, and the racial mix of its population. The downtown area features a unique combination of Old World essence and island modes with ultra modern buildings sitting indiscriminately cheek by jowl with funky shops crammed with brightly colored lava lavas (sarongs) in bold patterns.

Anyone who knows Tahiti will detect some similarities between Papeete, Tahiti's capital, and Noumea. To beat the heat, stores open at seven in the morning, close from 11:00 to 1:30 for siesta, and reopen for the afternoon. Wherever the French are, you can be sure of finding an abundance of bakeries filled with crusty white bread and mouth-watering, diet-defying pastries. Grocery stores display a wide selection of French wines geared to fit pockets and palates of various means and tastes. Modern supermarkets carry all the delicacies one would find in a French supermarket including a variety of cheeses, pate, about 15 kinds of canned mushrooms --- all beautifully displayed. The butcher shops are brimming with fine cuts of beef, pork and whole chickens complete with feet and claws scrubbed squeaky clean. With great curiosity, I stepped over to see if the rabbits still had fur on their paws as in Papeete, but it had been removed. When I saw the imported fruits and vegetables in the supermarkets, my first thought was that these old, shriveled specimens must be someone's idea of a joke. Not only were they past the point of being consumed they were terribly overpriced (but so were most other items found here).

Vegetables and tropical fruits, fresh and reasonably priced, are sold in the native market. Here they also sell fresh fish. This market gave me the first clue that Noumea has a dual economy, one serving Europeans, the other the indigenous Melanesians. Of all the native markets we've seen across the Pacific, this one was the smallest. The reason, no doubt, stems from the way the French have historically viewed the country, and how they have influenced its native inhabitants. In many respects patterns of the colonial past still persist today in New Caledonia. Consistent with other colonial economies this one was based on the practice of extracting raw materials from New Caledonia and shipping them to France. Hoping to develop a ready market in her colonies, France sent her ships back to them filled with French goods. The absurdity of this practice is most readily seen when the imports include fresh produce, dairy products and meats sent in from France! Any of these things can be grown in New Caledonia. Logically, we would expect a government to encourage self-sufficiency, especially in producing food. Formally, New Caledonia is no longer a colony. After all, colonial empires are an unpopular, outmoded concept. Yet, when you scratch the surface, the economic pattern appears to have remained fundamentally unchanged. The stores in Noumea are filled with European furniture, crystal, china, clothing, household wares and even French butter and cheese and eggs. Few, very few of the native inhabitants buy these high priced wares because they can't afford them, and in many instances because they have absolutely no interest in them or use for them.

Whereas the French Polynesians seemed to have made a more comfortable alliance with the French, the Melanesians of New Caledonia have continued to be very much at odds with them. From the beginning of French incursion, unrest and animosity between the two groups prevailed, and, as of the early nineties, had not yet subsided. The first European settlers were Roman Catholic missionaries who came in 1843. These missionaries were there even before France claimed the land as a colony. Four years later the natives drove them out.

Despite this defeat, the French persisted. In 1853, the French Navy returned to claim the main island for France. It became a separate French territory in 1860. Three years later nickel was discovered, and by the end of the nineteenth century thousands of French, attracted to the mild Mediterranean type climate and money to be made through mining and copra, settled in New Caledonia. As the French demand for land increased, many Melanesians were relegated to reservations. With this kind of disruption to their lives, it wasn't long before the Melanesian social structure, traditions and customs began to vanish. Embittered and angered, the Melanesians started retaliatory uprisings in the nineteenth century. The last of these was quelled in 1917.

Today few Melanesians live in Noumea. Traditional village life has been so squelched that the land is under populated to such an extent that it appears empty. Whereas the British promoted "bread and butter" programs in places such as Fiji and Papua New Guinea, the French never encouraged this kind of self-sufficiency among her colonists. As in Tahiti, New Caledonia is very dependent on French aid, which is largely spent on highly visible public works projects engaged in building roads and bridges. As in French Polynesia, the economic policy seems designed to keep the Melanesians quiet, in their place and unmotivated to develop their land for their own benefit.

In Noumea we crossed tracks with some of our old cruising friends and acquaintances --- many of whom we'd not seen for about two years. Among these were Pat and Larry on *Hallux*. Although we had met them in Tahiti, it was really in New Caledonia that our friendship blossomed. When Larry saw *Banshee* tied up on the wharf waiting to clear customs and immigration, he came roaring up in his dinghy, bringing us a baguette. Fresh bread is always one of the most craved for things when one makes port because often it will have been days since a cruiser has had fresh bread. The same day Larry loaned us some French Pacific francs so we could purchase things we might need before we had a chance to go to the bank.

A few days later, Larry offered us help of another kind. Our outboard was not running at full throttle. We had cleaned the carburetor twice, but this did not remedy the problem. Carefully, Larry disassembled the carburetor and blew denatured alcohol and air through the jets, showing us how to clean them. Voila! It was fixed.

With July Fourth only a few days away, the Americans anchored at Noumea decided to have a traditional Fourth of July barbecue on the beach. Yachties will use any excuse to have a party. The more the merrier.

So, we invited all the cruisers in Noumea, which included French, Dutch, English, Australian, German and New Zealanders. Noumea would not do for the barbecue, as there is no beach. We decided on Baie Maa, a very large bay about eight miles north of Noumea.

It was a perfect day for a sail on the morning of July Fourth. Moderate winds, on the beam, carried us northward past a landscape of mountains on the main island and tiny islands sprinkled around the lagoon. We were the sixth boat to anchor a quarter of a mile offshore in 13 feet of water facing a grand sand beach that sweeps around the expansive bay. Behind the beach we found a grassy area with a rough slab table and a fire bed. Eventually the inhabitants of twelve boats, containing 50-odd adults and children, gathered for a cookout worth writing home about.

When assembled, the long table was sagging with an overabundance of salads, rice dishes, potato delights, dips, chips, bread, pumpkin pie, chocolate cake, spiced cake and apple pie. The grill was sizzling with hotdogs, sausages, chicken, fish, pork, and steak. As dusk fell, the volleyball game ended and beach walkers returned to take their places on the grass. Soon everyone was eating and drinking. Laughter and joking filled the air. Sea yarns, whale sightings, fishing episodes were all part of the jovial exchange among people engaged in living afloat.

If we were a little more exuberant than such a group would normally be, it was because we had just received word over the ham radio that Dick and Sue and their two boys, Marc and Jason, had been taken onboard a freighter and were safely on their way to New Zealand.

This story had its beginning five days earlier when some of us heard Sue on the ham radio when she talked with *Hallux* at 8 in the morning. Although her transmission was poor, we could understand most of what she said. Their boat, *Fantasy*, a Valiant 40, was about 50 miles northwest of Noumea. She asked Larry why no one ever used the pass north of Amedée Light. Larry made some offhanded joke about people being like sheep and therefore all heading for Amedée Light. Sue's next words were puzzling. She asked Larry if he would notify Noumea Radio that they were a navigational hazard to shipping in the area. She also reported that they were having some "rig" problems.

Because the transmission was bad, Sue signed off, leaving the listeners to ponder what exactly was going on. "Rig" problems was an ambiguous term and its meaning was widely debated over the next few days. Ham operators often refer to their radio equipment as rigs. Sue's poor transmission could be an indication that she had a problem with her radio. Still another interpretation was possible. Sailors often speak of the rigging as "rig".

Everyone expected *Fantasy* would arrive the next day or so, but when they didn't appear and no one heard anything from them on the radio, we became concerned. Our anxiety was further augmented by the bad weather that arrived. In fact, on the day we'd last had radio contact with them, we had had winds of 40 plus knots in the harbor. Offshore it would have been more severe.

Scott ventured his fear that *Fantasy* had been dismasted. He had met *Fantasy* in Fiji and had observed that their rigging was very loose. He had even mentioned it to Dick, who responded that he didn't want to drive the keel through the boat, so he purposely left the stays slack. It was also known that *Fantasy* had left Australia twice. After experiencing some problems they had returned to Australia for repairs.

Why couldn't we reach them on the radio? It was possible that Dick and Sue used their backstay as an antenna. Therefore, if they had been dismasted and had no backup antenna, a dismasting would render them helpless to transmit. In fact, during the last transmission from *Fantasy* on the afternoon of June 30, they had reported being hove to in 60-knot winds and heavy seas.

Suspense and tension grew. Finally, after the third day without word from *Fantasy*, an Australian cruiser named Don spoke to the French authorities and gave them *Fantasy's* last known position. Now concerned for their safety, the French Navy spent part of the day flying over the coast on a search. However, they spotted nothing during their search.

On July Fourth when we heard the family was on the *Slurry Express*, a freighter bound for New Zealand, a big cheer went up. But as yet no one knew any details, and we all had a thousand questions. Did they have to abandon *Fantasy*? Did it sink or did they sink her when they left? Had they taken to a life raft? Why had they not talked to anyone on the radio?

Some of the answers came the next day when we heard on the radio that *Fantasy's* position had been given as a navigational hazard. From this report we concluded they had abandoned her and she was still afloat. Now some people were beginning to speculate that they could mount a search, find her and claim salvage. Soon thereafter we heard that the French Navy had towed *Fantasy* into a little yacht marina beside the navy base. That was a surprise. Later that day, Joy and I powered into the next bay to have a look. Sure enough, there was *Fantasy*!

As we looked, we could see one spreader was missing (as Dick had subsequently stated on the radio), but the mast was still standing, her inflatable dinghy was still tied onboard as were her fuel cans. Little by little we heard more pieces of the story. Apparently *Fantasy* had taken two knockdowns. She lost one spreader and all her batteries were overturned and lost their acid on the first knockdown.

Eventually, Dick and Sue and the two boys came to Noumea, and after some negotiation with the French Navy, they paid the salvage fee and repossessed the boat. We talked with them on several occasions and learned more about their experience. They were cleaning up the boat with the hope of selling her. They had decided to give up cruising and return to their home in the States. Dick would resume his former position in a law firm.

Damage to their boat was extensive. The inside suffered water damage and battering. Probably the worst damage was to the mast. It was bent the entire length into an "S" shape. This damage was not a result of the knockdown but rather occurred when the freighter, signaled by flares, came to their rescue. While taking the family on board, the ship rolled into *Fantasy*, smashing into the mast.

Miraculously, none of the family was seriously injured. On the first knockdown, Sue was thrown across the cabin and into the ceiling on the low side. The force of her body actually smashed through part of the overhead. Fortunately, she sustained no fractures, just some bruising. One of the boys was also thrown across the boat, but he too was uninjured. Dick, with a sprained leg, suffered the worst.

Cruisers, of course, have an avid interest in such experiences and want to know what went wrong and why and how it happened. Each of us knows it could happen to us. We asked Dick and Sue what their thoughts were. Both of them said that they didn't feel the conditions were that severe. Like them, most people who have done any blue water sailing will have experienced winds and seas as heavy or heavier than what they encountered.

Dick thought it had a lot to do with the hull shape of his boat. The Valiant 40 has a rounded bottom with almost no bilge. This feature makes the Valiant a very fast boat, but it also means that while it has good initial stability, it loses stability quickly once it goes beyond a certain degree of heel.

Sue said they were using an autopilot to steer when they were knocked down. They had wanted to steer a very tight course, which the wind vane could not do. The problem with using an autopilot in very heavy conditions, in our view, is that the autopilot is set to steer a compass course, and in strong conditions the autopilot may not be able to maintain control. Whether or not this contributed to the knockdown no one will ever know. Sue mentioned, though, that after the first knockdown, the autopilot was not performing right, so it may have been damaged in the first knockdown. Even so, they continued to use it rather than change to the wind vane or hand steer.

The enchantment of Baie Maa drew us back several weeks later. After a spirited sail with a following sea, we nipped into a protected bay opposite where we had anchored previously. Ashore, we found fresh water pools where deer come to drink. No more than 25 feet from the beach a dirt road winds through flat plains covered in knee-high grass. Here and there, coconut palms tower over the golden brown grass like giants in the midst of Lilliputians. A short distance up the road we paused to observe four graceful does feeding beside the pool.

Returning to the beach, we followed the curve of the shoreline as lengthening late afternoon shadows crept over the white sand. We found two coconuts and husked them with a rusting spike that poked up from a submerged wreck. As dusk descended softly, the buzz of night creatures swelled and the wind tapered to nothing. It was so still you could almost hear the twinkle of the stars as they appeared.

Chapter 3

THE ISLE OF PINES

We left from Baie Maa in the early morning. It was a still, hot day with a cloudless blue sky, promising a day of light winds. By the time we reached the Canard, a small island about eight miles along the way, I spotted --- perhaps two miles away --- what I thought was a board sailor with a black and white sail. But, after seeing it crash into the water, quickly recover and crash again in rapid succession three or four times, I realized it was no board sailor. It was a whale! Then it leaped again, rising straight out of the water. Three quarter of its gigantic mass was extended vertically; then the creature flung itself down with a mighty crash. This awesome behavior continued. In the end, the sperm whale which was coming our way, got within half a mile, all the time putting on this marvelous show. It was getting too near for comfort. We altered course, giving right of way to the whale. Fortunately, Baie du Prony, a huge crater at the southern tip of Grande Terre, lies roughly midway between Noumea and the Isle of Pines (Ile des Pins). This wonderful area has numerous anchorages convenient for an overnight stay.

Our ultimate destination for this part of the voyage was the Isle of Pines, considered by many to be the most beautiful island in the world.

What goes unmentioned is that this jewel is enmeshed in an elaborate network of reefs. In fact, the entire way from Grande Terre (the French name for the main island of New Caledonia) to the Isle of Pines is strewn with sand cays and countless tiny islands. To make matters worse, from a navigational point of view, the prevailing winds are normally southeasterly and the Isle of Pines lies about 70 nautical miles southeast of Noumea. It is best to attempt this passage when the wind has gone northerly. Even so, seventy miles is too far to do in a day as it puts you in the reefy area during the night.

By early afternoon we tired of the droning engine, shut it off, and put up the main and drifter. Sails might be slower, but the quiet was most welcome. Our course zigzagged around reefs and sandy islets topped by spiky trees that looked like pincushions. One such island is aptly named "Porcupine".

These strange trees, tall and slender, are the pines indigenous to the Isle of Pines. Sometimes they look like a perfect Christmas tree, but more often they are straggly. They resemble a Norfolk pine (to which they are related) but unlike these geometrically shaped trees, the island pine has a very large trunk with branches entirely too small in proportion to the enormous trunk.

Grande Terre, to our east, presented a spectacular mass of distant tall peaks of varying shades of blue and gray. Here and there silver trails of waterfalls glinted. Sadly, the monumental beauty of this island has been marred. Gigantic rust red slashes all over the hillside testify to the blasting carried out in search of nickel deposits. Without any effort toward conservation, the mining companies have simply walked away, leaving the bare earth to erode. The more distant triangular mountains were wrapped in haze. Amazingly, in this vast expanse of land, we saw no sign of human habitation. It could have been the moon.

As we approached Woodin Canal --- a natural slit between Grande Terre and Quen Island --- the water piled up between the two landmasses, creating a swift current. Along the shoreline coconut palms grew in sporadic clusters, but here also the hillsides bore their scars as rust clay patches that stood out like open wounds.

Just at the entrance to the canal, a large Mobil tanker was charging down upon us. We gave way. Once it passed, a local fishing boat overtook us. Not five minutes later, a pilot boat from Noumea came chugging through on her way home. All day we'd seen no boats and now, at the canal, the traffic was converging.

Baie du Prony branches off in several directions. To the north it narrows and snakes through the mountains. It was too late in the day to venture into this part of the bay. Instead we followed an arm reaching eastward. This area, called Bon Anse, comprises several fjord-like projections that have carved their way up to the edge of the jungle. Waxy-leafed mangroves form a tangled shoreline. We passed two little coves when suddenly the depth sounder showed nine feet! Only minutes earlier we had been in depths exceeding 100 feet! Now we could see the reef below us. Quickly I turned Banshee 180 degrees, and held my breath until I saw the depth slowly increasing. We returned to the previous cove and set the hook close to the shore in mud. On three sides mangroves with spindly legs and dense rain forest enclosed us. Large, lush trees stood erect and still. The only sounds were the gurgling of a stream and bird chatter.

As night fell, the sounds swelled in volume. Jason was transfixed. A million stars popped out of the cool night. Dew settled down as the darkness enveloped us.

Morning in the mangrove swamp was equally lovely. Nature and all her creatures were buzzing, singing, chirping, flying, skimming, stalking --- alive long before the sun peeked over the mountains, illuminating subterranean caverns lurking just under the surface reflections. In and around ghostly dead coral, big parrotfish and mangrove jack swam lazily. It was not a particularly pretty underwater scene. Rather it looked dusty like the interior of an old house that has been closed down and neglected for years. Still this muddy silt-covered bottom was home to these fish.

By 8 a.m., the chain was clanking as it speedily passed the gypsy on the windlass and fell into its locker. Then, abruptly, it ceased. The chain was tangled around a piece of coral. Once the silt settled we could see which way to steer to clear the chain. Free at last, we glided out of the sanctuary into the manmouth bay. A gentle breeze ruffled the surface.

Too little wind to sail, we powered out into the main part of Prony, heading past an extended coral reef where a lighthouse marked the end. A flat sea stretched to the horizon, dotted here and there by islands with stubby tops. We had expected to power all day, but by 10:30 a northeast wind stirred. With sail hoisted, we slipped quietly past tiny islands rimmed by crashing surf.

Toward early afternoon, we spotted another sperm whale leaping and thrashing through the water. This one was a mile or more away.

Several hours later, I noticed we were sailing directly for a leaping whale and quickly changed course, passing within a quarter of a mile of it.

Our principal navigational instrument was our knot meter. What we didn't realize was that the paddle wheel was fouled which made it record our speed slower than it actually was. As a result, we over stood our entrance. We only realized this when we took a bearing on Infernal Island, aptly named as it stands in the middle of the roadway. Our chart indicated that a bearing of 059 degrees true on Menunier peak would take us safely into the anchorage. Nga peak towers 262 meters above a verdant landscape. Nearby is a lower peak, shaped like a pyramid. It had to be Meunier. After identifying other landmarks, we were confident of our position. Because of numerous reefs in this area, good navigation is a must. In some instances reef extends as much as five miles offshore.

Most tropical islands are fringed by coconut palms. But the Isle of Pines is exceptional because its shores are graced not only by palms but also a number of *Araucaria cooki*, the unique species of pine indigenous to this island from which the island takes its name.

Soon we noticed two sailboats to our port on a converging course. Both flew Australian flags off their sterns. When within shouting distance, we exchanged greetings and were promptly invited to a fish feed that evening aboard the smaller yacht. Proudly they held up several large reef fish, as if to confirm their invitation and whet our appetites.

Several hundred yards offshore, we anchored in 25 feet of turquoise water on a sand bottom. I heard a splash and noticed a large turtle had swum close to inspect us. Since turtles are protected in New Caledonia, we saw many in these waters. Soon we had the sails stowed in their bags, and I went below to prepare a salad for our communal feast. Just about dark, we dinghied over to *Robbo* and met five Aussies who were buddy boating on two boats. It was fun to meet new cruisers and enjoy a meal with friendly people.

In the morning, the island was shrouded in mist. This condition would not deter us. We had decided to take our bicycles ashore and ride to Vao, the major town on the island. Initially, a very thick canopy of enormous trees lining the road protected us. Then a torrential downpour came. We hurriedly pushed our bikes through some tall grass seeking refuge in the jungle. Huddled under Joy's tiny umbrella we waited out the rain under a large banyan tree.

Proceeding inland, we passed miles of luxuriant rain forest. Gradually the road steepened as we approached another coast of the island. Our efforts were rewarded by an aerial view of breaking reefs, emerald lagoons, royal blue ribbons of deep water and hundreds of little round islands looking like heads with perfectly trimmed crew cuts.

Vao is more of a settlement than a town. It has one modern building --- the mayor's office --- a post office, and a magnificent European style Catholic church, in addition to several non-descript general stores. The real delight of the Isle of Pines is the powdery white sand beaches, which usually were deserted.

Several days after we had arrived, three American yachts came into Kuto Bay along with two Australian yachts and one French. For close to a week, we settled into a leisurely-paced life, sometimes going ashore to explore, to paint or draw, sometimes staying onboard doing boat jobs. Suddenly and unexpectedly, Paradise was disrupted. One evening a local launch came by to each yacht to inform us that on Monday morning (the next day) at 6 a.m., some French moviemakers were coming to do some filming in the bay and they wanted all the yachts out for the day. It was to be a one-day deal and we could return at 5 p.m. Needless to say, no one was very happy about this. Anchorages on the Isle of Pines are few and far between. Just for the day the only real option was to power out to one of the nearby little islands and anchor. But no one wants to go charging around reef-strewn waters at 6 a.m. when visibility is nil. To make matters worse, Monday morning dawned cloudy and rainy.

Joy and I still had no idea where to go. We just followed the procession of yachts out of the bay. When the boats split into two groups, we followed *Karinya* and *Robbo*, the two Australian boats. Incorrectly, we assumed they were going to Moro Island, but it soon became evident they were headed elsewhere. We powered up to *Robbo* to ask where they were going. Infernal Island. We certainly did not want to go there with limited visibility because most of the area around the island is unsurveyed.

The American contingency, headed to Ile Brosse, were now quite a distance from us. We decided to join them, but just after we made the turn to join them, it began to rain. Neither of us felt it was safe to continue to Ile Brosse. It seemed foolhardy to put *Banshee* in danger.

With that decision made, we reentered Kuto bay, intending to reanchor there. Suddenly a launch driven by a very large Kanaka thundered down on us at full speed as if to ram us! The hairs on the back of my neck stood up, but I told myself I needed to remain cool and rational. He stopped just short of hitting us. In limited English he managed to convey that we couldn't anchor in the bay. I tried to explain our predicament, as simply as possible, telling him we would not put our yacht in jeopardy. Unable to accept our explanation and possibly thinking I didn't understand him, the Kanaka indicated that he would bring someone out who could speak with us. Gunning the outboard, he sped to shore toward a group of people.

Immediately, someone jumped aboard and back they came, again just barely missing us as they splashed to a stop alongside. I was angered by their threatening manner. The Frenchman started speaking loudly. His English was heavily accented and almost unintelligible, only marginally better than the Kanaka's. He apologized, but requested that we leave immediately. In a typically dramatic French fashion, he waved his arms and his voice rose to a shriller and shriller pitch when I responded with a firm NO! This only made him more frantic in his body language. By now he was speaking only French at such a rapid speed I couldn't understand one single word.

Feeling even more frustrated and angry because of his overbearing manner, I exerted extreme effort to remain calm but firm as I explained again why we would not leave the bay. He just talked right over me, only shrugging his shoulders and saying he couldn't understand me. But the Kanaka understood, probably because he had not become enraged, but had listened. His rationality saved the day. He offered to guide us to the next bay, Kanumera, which would be protected in these winds.

Kanumera was an acceptable solution to us. We really had no desire to start a French-American war. We complied, knowing that in fact we were not compelled to move. The anchorage is for public use and cannot be usurped by someone wanting to film.

As it happened, the move proved to be good for us. We anchored next to *Shalmar*, a yacht flying a Kiwi (New Zealand) flag. Soon we discovered the owners were Kiwis who've immigrated to Australia. Stuart yelled over and invited us over for morning tea. We responded that as soon as we had *Banshee* put together we'd be over.

Both Wendy and Stu are cat lovers. They had seen Jason and remarked how beautiful he was. They wondered if he could come visiting. We ended up having lunch with them and when we left, Jason stayed behind to give them a little more time for their cat "fix". In the evening they came for drinks and brought Jason home.

The French filming, which was supposed to last for one day, stretched out to a week! On coming to Kanumera Bay, we had been told that the moviemakers would be asking everyone to leave the bay early again the following morning. Around 5 p.m., we watched the others return to Kuto Bay. Sure enough the next morning we saw the yachts in procession leaving the bay, but many of them came directly into our bay to anchor. The weather had deteriorated even more and Kuto was not a pleasant or safe place to be. In these conditions Kanumera was protected.

Kanumera proved to be good for about two days, but as the weather system went through, it became an untenable anchorage. Several of us dragged anchor. Of course, it happened to us at the worst possible time. We had only just discovered that for some reason our engine was not charging our batteries. That meant that it would be extremely difficult if not impossible for us to get our anchor up by electric windlass before we dragged back onto the fringing reef! We have a manual windlass for emergencies and would have resorted to that had not Stu seen our predicament and rowed over to help. In a flash, he jumped on deck and manually pulled up our chain. This is a feat that even Joy and I together cannot do as quickly as Stu. Meanwhile, I stayed on the wheel, and with the engine running, kept us pushing hard enough into the wind to keep us off the reef.

We reanchored and Stu went back and had to reanchor *Shalmar* as she was also dragging. As the day progressed, the fetch increased tremendously. All of the boats were bouncing around like bucking horses. I was becoming more and more irate at the whole situation. I knew Stu felt the same way, as did Roger on *Lazybones*, but thus far no one else seemed to object to what was happening. Joy and I had decided that we would not wait until until 5 p.m. to go to Kuto Bay. The wind was increasing and becoming more westerly so that we had no protection where we were. Finally I noticed Stu and Wendy were picking up anchor. By now Joy had finished making the repair --- a wire from the alternator had broken. With the repair done, we decided we too would pull up and return right behind *Shalmar*. No sooner had we exited than Roger was right behind us. Then one by one, as if on cue, all the boats followed!

We wondered what the response of the French would be. I knew Stu would stand his ground, so would I and so would Roger. But what about the others who seemed so unwilling to consider "civil insurrection"? As we rounded the corner, we saw Stu anchoring. We watched for the speedy launch, but it did not appear. By now the French could see at least half of the yachts coming back home. I didn't think they would take us on. For once they showed more prudence than emotion!

Still, the filming was not finished. The next day the Frenchman came around in the launch, telling people to move after lunch to the opposite side of the bay. *Shalmar* and *Lazybones* had left to return to Noumea. Having no allies for civil disobedience, we joined the herd and moved yet again.

The last straw came the next day. Joy and I had gone ashore early in the morning to fill our jugs with fresh water. From shore we saw the dreaded launch making its rounds. What now? We were very tempted not to go back, but we did. Just as we were approaching our yacht, the launch came over. Aboard was the familiar Frenchman and with him an arrogant, self-impressed teenager. They told us we must remove all the blue canvas --- they had been requesting this of all the yachts! But we had the most blue canvas of any boat --- our dodger, sail bags, awning, and mainsail cover! It would mean several hours of work to remove everything and then several more hours to put it back! Joy exploded. The arrogant teenager responded, "If you don't comply, we'll have the harbor closed!"

That we both knew was an outrageous, empty threat, but we decided not to challenge it.

Back onboard we debated what to do. Everyone else seemed to be complying. Wouldn't anyone stand up to them? Finally we decided on a compromise. We removed some of the blue canvas and covered up the rest with bed sheets! What a sight we must have looked, a yacht sitting at anchor with bed sheets blowing about! There were no repercussions and after several hours we removed those and put back the blue canvas. Out of three weeks in the Isle of Pines, one week had been wasted moving around to suit the filmmakers.

One fine day --- after the French occupation --- we decided to do some exploring and take *Banshee* to a nearby island. To find a place to anchor, we had to wind our way through reefs until we found a large patch of sand. Ashore we explored much of the circumference of the island whose interior was impenetrable jungle. Walking along white sand, soft as flour, we spotted six black and white banded sea snakes tucked up into crevices along the shoreline. In the water the snake is black and white, but dried out they were pink and black. One brazen snake swam ashore landing almost at my feet. I moved a healthy distance away and watched it land and wiggle along the sand right across my deep footprints.

The bite of these snakes is deadly, as there is no antidote. It is said because their mouths are so small, they can only bite a human on the ear or between the fingers and toes! I'm not adventurous enough to test this theory.

Because the Isle of Pines is so outstandingly beautiful, it would seem to be the perfect setting for resorts and all kinds of tourist attractions. Fortunately, this kind of development has not happened. Tourism has declined drastically in New Caledonia since the open hostilities that occurred several years ago between the French and the Kanakas who were striving for their independence. In fact, the Kanakas have actively deterred tourism to some extent. One of the hotels being built on the Isle of Pines at the time of heated disputes was destroyed, leaving intact only some concrete block walls decorated with political graffiti. The message: "We don't want our island thronged with tourists." Seeing the island as it was, we had to agree. It is quaint, tranquil and natural. There are no noisy people crowing the beaches and jamming the little road with cars, vans and buses belching clouds of poisonous carbon monoxide. There are no tourist attractions, no blaring discos, no shows, no nightclubs, just a few low-keyed restaurants. The entertainment consists of exploring this gorgeous spot and savoring the natural, unspoiled environment.

Strangely enough, yachts, as long as there are not hundreds, seem to be welcome. All our encounters with the inhabitants were pleasant. Aside from the French military on the island, all the inhabitants are Melanesians. Some live in towns located at various parts of the island, but most live scattered about the countryside, supporting themselves from their gardens and keeping several goats or cows. Within walking distance of Kuto Bay was a store that sold fresh French bread daily, from a bakery just a bit further down the road. The store carried a limited supply of canned goods and an even more limited offering of fresh produce.

Before leaving the Isle of Pines we went to visit the remains of the prison. France initially took possession of New Caledonia to establish a penal colony modeled after the notorious Devil's Island in French Guiana. The first prison was located in Noumea, but ten years later it was moved to Ile Nou, a small island in Noumea Bay. The Paris Insurrection of 1870 left the French government with almost 4,000 political prisoners, too many for the small prison on Ile Nou. Consequently, these prisoners were sent to the Isle of Pines and to Maré, one of the Loyalty Islands. Twenty-four years later, the penal institutions were closed down. It was to this prison at Ouro, north of Kuto, we rode our bikes. We wandered through thick-walled rooms, now crumbling and heavily overgrown with plants. Many windows with iron bars are still intact.

I couldn't shake off the heavy sense of oppression and pain of this place. Some of the iron rings to which prisoners had been chained were still in place on the walls. I wondered how many people had succeeded in hanging themselves here. It was the kind of place where death would be more welcome than suffering the privations of confinement and abuse in these cells.

Now we had seen both the dark and light facets of this famed isle. We could only hope that its future would not be clouded by pollution, financial exploitation or human brutality and bloodshed. Nature has created an island of unsurpassed beauty to share with those who tread lightly.

As for the early history on this lovely island, archaeologists have made some important discoveries at the southern end of the island at Vatcha. Digs here have uncovered a remarkable Lapita site. The so-called Lapita Culture, named after a special type of pottery, refers to seafaring colonists who rapidly moved through Melanesia during the second millennium B.C. and into Polynesia. It is conceivable that these pottery makers were Polynesian. Detailed investigations into the spread of this type of pottery have shown its distribution extended from northern

New Guinea to Samoa from roughly 1500 B. C. until the first century A.D. when it ceased being produced. Lapita sites are always found in coastal areas or on small offshore islands. The pots from the Vatcha site are unusually well preserved.

As for its archaeological wonders, the Isle of Pines possesses an unresolved mystery. On the interior plateau are about 300 earth mounds that contain cylindrical cores of lime concrete with ironstone and coral aggregate. One such mound is over 9 feet tall. No one knows what purpose these mounds served. Similar cylinders are also located just north of Noumea. Moreover, it isn't even known if these mounds are naturally formed or man made.

August 11 was the beginning of a four-day weekend celebrating the Assumption of the Blessed Virgin Mary. Wanting to clear Noumea over the weekend, we went in to Customs and Immigration on Friday afternoon to get our clearance in advance. Sunday was a cloudy, squally day. With the wind from the west, we had a fast sail down to Woodin Canal. Even before we reached the narrow part of the canal we could see the white water turbulence caused by the 20-knot wind blowing against the incoming tide. What a sight and what a heart-thumping episode as the seaway pulled *Banshee* this way and that across overfalls.

Once we passed through the rough water, the canal became absolutely calm, almost glassy even though we still had the full wind astern. By now the sun was shining and the tall green mountains disfigured with red slashes contrasted sharply against a cloud-swept cobalt sky. At the end of the channel, we sailed into the broad expanse of Baie du Prony and headed for the far reaches where the waterway narrows into winding fjord-like fingers. On the VHF we contacted Larry, this after I thought I saw the tall mast of *Windward Passage I* projecting over one of the tall peaks in the cove. Also anchored in the same cove were our friends Peter and Kathleen on *Wild Spirit*.

Soon all three boats came into view. We anchored nearby in 30 feet, but as the chain stretched out the depth sounder showed 10 feet even though we were a good half mile from shore. Obviously, we were over a patch of coral, but it was impossible to see it, as the water was opaque green.

All our friends were gathered on *Windward Passage I* , enjoying their day's catch of oysters. Tired from our rigorous sail, we opted to put the boat to rights, have an evening drink and an early dinner on *Banshee* rather than joining the others. The following day we joined in the evening festivities, eating raw oysters, smoked oysters, oysters Rockefeller and barbecued prawns with wine.

After *Windward Passage* and *Wild Spirit* had returned to Noumea, Larry and Pat and the two of us decided to take our boats up to the top of the bay to Grande Rade. This truly picturesque spot with a waterfall is considered to be a hurricane hole. We didn't know it when we went there, but several days later, after *Hallux* had gone, the opportunity to test it occurred.

Fortunately, we had sufficient warning. The weather fax map showed a double headed low coming right onto New Caledonia. Well, we were in the best place we could be, right? Anchored in mud alongside mangroves, tucked up into the top of Prony. But, there was one factor we hadn't attended. We should have let our more anchor chain in anticipation of the blow. That afternoon a Kiwi boat came in and anchored close astern, thus hampering us from letting out more chain. We really should have said something to them, but, wanting to be polite, we said nothing. That was a mistake.

By midnight it was gusting up to 65 knots. The wind was accelerating down the steep mountains, creating considerable fetch. *Banshee* was slamming back and forth, rocking with a fury as the wind pummeled the mast and rigging. Sleep was impossible. I kept hoping it would calm down and questioned how we could possibly hold in this kind of blow. Then around 3 a.m., Joy looked out and screamed, "We're dragging and we're almost down on *Geminis*." We both bounded topside, not even taking time to put on foul weather gear. There was no time for that. It was raining so hard we could hardly see the nearby shore.

Immediately we turned on the engine and Joy tried to raise the anchor, but the wind was pushing so hard the anchor was not coming up. By now we were parallel to the Kiwi yacht. Thus far I had been able to avoid collision by using the engine to maneuver us back and forth. Finally someone had come on deck. Joy was yelling to him to fend off, and I was trying to power us away from the boat. I was succeeding, but we needed to reanchor, and I didn't know how we were going to accomplish this. Finally I said to Joy that we should try letting out more chain so we could swing by him and then set the anchor when we were astern of *Geminis*. She yelled our plan to him, but I doubt he could hear what she said over the roar.

By this time I had managed to work us a bit to windward of the other vessel. I thought if Joy could let out more chain we would just have enough room to scoot past him. The idea was that with the additional chain out --- almost 300 feet --- our anchor would set. We were moving good, but at the last minute before we cleared his stern, *Banshee* responded by turning beam to the wind. This is exactly how a boat responds when there's a lot of slack chain and the anchor has not yet caught. If we continued in this direction, our bow would come crashing down on his stern.

I shifted into reverse and then used full throttle. We were in luck. Our prop pulls us to port, initially, regardless of the position of the wheel. It was to port we needed to go. At the very last second, with only inches to spare, *Banshee* responded; miraculously our bow pulled back and away. We were clear! Now the question was: would the anchor dig in and hold us? It did. But our job was not yet finished.

We needed to set another anchor off the bow. We have a second 35- pound CQR sitting on the bow in readiness. Joy cut the line lashing it to the pulpit and, after readying everything, I powered up about 150 feet and she dropped it over. It, too, caught. Actually the two anchors were better because they dramatically decreased the mad swinging and thrashing that we had been doing with just one hook out.

The horrible night was not yet over. Two hours after we dragged, *Geminis* returned the favor. At almost 5 a.m., we saw her rapidly falling back on us. There was no one on her deck! The owners were below, probably sleeping. Joy must have yelled herself hoarse, but still no response. The tempest, now into its grand finale, saluted us with a display equaled only by Hollywood film pyrotechnics! No one could hear anything. Suddenly it came to me. Shine our bright diving torch into their cabin. If the bright light comes inside, it will surely wake them.

It did. A head came poking out the hatch, but it was an eternity before anyone came on deck. He must have been dressing! He finally came out, fully clad in foul weather gear. Somehow, incredible as it seems, he got his engine going and at the last possible moment pulled away and powered up the bay a good distance from us.

When the sun arose two hours later, the world looked washed clean. The sky had cleared and the wind had shifted. The front had passed. However, Noumea Radio was calling for strong westerly winds coming up after noon. Hearing this we postponed our departure and moved into a smaller extension of the bay, one totally protected in westerlies.

One day later we talked with Larry and Pat on the VHF. They were tucked up in a bay directly west of Ile Casy. We decided to join them, not only to see them once more before we left, but because it would bring us closer to our point of exit. As we came into their cove, it was raining hard and blowing a gale. Larry spent the afternoon rebuilding our large salmon fishing reel. On our last night in New Caledonia, we had one more gourmet feast aboard *Hallux:* Caesar salad, marble soup, and escargot with pasta. There's nothing like a full stomach and an evening of good company to prepare one for sea.

Chapter 4

VANUATU: ENCHANTED LAND

The morning of departure for Vanuatu dawned clear. Though stiff, the wind had lessened from the previous day. Because of strong tidal currents, rips and overfalls in the Havannah Passage, the *Sailing Directions* recommends transiting it at slack water. With this timetable in mind, around noon we pulled up anchor and waved to Pat and Larry as we sailed by them. Under reefed main and staysail, it took two tacks to clear the lighthouse at the end of the reef. Despite our attempts to retard our speed, the current carried us along so fast we came to Havannah Passage over an hour before slack water. Even with the wind and tide in the same direction, the overfalls and slicks were awesome enough to set my heart racing! The turbulent water was frothing and swirling, forming giant whirlpools. A short chop slapped the sea into sharp peaks. As we entered the pass, a strong northerly current grabbed us. To compensate, we steered 50 degrees high of our course and turned on the engine to combat the current.

At daybreak the following morning, we saw a shadowy line on the horizon. It was Maré Island, the southernmost of the Loyalty Islands. It projected above the horizon, resembling a gigantic lizard poised for the kill. We had planned to visit one or two of these islands on the way to Vanuatu, but Customs told us if we visited, we would have to return to Noumea afterwards for a final clearance. It would mean a round trip of around 400 miles, which we had no intention of doing.

Not going to the Loyalties meant we would miss Ovea Atoll, a group of closely connected islands and reefs that boasts pristine white beaches. Several years ago when the Kanakas (native-born people) were pressing hard for independence, Ovea became the scene of political violence. Some revolutionaries captured several French military men and imprisoned them in caves on the atoll. Later, when their demands were not met, they killed some of their captives. From various sources we heard that since then the locals have been less than friendly to whites, especially the French. Perhaps it was just as well we did not go.

As we drew closer, Maré Island took on a flat shape. Large trees, widely separated, stood gauntly above the stark landscape. Around noon, a fish hit the hook. We landed a beauty, a ten pound rainbow runner, descriptively named for the band of colors running along its body. Joy streaked it, and for dinner we enjoyed some of the fish prepared in herb butter sauce, while Jason ate his share raw. We dined in the cockpit, watching the sunset and glimpsing the last of Maré as it shrank and then disappeared altogether when night crept over the sea.

I had the sunrise watch. When the red-orange ball bobbed up, the trade winds started blowing lightly. Soon the smell of coffee, a brew of dark New Caledonian beans, filled the air along with the strains of a Bach Violin Partite. A couple of hours later, we landed a skipjack, a perfect fish for sashimi. That night's menu: sashimi, cole slaw, rice salad made from pilaf with mushrooms, green pepper, olive oil and parsley, another delicious dinner under the stars. This night was one of the most memorable at sea. While balmy trade winds pushed us over a silvery sea, we smelled the sweet scents of land from Erromango Island, which lay thirty or so miles off our starboard.

At sunset on the third day after leaving New Caledonia, we spied Pango Point on Efaté Island, Vanuatu. Good thing we got there before total darkness. The navigational light on this point is not working because of a land dispute whereby the owners will not allow the government to operate the light on their land unless the government pays the fee the owners are demanding. A good swell was running here around the point. Port Vila, the capital, lay just inside the bay, but it was dark before we could make port. Normally we wouldn't attempt coming into an unknown port at night, but Vila has very good leading lights. By keeping these lined up, we came through the narrow channel.

The radar was on, giving us a bleep just a short way in front of us. The bleep, we soon discovered, was the quarantine buoy located directly in front of downtown Vila. The twinkling lights from land were a comfort. Easing up to the buoy in a flat calm, we tied to it for the night.

Early in the morning we called port control, requesting clearance. Our yellow quarantine flag sagged limply from its halyard on the starboard spreader, for lack of wind. A young Customs officer, delivered by another cruiser, competently filled out the papers. Just as he finished, Immigration called on channel 16, saying an official was waiting for us at the quay. Perfect timing. We were just going there to land the Customs officer.

We had our first greeting from friendly Ni Vanuatu when we tied up at the quay. Ten or 15 people stood there, eager to take our line. Big smiling faces greeted us. They eagerly talked with Joy while I filled out more papers. Here we got the question, which was to become the leitmotif in Vanuatu: "Only two woman?" (There are no plurals in Bislama, the type of pidgin spoken here.) "Where your husband?" We soon learned to respond, "Boat blong two woman. No man." Everywhere this answer brought a boisterous laugh from the women and an incredulous gasp from the men. Often both men and women would respond with "True?" rolling the 'r' heavily. Spoken as a question, the inflection signified surprise.

One of the things I had dreaded about coming to Port Vila stemmed from having read Alan Lucas's cruising guide. He said we would have to tie stern to at the quay, which was completely unprotected in the prevailing southeasterly wind and swell.

As it turned out, we went alongside, not stern to. I could see there were no other yachts tied up at the quay. Through the binoculars I had seen a few tied stern to, in another part of the harbor. Not many, though, and we wondered where all the yachts were. We soon learned that many of our negative impressions, gleaned from Alan Lucas's cruising guide, *Cruising New Caledonia and Vanuatu,* were erroneous. Perhaps in the ten years since the book was published, there have been some changes, albeit only minimal. My impression is that Lucas did not care for Vanuatu and spent little time cruising in this country.

In fact, Lucas's negative press has probably been responsible for yachties simply using Vanuatu as a waypoint on their way to the Solomon

Islands. At first we had fallen into this trap, planning to spend only one month in Vanuatu, sailing rapidly up the chain of islands en route to the Solomons. Lucas's bias shows in his opening statement on Vanuatu: "I should make it clear from the word go that Vanuatu (formerly the New Hebrides) is not the cruising paradise most boatmen are advised of it being." Several paragraphs later he continues, "Why then, is it not a truly great cruising ground? Anchorages! That's the answer plain and simple." Pretty damning words. Surprisingly, almost everyone accepts his statements as gospel!

Soon after arriving in Port Vila, we abandoned our plans to pass through hurriedly and move on to the Solomon Islands. For one thing, we fell in love with Port Vila, with the mellowness and charm of the town. A small museum in Vila was a strong factor in persuading us to stay longer. This informative exhibit and a film of some of the outer islands opened our eyes to the magnificent array of cultures found in Vanuatu. Many intriguing and mysterious cultural links to an ancient past still linger. We could not pass through without pursuing some of these.

On second thought, perhaps Lucas did a great service to this country and to some cruisers. Because few yachts come here --- and those that do stick to a well traveled path --- this country has remained virgin cruising grounds. Few yachts mean friendly and helpful villagers who have not become jaded and opportunistic in their dealings with outsiders.

By reporting on our adventures and wonderful experiences in Vanuatu, may well be endangering some of the features that make it and its people such a delight. Masses of people descending upon any area of the world have the adverse effect by destroying those very qualities that people come to enjoy! So, it is with certain misgivings that I write about our wonderful experiences here

After completing formalities with Immigration, we left the quay and powered toward the six yachts tied stern to in front of a lovely open-sided palm thatched structure. This well-known establishment is the Waterfront Restaurant and Bar. It is also the headquarters for the Vanuatu Cruising Yacht Club. Directly across from the restaurant and bar, a distance of only several hundred yards, is the small, thickly wooded island of Irikiriki, home to a resort with individual palm thatch dwellings set back from a sand beach against a background of tropical trees and vines. Anchored in front of this resort were five or six boats. Scattered about the deep waterway that meanders between Vila and Irikiriki were a dozen or more moorings, most of them occupied by yachts.

Before deciding where we would stop, we wanted to power along the channel to see if anyone we knew happened to be here. Then we saw *Big Smile*, a Dutch yacht we had met several years previously in Tonga and New Zealand. Seeing us, Fred waved excitedly then dived over the side, yelling for us to follow him. He led us to an empty mooring about 50 feet from shore (it was deep right up to the shore) and dived down to retrieve the line for us. He said the mooring belonged to the diving company and they wouldn't mind if we used it. The only catch was that if very bad weather developed, we would be asked to move off for one of the company boats. During the three weeks we were there we did have to move, but the owner of the dive shop came out and personally led us to another mooring we could have for the duration. There was no charge for the mooring.

Here in this quiet spot, with crystal clear water, we could dive over the side at any time for a swim. Fresh water showers were available at the Yacht Club, and when going to town, we left our dinghy at their dock. Fresh water was handy at the yacht club and diesel fuel was available at a small resort dock next to the club. With all these amenities at hand, it wasn't long before we felt very relaxed and mellow.

Port Vila, Vanuatu's only real city, possesses a casual sophistication appropriate to its tropical setting. Even in 1990, a decade since the English and French ruled in an unusual joint administration --- referred to as a condominium government --- a hint of this binational presence still lingers. Both English-speaking and French expatriates are scattered over the islands, but the majority have settled in Vila.

Much of the environment and atmosphere mentioned by early travelers to Port Vila --- the tropical torpor, picturesque large wooden houses with encircling verandas --- have been replaced by the bustle of a modern town. Sidewalk cafes, a number of restaurants and a town full of duty free shops and tourist boutiques present an up market facade. Yet, in the center of town, along the waterfront, the traditional

Melanesian market opens just after sunrise three mornings a week. Here knots of women sit together on the ground, their wares spread before them on banana leaves. Among the foods sold are yams, kumala, taro, manioc in addition to western vegetables and many varieties of fruit. In the market are the greatest variety of bananas of every size, shape and color --- ranging from deep green to yellow and bright orange. Seashells are sold here also.

Vila is a major port and sits in the midst of fringing reefs and a seascape to rival that of any South Pacific resort. Stretching as far as the eye can see are dazzling blue and green waters. Many ports are dirty, grimy holes gasping their last breath amidst oil-clogged water, stagnating in the harbor. But not Port Vila. The harbor waters are sparkling and clear.

Vanuatu is a young country. It has only had its independence since 1980. Yet it is an old land, having been inhabited for at least three thousand years, possibly longer. Although the people are called Melanesian -- literally meaning "black islands" --- the term is misleading because the inhabitants of the Vanuatu chain are of various origins. In general, the Melanesians tend to be light brown, medium build and muscular. Most anthropologists agree that they are a mixture of Indonesians, Australian Aborigines, Papuans and Polynesians. Probably this ethnic mixture was well established by the Neolithic period.

Vanuatu comprises some 80 islands that form part of a volcanic chain stretching to New Zealand in the south, north through the Solomons and westward to the islands of New Guinea. Vanuatu is one of the most complex geological archipelagos in the South Pacific. Land formation was brought about by a succession of powerful volcanic movements alternating with periods of sedimentation. Coral platforms were raised, broken into blocks and then covered in lava and ash, thus alternating with calcerous reef formations.

Today volcanic activity and frequent minor earthquakes still occur. There are three active volcanoes: the Benbow of Ambrym, the Yasur of Tanna and the Lopevi (a solitary volcano rising out of the sea). Those of Aoba and Gaua are semi-active, belching smoke and possessing sulphur geysers and springs near their craters.

Sixty-six of the islands are populated, but most of the population live on 16 main islands. About 93 percent of the population is Melanesian, the remainder being European, Chinese and Vietnamese. Polynesians occupy two small islands, Aniwa and Futuna, and one corner of Efaté.

The social and cultural aspects of the people vary enormously from island to island and sometimes even from village to village on the same island. Their differences are quite evident linguistically. Over one hundred different languages are spoken in Vanuatu! Myths, legends, rituals, house design and many other cultural manifestations are also unique to each tribal group.

The two greatest unifying forces for these people have been Christian religion and Bislama, a form of English based pidgin. Over time Bislama has become the national language of the republic of the people who call themselves Ni Vanuatu. It is spoken by 130,000 inhabitants. Currently, however, the country is making considerable effort to teach English in the schools. Ironically, before the development of Bislama, most of the tribal peoples of Vanuatu could not communicate with each other. Statistically, there is a distinct Melanesian language for every 1200 people in Vanuatu, resulting in this country having one of the highest language densities in the world. Without Bislama, communications would be very limited in Vanuatu.

Culturally, Christianity also has provided many unifying features, primarily by lending a common frame of reference. Still, religion has not yet eroded all the traditional beliefs or customs of these diverse peoples. Even now, in the interior of some islands, custom villages exist where people have not embraced any form of Christian religion. As long as the people remain tied to their land, engaged in subsistence farming --- as most of them are --- many old customs will persist.

No doubt change will come faster in the next generation because of the rise in literacy and as a result of expanding contact with people from industrialized countries. Today, all children may attend school, paid for by the government, for six years. The only exceptions are repeaters. A child may repeat a class once, but if she or he fails the grade a second time, that child is dropped from school.

Higher education (meaning schooling beyond the sixth grade) is still the prerogative of only about 20 percent of the Ni Vanuatu who extend their education from one to four years beyond the initial six years. Only a very few, the quickest and best students, advance to an additional two years and perhaps a college education. Secondary schooling is paid for in part by the parents, and for most of them it is a hardship. One of the problems facing this country, one that is common to most of the Pacific island nations, is what happens to educated young people. A few coveted jobs number too few to accommodate all the young people wishing to escape village life. The sad fact is that most of them, having been intellectually stimulated and having been seduced by modern technology, will have no place to go but back to their villages to grow yams. During our travels in Vanuatu we met many young people suffering this very plight. They would do almost anything to get to Australia or New Zealand to find a job. But, they have no *vatu*, the local currency, and no way to raise enough for transportation, even if they could get a work permit for one of these countries.

The development of Bislama is a fascinating phenomenon. It evolved in Vanuatu during the nineteenth century when South Sea Islanders began to work on whaling ships and European-owned plantations. It arose as a kind of jargon used between the islanders and the Europeans. Of course, it also enabled the natives to converse with each other. Still, Bislama is not as provincial as it may appear. Variations of pidgin occur in the Solomons and Papua New Guinea. Some words used in Bislama are common also in the West Indies and some of the southern states of America. For example, the pidgin word "pikinini" (child) appears to have been coined by the West Indian black slaves who took the word from Portuguese or Spanish pequeno "little". In southern black dialect in America the word "pickaninny" was still commonly used into the 1940s. I often heard it as a child. Today, in the States, it has deteriorated into a pejorative term, considered to be a racial slur, especially if used by a white speaker. So for me, a native southerner, it was difficult to use this word in Vanuatu, even though it has no negative connotation there.

The cadence of spoken Bislama is Melanesian rather than English. Basically grammar and syntax are also Melanesian. Most of the vocabulary is English derived, but French, Spanish and German have also contributed.

One of the best indicators as to how much of its tradition a society has retained can be determined by the vitality of its oral tradition. Unfortunately, after people become literate, gradually they tend to forget their oral tradition --- their histories, stories and myths. As recently as three decades ago, the oral tradition was still fairly healthy in Vanuatu as the following account illustrates. Some people of Efaté tell of the arrival of new immigrants before a cataclysmic volcanic disruption that exploded a large island and left behind many small islands south of Tongoa. The natural disaster that created the Shepherd Islands occurred around A. D. 1400!

High-ranking peoples who introduced a matrilineal form of social organization governed these newcomers, who settled on Efaté, Makura, and Tongoa before the eruption. One of the important leaders of this group was named Roy Mata. When he died he was buried on Retoka, a small island off the coast of Efaté. Many of his followers sacrificed themselves voluntarily, and others were forcibly murdered and buried.

These events, retained in the oral tradition, were actually substantiated in 1967 when French archaeologist José Garanger began excavating this area after informants took him there. The man thought to be Roy Mata was on his back in a pit, which also contained a male and female side by side, and a single male --- each body positioned beside Roy Mata --- and across the feet of these four parallel bodies was a young girl. Between Mata's legs was a bundled secondary burial, perhaps a predeceased wife of his. Around this main gravesite, marked by two slabs of stone and large marine shells, were shallower burials of 35 individuals, 22 of whom were men and women buried together. The attitudes of the female bodies --- clutching the male by the neck or arm and clenched fingers and toes --- suggests the women may have been buried alive, while the males had been relaxed by previously drinking kava, *Piper methysticum*, a locally used narcotic. The presence of pig bones and cannibalized human bones suggests important rites occurred at the time of the mass burial. Moreover, the carbon dating of the burial site in A.D. 1265, plus or minus 140 years supports the oral tradition.

Sacrificial burial of this kind in Oceania, according to Peter Bellwood in *Man's Conquest of the Pacific*, is quite rare. A similar burial of ten bodies with a chief in Uvea (Wallis Island) has been found and one from Chuukk (Truk) in the Carolines. More common was the burial of one or more of a chief's wives with him when he died.

Our three weeks in Vila passed all too quickly while we reprovisioned, picked up and sent mail and made phone calls to the States. Pleasant as it was here, it was time to move on. Just as we were ready to depart, Joy developed a sore throat. When it didn't improve after three days, she went to see a western trained Ni Vanuatu doctor. He prescribed an antibiotic and several days later, with her condition much improved, we were off to explore as much of Vanuatu as time would permit.

Little did we know we would soon be entering a world still very much bound to the past, a world where money has not yet become the primary concern. For the Ni Vanuatu, life's necessities and pleasures are important adjuncts to friendship and sharing. Still very natural and spontaneous, these people readily show their feelings on their faces.

In many respects, we were not at all prepared for such openness, coming from a culture where we are taught restraint of emotions. An encounter with people still unspoiled by our occidental preoccupation with "success" and acquisition was novel and at first almost disarming. More than anything to date, our encounter with these people would open our eyes to the value of a society which operates on the basic assumption of communal good and responsibility to the community rather than an emphasis on individualism. To be sure we were not discovering paradise or a world devoid of problems, but a world whose problems primarily are the direct result of their contact with European "civilization".

Chapter 5

ISLAND HOPPING

About 9 p. m., we arrived and anchored along with *Ahimsa*, *Belle de Jour* and *Shiraz*, three Aussie boats we'd met in Port Vila. The four of us had been anchored off a sandy headland in Havannah Harbour, a large bay at the northern end of Efaté. After Peter from *Belle de Jour* had picked up a weather report that a front would be coming through that night, he suggested we move to the top end of the bay between Moso Island and Efaté, where it would be safe. With his radar, he led the way through the dark; and with our radar on, we brought up the rear. Having just come from this area, these people knew where to anchor.

As if to warn us of the impending storm, heat lightning frequently lit up the sky. We dropped our anchor near the mouth of a broad river while lightning flashes revealed a shoreline choked with jungle.

Now in bed, we could hear the rumble of distant thunder gradually creeping closer. Later fine rain sprinkling on my face through the open hatch woke me. Thunder boomed nearby, and then I heard the sound of rain, becoming louder and louder until the cloudburst was upon us, pelting down with a deafening roar. With the hatches and ports closed the boat's interior soon felt like a Swedish steam bath.

Morning broke sultry and cloudy. Soon, a steady procession of outrigger canoes paddled by. We were greeted with smiles and hand waves. Unknowingly, we had anchored in the middle of the "freeway". The islanders were coming from their village on Mose, going to their gardens on Efaté! Some people stopped for a friendly chat and several asked if we wanted any fresh fruit or vegetables. Most of the visitors told us that their gardens supplied the vendors in Vila.

From 7:30 to 10:30, the canoes came so steadily we could not do any chores. Although many locals inquired if we wanted anything, we only asked Rowland, a muscular young man who was the first to ask us, to bring us some green tomatoes and bananas. Finally we were alone, really alone because the other three yachts had said goodbye and sailed away, and the commuter traffic had ceased. We had two major jobs to do that day: patch the dinghy where a previous repair on the keel had broken away and restitch some seams on the mainsail.

True to his word, around four o'clock, Rowland returned with lovely tomatoes, a stalk of green bananas, a pawpaw, some limes and a very large pumpkin. In exchange he took a shirt we offered, preferring it to money.

Rowland wanted to talk. Several times he said with wonderment, "You two sailed from America to Vanuatu! No man!" His eyes gleamed and his smile spread over his face. Joy told him about the Australian woman, Kay Cottee, who had sailed around the world alone. But this information did not faze him. He looked at us steadily and said, "You are here. From America to Vanuatu!" We were real to him. He could see us, talk to us.

When Rowland asked us if we would show him how we came into the harbor at night, we knew word had traveled. That morning we had explained to eight men who came aboard how the radar worked. Every time visitors saw the radar screen, they thought it was a T.V. and asked if we had video. Apparently they didn't know about radar. We showed them how it worked. With childlike amazement and wonder, their faces lit up when they saw the land mass pictured on the screen just as it was all around them. We explained how we had used radar to come into Port Vila at night and also to come into their island at night to anchor. Rowland was captivated by the radar. It was magic.

During our four-day stay at Havannah Harbour, the villagers stopped by in increasing number. We began to realize that they enjoyed not only the exchange of gifts with yachties but really desired contact with people outside their environment. Certainly they are interested in various kinds of equipment found on yachts, but additionally a visit affords them a vicarious escape from their regular routine.

Much of their curiosity is aroused by the shear amount of possessions we have. Not just a yacht that is worth an absolute fortune to them, but all the additional things --- books, dishes, pots and pans, cassettes, tools, radios, sails, dinghy, outboard, refrigerator, clothing --- are simply staggering to them because they have so few belongings. Most of them have no more than a few changes of clothing and several pots for cooking. Their most valued and essential possessions are a bush knife and their outrigger canoes. At about age 10, boys learn how to build their own canoes. Theirs are smaller, but exactly the same design and construction as the adult models. Even the lashings on most canoes are made from coconut fiber because store bought rope is expensive. By contrast, girls are taught gardening, cooking, childcare, washing and weaving, thus perpetuating gender divisional tasks.

Amazingly, these people are still almost entirely self-sufficient today. When the missionaries introduced them to Christianity, they insisted the native people replace their simple clothing made from plant fiber, leaves and feathers with western clothing. In place of a penis wrapper for the men, grass skirts and bare tops for the women, they now dress in "Mother Hubbard" dresses, introduced by the earliest missionaries, and shirts and long pants or shorts for the men. However, it is now acceptable for the men to dress comfortably in shorts and go shirtless, but for modesty's sake, women must keep their bodies totally covered in this very humid and hot climate. Not only is the clothing required for the women physically uncomfortable and impractical, it represents a major expense for people living outside a money economy.

The only other commodities that require a lot of money are materials for housing. In Moso village, most of the houses are made of cinder block with corrugated iron roofs. Such houses are considered prestigious, and people who own one are very proud of it. The traditional buildings of palm and woven bamboo, which are both more attractive and cooler, are being rapidly abandoned. There are two advantages of these modern structures over the traditional. The iron roofs provide water catchment, and the cinder blocks better withstand cyclones, although if the corrugated roofs come loose during high winds, they could be very hazardous.

But, as with clothing, buying materials to build houses requires much time and effort and years of saving. Add to this the expense of paying for their children's education, and it becomes evident that the Ni Vanuatu must struggle very hard to keep up.

Our second day at Havannah Harbour began at 5 a.m. Rowland had told us we could buy bread from a truck if we landed at a nearby cove and then walked a short distance up to the road. The truck would come around 6:30.

At the cove landing we found a cement block copra-drying shed. Old discarded coconut husks lay heaped up on one side of the shed. As soon as we got ashore, a cloud of flies encircled us and clung like fog. Following a path through the bush up to a pot-marked dirt road, we arrived just as the truck was coming around the bend. The driver pulled to the side and handed out the two loaves we requested. All the way back to the boat we swatted flies.

We had just completed an early morning breakfast of sausage, toast and jam when the villagers appeared in their outriggers. Some we had met the previous day called out "good morning" in passing. Others stopped by to chat. Much to our dismay, we noticed that with the villagers came hundreds of flies. They were surrounded. Even more disconcerting, when they left, many of the flies stayed behind.

While Joy was washing dishes, I went outside on deck to do a watercolor. To my amazement I had an audience. Several canoes hovered and watched in silence with curious expressions. Probably they had never seen anyone painting a picture!

This morning we learned that many of the callers came to see Jason. When they saw him their eyes widened in surprise. As they explained, he was the biggest "puskat" they had ever seen! In fact, most of them seemed afraid of him. Village cats are quite small, usually half starved and mangy, pathetic creatures because they are never fed. Dogs unfortunately don't fare much better even though they are used to hunt pigs and herd goats. We wanted to say, "If you would feed your cats, they too would grow large."

Some of our visitors said we could wash clothes up the river in fresh water and also take a bath there. Around ten a.m. we set out to do a little exploring up river in the dinghy and check out the laundry situation. The river mouth was very wide but quickly narrowed and became shallow. Lush mangroves lined both side of the stream, their waxy green leaves flashing in the sun. It was a falling tide, and the further upstream we progressed, the shallower it got. Soon we lifted up the outboard and started paddling over a sparse trickle of water that snaked through the jungle. Low overhanging foliage shaded us as we penetrated deeper into the wilderness.

Just as we came to a bend in the stream, we heard voices and saw a group of women and children gathered at the top of a bluff in front of a house. Some of the women squatted while they scrubbed clothes on a board. Others were hanging out clothes. They saw us immediately and greeted us excitedly as they came down to the shore.

Most of them spoke little English, but with our limited Bislama and their limited English we could converse well enough. They welcomed us to do our laundry there at the spring and bathe. It took a while to comprehend something they were trying to tell us. Finally we grasped that they were telling us to come back around one o'clock when the tide would be out and the salt water not intruding on the spring water.

When we returned at low tide, we had to walk the dinghy up parts of the river. At the laundry area, what they had been trying to explain became immediately evident. The salt water had receded a considerable distance from shore. Someone had placed a barrier of rocks extending in a semicircle about 15 feet from the shore. This barricade effectively walled up the fresh water bubbling up from the sandy bottom. A healthy stream of cool water literally gushed out from a rocky ledge by the shore.

Here we encountered heaven and hell at the same time. The pesky flies left us alone only momentarily when we threw the cool water over each other. Seconds later the flies alighted again, hundreds of them. We bathed and washed our laundry in record time, eager to flee the flies as quickly as possible.

A 17-year-old young woman, Edna, sat on a rock and chatted with us as we hastily washed and rinsed our clothes. She was very well spoken and talked extensively about Vanuatu's educational system.

As we finished, she asked if she and her family could visit us on our yacht. We said they were welcome and invited them for later in the afternoon. Of course, when a villager says family you have no idea how many people might show up. It could be three or fifteen! We should not have worried. Edna and her family never came.

Later in the afternoon, Andrew, a well-spoken 20-year-old we had met the previous day, came with two younger boys, ages 14 and 15. They wanted to visit and play our guitar. Their selections consisted mostly of religious songs sung in Bislama. They were only too happy to teach us some Bislama by translating the texts for us.

We were surprised to learn that Andrew was Edna's brother. I asked him if she was coming. He said yes. When I asked him why she hadn't come with him, he had no answer. I suspected it was the same behavior we have encountered elsewhere: brothers do not want to take their sisters with them. As we soon learned, Ni Vanuatu women do not enjoy any more liberty than their South Pacific island sisters. Basically, women are very isolated from the outside world and from visitors who arrive in yachts. Men and boys have outriggers and are very eager to come out and meet strangers. Women and girls do not generally own outriggers. Occasionally, they may borrow one from a brother, father or husband, but most of the time women and girls remain in the village. On rare occasions, when they accompany men in the canoe, the men do all the talking; the women, it seems, are expected to remain silent. We soon learned if we wanted to become acquainted with women or girls, we would have to go to the village and make a concerted effort to speak with them. Even then, some of them are so embarrassed and shy they do little more than giggle when spoken to. Whenever we found women to converse with, they were interesting and interested.

Andrew and Edna, both exceptionally bright, conveyed their yearning for a different kind of life, a way to escape the village. Andrew mentioned dejectedly that there were very few jobs in Vila, where all the young people want to go. He would like very much to go to Australia but he can't afford it.

Moso village is one of the more prosperous villages in Vanuatu because of the steady income from produce sold in Port Vila. Their relative prosperity is also evident in that most of the houses in their village are cinder block, rather than traditional thatch. Even so, these people are still very poor. Out of an entire village of about 250 people, only two owned outboards and a commercially built western type speedboat. The others have an outrigger, a dugout lashed to a second small solid piece of wood, which functions to stabilize the canoe. In common with other Ni Vanuatu, they still live a subsistent life. As Andrew said, "Everyone has a garden. If you want to eat, you must have a garden."

In contrast to the Fijians, the Ni Vanuatu spend more time working in their gardens and grow a much larger variety of plants. But, unlike the Fijians, the Ni Vanuatu appear to have no concept of the need for birth control. Many of the people I talked with had ten or more siblings. The birth rate continues to climb even though life expectancy hovers around an average age of 60 for men and 62 for women. When asked the cause of most deaths in Vanuatu, one doctor responded without hesitation, infection.

Medical care is not readily available to people living outside Port Vila or Luganville on Espiritu Santo although there are some clinics and even some minimal care facilities called hospitals in a few villages. But doctors and medications are too expensive for most Ni Vanuatu. In our experience villagers do not seek medical attention unless the situation becomes desperate. In part this may be because they cannot afford the expense, but it might also be because they are not well enough informed about health care. As we learned in Western Samoa where many people become blind because of cataracts, Samoans expect to become blind somewhere between 50 and 60 years of age! These same people do not know that eye surgery can remove cataracts and restore vision. Generally speaking, this type of treatment is not routinely available in Samoa. Acceptance of one's living conditions usually corresponds closely to one's expectation. Lice, scabies and various other parasites are endemic in Vanuatu, therefore expected and accepted.

Talking to Andrew and Edna made us very aware of a great irony. Joy and I and other cruisers we've met want to escape the clutches of the consumer world and many of its dire consequences --- depletion of natural resources, pollution on a massive scale and obsession with possessions. Andrew and Edna see only the glamour of such items as television, videos, ghetto blasters, cars, flashy clothing, and refrigerators. But is their view really any different from that of Europeans and Americans who idealize the life of Pacific islanders, seeing them as living in paradise? It doesn't take much time in the typical Pacific island village to recognize the fallacy of the paradise concept!

Initially, it seemed a very positive example for us to sail into these villages, showing women and men that women can do things categorically reserved for men. Yet on another level, I found myself becoming impatient with the roles that each of us is cast into not by choice but by virtue of our different backgrounds. I am a product of my society just as they are of theirs. I don't fit in. I am always something of an oddity in their eyes. I object strongly to the role of women in their society, and therefore I consider it important that they see the two of us as being independent women. But also I didn't want to relate to people exclusively as a role model.

However, the problem was even more complex than this. For them, both men and women, there was another anomaly about two women on a boat. Their society is communally oriented. No one does anything alone. Consequently they continually asked us where is your family, your mother, father, sisters, brothers, children?

After several days of doing our chores, having done laundry and repaired the mainsail, it was time to say goodbye to Moso village. We left at 9:30 a.m. Light winds astern pushed the main out until the boom was perpendicular to the beam. We ghosted along slowly to the pass between Lelepa and Moso. It wasn't until we cleared the pass that a true sailing wind came up. It was northerly, naturally, just where we wanted to go. Over the next hour the wind increased until by 1:00 p.m., it was blowing 20 knots. We reefed the main, and then clipped along at five to six knots, tacking back and forth between the northern end of Efaté and the steep rugged face of Ngouna Island whose eastern end was our destination.

Around 4 p.m., we arrived at our anchorage. Immediately two outriggers with three teenage boys paddled out. They were surprised to find two women with a cat. Such a big cat, too! We were tired and had sails and lines to put away, so we did not invite them aboard, but talked with them as we worked. When finished, we said we had to go below to rest. They were polite and left, if reluctantly.

As soon as the sun was up the next morning, we set out for Kakoula Island across the bay. It is uninhabited and we hoped for some time to ourselves away from villagers. The island is totally surrounded by reef, which at one end actually connects it to Efaté.

Amongst the reef we found a nice sandy spot to drop our anchor, almost a mile off the island. Solid reef prevented us from coming closer.

After lunch we dinghied ashore. Immediately, three outriggers approached us. Teenagers on two asked if they could see our yacht. We said they could, but asked them not to go aboard. After checking out *Banshee,* they departed. A very old man in the third outrigger paddled ashore to talk with us. Speaking Bislama, he rattled it off so fast we could barely understand him. His single tooth jolting up and down, projected like a stalactite in a cavern. The lack of teeth also made his speech mostly incoherent. He was concerned about the two outriggers going over to our boat. We assured him it was okay for them to look, as long as they didn't go aboard.

Shortly after we left the old man, we saw an outrigger under sail, darting toward shore a little distance from us. It looked so graceful and swift. Since it was the only sailing outrigger we had seen, we were eager to meet this person and learn about his boat. We caught up to him soon after he landed. He had come ashore to tighten the lashings on his rigging. Sammy Shim, a very well spoken, educated man, was returning to his home on Emau, a very small island a few miles east of us. He had recently returned from Hawaii where he'd been teaching linguists about the language of his island. For years he has been sailing his outrigger, making canvas sails and rigging with line. He said most people no longer know how to rig or sail a canoe. He invited us to come visit his island. Because he was sailing into the wind, he had to hurry along. It would take him most of the day to get home.

After returning to *Banshee,* we donned swimsuits, masks and fins and swam toward shore to view some of the spectacular reef. Unlike so many reefs in Vanuatu, it was not damaged. Suddenly, both of us realized how strong the tide was. Initially, we hadn't given it a thought, but now it was pulling us toward the pass! With determined swimming, we finally made it back to *Banshee,* exhausted. Without the fins it would never have been possible to swim against the current.

Some time after dark we heard indistinct, loud noises from shore. It sounded like an angry crowd, arguing and shouting, but all we could see was a fire on the beach. Perhaps some of the islanders were having a cookout. But it didn't sound like a pleasurable gathering. I listened for female voices in the din but could not detect any. Joy and I thought perhaps the men were having a *kava* (a native narcotic drink made from the pepper plant, *Piper methysticum*) party. With some concern, we wondered whether they might decide to come visit us. The prospect was unsettling. We certainly hoped not because their behavior, if they were indulging in a narcotic, might be unpredictable.

We were tired and had to get up at 4 a.m. to get an early start for our next anchorage on Epi Island. Even though the commotion had not abated, we decided at 9 o'clock to go to bed. But the melee on shore was not conducive to sleep. Our nerves were on edge. The shouting had risen in volume, and suddenly, I recognized some of the words: "Hallelujah, Oh Jesus, sweet Jesus!" Most of the noise was a jumble, but these words were repeated over and over. Maybe it's a religious meeting I said to Joy. I also wondered if they had fallen into a religious trance, a kind of self-induced religious ecstasy. Were they speaking in tongues? Still it was unnerving, not knowing what was happening, if or when it would end. Joy thought it might be a funeral. Perhaps she was right. Some of the voices were screeches and wails not unlike a ceremonial lamentation.

Finally it changed. A few people began singing in harmony, and gradually the screaming and shouting subsided as more voices joined in singing the hymn. After a time the singing faded away and all was quiet.

Adult booby with chick at Chesterfield Reefs

Jeannine at *Banshee's* helm

Jason with Joy and Jeannine in sailing dinghy

Jason

John Wayne and sons in Solomons with skulls

One way sailing canoe in Vanuatu

Nan Madol structure in Pohnpei

School children in Ontong Java

Stilt house in Lilisiana in the Solomons

Ngatik sailors racing native canoe

Ngatik elder sailing with young boy

Chapter 6

GROUNDING ON DICK REEF

The alarm jolted me awake from a dream about grapefruit that grows on vines. It was 4 a.m., still dark. But for the enticing aroma of coffee, I would easily have slipped back into my dream.

Fifteen minutes later, sipping coffee on deck, I saw a sky filled with stars and a radiant half moon. Glancing over the side, I saw what I first thought were clouds reflected on the water. But something didn't seem right. There were no clouds overhead. I was seeing patches of coral in the dark in 20 feet of water! That's how clear the water was off Kakoula Island.

Jason, eager to be fed, was chasing madly about the deck, his tail puffed out, his back arched. Feeling groggy, we were still fumbling around and momentarily ignored his meows for food. Normally, for a one-day passage, we don't arise so early. Today was different. Our destination, Ringdove Bay at the north end of Epi Island, was 56 miles away. To make it in daylight we would need a good 12 to 14 hours. With only 13 hours of daylight available, we had to start early.

Already the eastern portion of the sky glowed rosy. The dark peaks of Ngouna and Pele pierced the pale sky. Behind us our little island was absolutely silent, innocent of the previous night's raucous activities. Efaté and Moso, off to our left, closed the other side of the circle. Distant volcanic cones towered above the nearby islands, their shadowy shapes standing out against the first gray light.

By five after five we had finished a light breakfast and were raising the anchor. Windless, the sea stretched out flat, an endless silky gray splashed with pastels. The sharp putt-putt of the diesel cracked crisply, echoing across the silent panorama. Soon the sun flooded the horizon, setting the sea aflame. The air became searing. Still there was no wind apart from that which we created as the prop pushed us over the glassy surface. The day turned hotter as the sun climbed. For some relief we put up an awning.

About midway in the passage lies Cook Reef, also called Pula Iwa. To avoid it we altered course slightly to the west, planning to miss it by a couple of miles. By 2 p.m., the first light breeze stirred, bringing some relief from the blazing sun. By now, nearing the reef, we kept a sharp lookout, either standing on top of the overturned dinghy or stepping up onto the pinrails. We had been plotting fixes from the satnav, but the best insurance is to watch. By the time the satnav works out the position, it tells where you were approximately half an hour earlier. Another problem with satnav navigation when close to land is that some charts are inaccurate by several miles. This is hardly surprising since many charts in this area are based on surveys made several hundred years ago. A still further consideration is the current, which often is quite irregular and unpredictable around islands and reefs. Considering all these discrepancies, keeping a good watch is prudent, especially when there are known hazards.

Gradually the breeze filled in off the quarter. Eagerly, we hoisted the main and shut down the engine. Finally we saw a slight ruffle of surf about one and a half miles off. It was the only indication of Cook Reef, and we were well clear of it.

After a couple of hours, the fickle wind lightened. To keep up our speed, we turned on the engine again. It was already mid-afternoon and we were concerned we had not made better time toward our destination. After about three o'clock, the sun is too low to see coral. Another nagging thing was that we had no adequate chart of Epi Island. We were using a small-scale chart, which contained most of the southern islands of Vanuatu. We dug out the *U.S. Sailing Directions* to read a description of Ringdove Bay. There are other anchorages on Epi before Ringdove Bay, but all are open to the prevailing southeasterlies. We had also been told that Ringdove was the first secure anchorage on this side of Epi.

Before we knew it, it was five o'clock. According to our reckoning, we were abeam Ringdove Bay, but we were uncertain how we should approach the anchorage. From the chart it appeared there was a fringing reef on the south side of the bay that projected out, perhaps as far as a half mile offshore. But on this chart the location of the reef was inexact. By now, the sun was too low to detect depths by the color of the water. Even a slight breeze would cause the water to break on coral, but there was no breeze, only the gentlest swell.

At last, we thought we had the lay of the land. With my eye on the depth sounder, I turned shoreward. We dropped the main and Joy went on deck to furl the sail. In a split second, the depth sounder went from 48 to 24 feet! Then Joy was frantically screaming at me, "We're over reef! Turn around." I put the wheel hard over to port and about 10 seconds later we smashed hard and stopped dead! I put the engine in reverse, hoping to back off. We didn't move. Looking over the side, I saw we were perched on a massive coral head, a beautiful live one. The depth sounder read 19 feet! One side of the boat was on the reef and the other was over deep water. The keel and the rudder were grinding against the abrasive surface, making a horrific noise each time the gentle swell lifted us up and down. Suddenly there was the slightest breeze and I suggested we hoist the sail again. Perhaps that extra slight heel with the wind pressure against the sail along with our weight would carry us off the reef. It worked! But 30 seconds later we went right back on. This time even worse!

It was eerie. We could see every single detail of the coral below, including the fish, but we couldn't see anything under the water five feet in any direction away from us. It was getting darker. We had only about 30 minutes of daylight left.

We were about three-quarters of a mile offshore, roughly right in front of the cove where we wanted to go. What we didn't know then was that we were on a detached reef. Except for that little fish-hook-shaped reef, the water was clear up to the onshore fringing reef! If I had turned right instead of left, we wouldn't have gone on the reef.

On shore were some buildings. We could hear voices and see children playing on the beach. One of us had to go ashore in search of someone who knew the reef and one of us had to stay aboard, otherwise it would be abandonment and anyone could claim the boat for salvage! We agreed Joy would go ashore and I would stay with the boat. By the time we had offloaded the dinghy, put the outboard on, loaded in the oars and got reef walkers and a flashlight for Joy, it was almost dark. I wished her well and she was off. All this time *Banshee* banged and crunched as the keel bumped along the coral. The mast and rigging shook with such horrendous sound and motion I thought they would collapse. Each time the rudder hit the reef, the wheel spun and shuddered. All this in calm conditions! What would it be like in heavy surf with wind? A piercing cold dread struck me in my stomach. Periodically, I checked below to see if we were taking on water. So far, so good.

Jason knew something was wrong. He was frantically charging around and looking over the sides into the water. I tried to calm him, but he jumped out of my arms and continued to chase around in a frenzy. Suddenly, I realized the main was still up and a breeze was beginning to blow off the land. I had better get it down so the wind wouldn't push us harder onto the coral.

It seemed an eternity had passed since Joy left. What was she doing, and would she find anyone who knew the reef and could help us find clear water? I continued to circle the decks, peering down, trying to determine if we were moving, hoping desperately that we would float free and drift into a clear area where I could anchor.

Just as the last light faded, I saw our dinghy returning. In it were three figures. Preceding them was an outrigger. Soon everyone was alongside, scrambling aboard. Apia, a large and handsome bearded man who came with Joy, was a natural leader. Daniel, the other young man who came with Joy, seemed quiet and competent. Ruben, the man in the outrigger, was to prove very talented in maneuvering his canoe.

By now it was totally dark. Fortunately, we had two very bright flashlights, one of which we had just purchased prior to leaving Port Vila. The first step, Joy and I decided, was to attach our stern anchor, a Danforth 22 pounder, to our main halyard. The men pointed to the direction clear of the reef. It was about 20 feet away where the depth dropped to about 30 feet. Daniel and Ruben got into our dinghy, and we loaded the anchor, chain and line down to them. It was attached to the main halyard. In a rapid and loud voice, Apia shouted directions to the two men as they rowed toward clear water and then lowered the anchor. Apia spoke English very well, but when speaking to his companions, he used their language.

With the anchor dropped, we began winching in on the main halyard, which tipped the boat over, and almost immediately we floated free. We then tried to retrieve our anchor and halyard, but could not raise the anchor. We pulled the halyard free of its sheave at the masthead, tied another line onto it and attached a buoy so it would float and we could return later to recover it. The only problem now was propelling the boat. With so much line in the water we didn't dare run the engine for fear of fouling the prop. Joy thought she could tow *Banshee* with the dinghy. She tried, but it pushed us back on the reef!

Apia asked if we had a "long stick". We got him a very long boat hook. He smiled and said: "We do it the local way." Ruben jumped into his canoe and after tying a line to our bow he began paddling. Apia pushed off with the boat hook, and voilá, we floated free again. Relieved and excited, we all cheered. Apia grabbed one dinghy oar and Daniel the other. Standing at the bow, each paddled on his side of the boat. Joy focused her flashlight on one side and I held mine on the other. Both men paddled rapidly while Apia called out directions to Ruben who continued towing us with his outrigger. It was most amazing, with two oars and an outrigger they were moving 11 ton *Banshee*! The men were proud and delighted their method was working. Only when we were well clear of the reef and the line did we fire up the diesel. I steered, as Apia directed, until we got to an area where they said we could anchor.

In 35 feet, we anchored. And let out a great sigh. What a relief to be free and apparently without any major damage. We had not been taking on water, the mast and rigging were intact and the rudder steered fine. Apia sat down in the cockpit with a very satisfied smile and said, "Black men do good job!" "Yes," we both agreed enthusiastically. It was now three hours since we had gone up on the reef. Joy and I were emotionally drained, but ready to celebrate with a beer. We offered beer to the three men. Apia and Ruben readily accepted, but Daniel doesn't drink anything alcoholic. He had a coke. Relaxing for the first time since our three helpers had come aboard, we could finally talk with them. Apia told us he is the government treasurer, working for

Public Works at Ringdove Bay. Also government employees, Daniel is in charge of sanitation and Ruben is a driver.

We were too tired to get out the gifts we wanted to offer them, so we asked if they could return the next morning. Only Apia thought he would not be able to return the next day as he had other obligations.

Once they had gone, Joy and I had some toast and cheese, then we crashed. While unwinding, Joy told me about her experience on shore. The first few women she had tried to talk with just giggled and left. Feeling a bit dejected, Joy finally found a bright young woman, Lume Mawa, who spoke English and immediately comprehended the problem and what Joy needed. Joy found it a bit humorous as Lume looked around at various men, saying, "He's useless," or "He can't help," etc., until at last she spotted Apia and said, "That's the one you want." Right she was!

Neither of us slept very well. We were too hyped up. Filled with anticipation, Joy woke before sunrise. Her movements about the boat woke me, and soon, I got up too. We had a light breakfast, picked up some of the disarray from the previous night and then began gathering equipment for Joy's dive. In addition we pumped up the Avon dinghy, which Joy would use as her diving platform.

Sometime during these preparations a young man paddled up in his canoe. We spoke to him, but other than his good morning, he said nothing. Joy mentioned something to him about the three guys who'd helped us the previous night and that we were going out to get the anchor. He smiled but said nothing. Somehow I was sure he knew what had happened because nothing is a secret in a village, especially an event as exciting as this one. Later, we learned his name was Tom and that he spoke French. He could understand most of what we said, but he didn't speak English.

We continued our preparations. A little later I looked up and saw Tom was paddling out toward our buoy. We left in our dinghy towing the Avon behind with all the diving gear. Tom was waiting for us at the buoy and by sign language he expressed his willingness to help. We pulled on the line. It was still firmly attached to the bottom. We could only pull in about 20 feet into the dinghy. I continued to hold it while Joy got in the Avon to suit up. Then she realized we had come away without her regulator. Since I was holding onto the line, Tom volunteered to take Joy back to *Banshee* on his outrigger.

Even though it was still early --- about 6:30 --- there was a bit of wind. The sea was breaking on the reef and a strong surge rocked the dinghy, sometimes a bit more boisterously than I liked. I tried to take up more line and found that though it was difficult, I could. Slowly, I continued working it up until I got about half of the wire portion of the halyard into the dinghy. I didn't want to put too much tension on it, fearing it might be pulled taut against a piece of coral and become damaged. I eased out the wire completely so that once more I was holding onto rope.

I looked up and was startled to see another outrigger coming toward me. It was Daniel. When he came beside me, I told him what had happened. Soon Tom and Joy returned. Joy eased herself into the water and Tom helped her put on her tank. Then she dove down. Without a word, Daniel slid into the water with a mask and snorkel. He swam over to the side of my dinghy where the line was. As Joy freed line from the bottom, he handed it up to me, making my job ever so much easier. I was very impressed with the quiet, unassuming way these two men helped.

This experience is quite amazing when you look at the situation from their perspective. In their society, women rarely even paddle an outrigger. No woman dives with a tank or a snorkel! It's men who engage in this type of physical activity and exertion. Yet, somehow they seemed to accept what we did, even though it shocked them.

Within ten to fifteen minutes, the anchor was up, sitting securely in the dinghy. We invited the two men to come back and have morning coffee with us. They eagerly accepted. We gave Daniel a large hank of line, which seemed to please him immensely, as he smiled from ear to ear. We also gave them fishhooks, swivels and steel leader and t-shirts. They drank coffee with milk and sugar with us and ate cookies, all the time smiling and talking, at first shyly and then more confidently. For them, coffee is a special treat. Even though it is grown in Vanuatu, the villagers usually drink tea, which is not as expensive. Undoubtedly, much of the pleasure for these young men was that their family and friends knew they had spent time on the yacht after helping two American women.

Daniel and Tom told us they were going a few miles up the coast to Lamen Bay that afternoon for a soccer match. Since we had planned to go there, we asked if they would like to go with us and bring some of their friends. This suggestion seemed to please them very much. Off they went to get their soccer shoes, shirts and their friends. Before we could leave, we needed to dive down and check for damage under the waterline and go aloft and rerun the halyard.

Imagine our surprise when they returned with the entire soccer team! The 'Black Rustas'! The first team members began arriving singly or in pairs while Joy was at the top of the mast rerunning the halyard. They were brought out in canoes by a younger brother or a friend. With them came an assortment of gifts for us --- coconuts, papayas, yams and bananas. Some guys had no transportation, so Joy made several trips ashore to bring them out in our dinghy. Few of them had ever been on a yacht. When we left, there was so much whistling and hollering as they waved to friends and relatives on shore, you would have thought we were bound for a long voyage. It was only a one hour trip.

Once we got underway, they entertained by playing our guitar and singing. By turns one or two chatted with us, each expressing his surprise at seeing two women who had sailed from America to Vanuatu. Everyone wanted to know how long it took. We explained we had been gone for over four years but had stopped at many islands along the way. Many were curious about our ages. Everywhere we've gone, the local people seemed very surprised when we told them Joy was in her late forties, and I in my early fifties. They couldn't believe it because they think one is old at that age, and they didn't think we looked old enough to be grandmothers!

The Black Rustas were kind and mannerly. All were careful of equipment, helpful and polite. There was no bravado or aggressiveness. Probably, it was a very strange experience for them. Certainly they would never associate with Ni Vanuatu women as casually as they did with us. Most likely it was their first experience relating to women who knew more about something technical than they. Although many of them are sea wise, they are totally ignorant about sailing or handling yachts. In their culture most activities are divided according to gender with very little overlapping of roles.

Unfortunately, Joy and I were too tired to attend the soccer match in Lamen Bay. More rested, we went ashore the next day, a Sunday. Lamen Bay is a small village, but an important one because it has a high school going up to fourth form (equivalent to eighth grade). It is one of several high schools in Vanuatu. Students come from islands throughout the country and live in quarters on the campus. No one is pampered. Students assist in the preparation of meals and grow their own food. They are also responsible for their own laundry. Parents must pay 10,000 vatu per term, about $100 U.S. For most Ni Vanuatu this sum represents a lot of money. The government supplements the cost of running the school, paying teachers' salaries and various other expenses. The 142 students attending this school are only a small percentage of high school students in the country. Others attend schools located on other islands, some being more prestigious than others.

Lamen Bay, an attractive, unpretentious village, mixes traditional thatch and modern concrete buildings. It is clean and neat and --- the biggest bonus --- free from flies. (Daniel must be doing a good job as sanitation inspector.) A coral road curves around gently rolling land, covered with green grass, gigantic trees and numerous flowering plants around the school grounds. The road runs parallel to the shore and then turns inland where it is swallowed up by thick jungle.

On our walk through the village, we encountered many women and girls who shyly smiled and nodded in response to our greetings, but not one of them stopped us or would say anything beyond a simple hello. As we passed by the school, we noticed four teenage boys huddled together examining a kite. In a few moments two of them, each with a string in hand, ran a short distance trying to get the kite airborne. They made several tries but each time the kite shot up about six feet, then nose-dived.

A tall, slender young man and a shorter fellow observed our interest and walked toward us. The tall lad was Jonathan; he was 17. The shorter fellow was Malcolm. We inquired about the problems with the kite. Two younger boys, the kite fliers, now came over. Joy immediately spotted three problems: there was a tear in one seam, the kite had no curve or bow in it and the tail was much too short. Under her directions the two younger boys ran to the school for a needle, thread and something to cut with.

69

After ten minutes or so Joy had the kite put together properly, but still lacking was an adequate tail. Several attempts to launch the kite proved it needed a longer tail. All this time Jonathan was talking with us. His questions, mostly, were what we had been asked by everyone we saw: where are you from; how long did it take to come from America to Vanuatu; just the two of you; you have no husband; how many brothers and sisters; how old are you? From Jonathan came two new questions: do you smoke and do you play sports?

Later, when we were back on the boat, many people came in canoes all asking the same questions over and over. This behavior struck us as strange. We knew the news of our reef rescue and everyone up and down the coast of Epi and on offlying Lamen Island knew of the transport of the soccer team. (As is true in so many areas of Vanuatu, the village is located on the small island and the gardens are on the main island.) Since we were anchored in the bay, in full view of both the village on Epi and the one on Lamen Island, there was no mistaking who we were. There was no doubt that everyone knew that we were two women "alone". Still, they had to come out and see and hear for themselves! The steady stream of canoes and the repetitive questions, especially two: only two of you, no husband, were beginning to make us feel as if we had landed from outer space. We hoped our presence would testify that women are capable of doing anything they want to do. But in fact it appeared we were a rare and idle curiosity, perhaps akin to the snake woman at a carnival rather than mature, adult women charting our own destinies.

How do you get the right message across? One way is to make people aware of their own contradictions. For instance, three very bright 13-year-old boys from the school came by in their canoe to chat. When they expressed surprise that Joy and I did not have husbands, I followed up with: "Do you think that different?" Their response: "Oh yes, very different." I came back with, "Does everyone in your village get married?" "No. Some die and have not married." "Well," I said, "then we are not really different because we're not married, are we?" They had to concede that our difference was something apart from not being married.

One of the most interesting conversations I had with anyone in Vanuatu occurred that Sunday ashore. It was with George, a French-speaking teacher at the school. We had been talking about this and that, and then George mentioned he was from Paama Island, a smaller island near Epi. Paama Island is reputed for excessive shark attacks. Many Ni Vanuatu had mentioned it to us. Since George was the first resident of Paama that I had met, I could not resist asking if the sharks on Paama were as bad as their reputation.

His response was very involved, combining folk tradition and Christian belief. He is an educated man who speaks fluent French and English, as well as his native language and Bislama. Even so, he still accepts some of the superstitious views of his own island. The shark attacks, he said, are believed by many (himself included) to be the result of witchcraft. When I asked him to clarify witchcraft, he explained that there are followers of witchcraft on the island. For whatever reason, they may decide to kill someone, which they do by making a slash across the abdomen or perhaps by cutting off a leg. In both cases, the person bleeds to death and is, in fact, dead. However, the witch can revive such people and make them whole again. They do this by putting banana leaves or some other vegetable material over the damaged area and then working their magic. In such cases the revived person is compelled by magical means to go to the sea the next day. It is arranged by the witch that the victim will be attacked and killed by a shark. But, George emphasized, it is not really a shark that kills. Always the person attacked is near the shore and the shark never bothers others who are swimming in the area. Also, when recovered, the victim is always dead. In true shark attacks, a person may survive. Real shark attacks occur infrequently, whereas the witchcraft shark attacks happen at least once a year, sometimes more.

Now comes the Christian veneer or rationalization. These shark attacks, said George, result from witchcraft. This power is derived from Satan. The witch actually turns himself into a shark. "We believe Satan exists and is an evil force." The cessation of shark attacks, however, is attributed to the powers of a traditional practitioner. According to George, there have been no shark attacks for the last two years because a man from another island, a *kleva* (traditional healer) came and expelled or made the witches powerless.

****

We stayed almost a week in Lamen Bay. On our second day we became acquainted with John, the headmaster, his wife, who is also a teacher at the school, and Patricia Lowe, a Kiwi teaching science. One morning Joy and I jointly taught with Patricia. After class, a student asked me if I would give him a music lesson. We borrowed a battery operated electronic keyboard from the headmaster and had a music lesson on the beach in the shade of a large tree. A curious audience of interested students sat quietly taking it all in.

Just before leaving Lamen Bay we discovered we had lost almost a full tank of diesel. We found and fixed the leak in one of the fuel filters. With only 12 and a half gallons of diesel in our jugs, we were reluctant to leave for Port Sandwich where fuel may or may not be available. John said diesel was available at a small store at the far end of the village, if we were prepared to pay extortionary prices! We had only American dollars on hand. Twice a week someone came to act as a banker for the nearby villages. Unfortunately, the banker couldn't change dollars for *vatu*, as he didn't know the exchange rate. Fortunately, a New Zealander overheard the difficulty and he was willing to exchange the money, based on what Joy knew the exchange rate to have been when we were in Vila. His kindness and trust saved the day for us.

Other than Sammy Shim's sailing canoe, we had seen none in Vanuatu. Why, we wondered, would this important aspect of their culture have almost entirely disappeared? Sailing, after all, is physically easier than paddling. On the flip side of the coin, building a sailing canoe is complex. Building a paddling canoe takes less time and skill, the biggest part being cleaving the wood out of the log, which is done with an axe and adz. The outrigger itself, much smaller than the hull, is a simply shaped solid piece of wood. Branches and saplings are used to lash the hull and outrigger together. No high technology here.

In contrast, the sailing canoe requires considerable knowledge of materials and engineering. Building a mast, staying it, making all the moving parts, the boom, the rigging and the sails, takes much time and thought. If everything is not done correctly, the vessel will not sail and will not withstand the pressures of wind and sea. In short, sailing canoes represent advanced technology, while the dugout is primitive.

So, we were greatly amused one day in Lamen Bay to see an outrigger approaching that, from the distance, looked like a palm tree floating upright on the water! As the outrigger came closer, we could see that a number of palm fronds had been cut off, loosely tied together then splayed out like a fan. This makeshift sail could only operate downwind as there was no way to maneuver the sail for any other position to the wind. Within half an hour, we saw other Lamen Islanders returning home from their gardens under variations of the palm frond sail. One or two had whole trees and some used branches from other trees. The people called them "one-way sailing canoes"!

Chapter 7

MALEKULA

The first hint that Malekula, a high island of 2,024 square kilometers with just over 11,000 inhabitants, was still tribal in its interior came from Curt Hoffman, the curator of the Vila Cultural Museum. A heavily wooded and mountainous terrain have acted as a tough barrier against intrusion by outsiders, especially zealous missionaries. Hoffman indicated that cannibalism occurred here as recently as the 1960s. Four or five hundred Small Nambas, living in the interior of southern Malekula, have managed to keep their traditional society mostly intact. Their name comes from the word denoting a small penis wrapper (*namba*) made of banana leaf. These peoples are known for their colorful masks and body paint worn during funeral rites.

The Big Nambas, living on a plateau on the northwestern part of Malekula, once known as very fierce tribesmen, have mostly moved to coastal villages. Some of their rites and customs continue today. Not surprisingly, many of their customs concern women. For example, they still pay a bride price in yams and pigs, and when a wife is highly valued, her two front teeth are knocked out! Occasionally one of these tribesmen, clad only in a penis sheath, may be seen downtown on the streets of Luganville on the island of Espiritu Santo.

The pig plays an important role in the tribal rites of the Nambas. The upper canines are removed from young animals to allow the tusks to grow around in a full circle. Sometimes these tusks force their way up through the jawbone and continue growing. To signify their progress through the hierarchy of male fraternities, men once wore pig-tusk bracelets. One sign indicating just how far the old society has eroded is that the pig tusk is now one of the most sought after souvenirs. All of the boutiques in Port Vila display many highly polished tusks --- some gold tipped --- selling for astronomical prices. Also available, albeit in lesser numbers, are the entire jaws with the tusk that has grown through the jawbone.

In villages, where tribal societies are still intact, men and women live in separate areas, each in their own huts. Male religious activities remain secret and completely taboo to women; even the paths to the men's huts are forbidden to women. The Nambas are noted for their elaborately carved headdresses made out of tree fern, fashioned with bulging eyes and curved pig's tusk. These masks are gaudily painted. Perhaps one of the most curious customs is that of death masks made from vegetable matter pasted over a human skull. Formerly, they played a part in fertility rites enacted to increase the yield of yams.

We wanted to sail to Malekula, but we ruled out trying to go inland in search of the Small Nambas. For a considerable sum, it is possible to locate a guide to take you inland. But this situation struck us as a bit phony, trekking in for one day to stare and take photos. (In normal circumstances I am reluctant to take my camera into a village the first time I go, and I never take pictures without permission.) In our circumstances such a journey, requiring several days packing inland, would mean leaving *Banshee* unattended, a prospect not to our liking because of the possibility of bad weather, vandalism or theft, although we had no reason to fear the latter as everywhere the Ni Vanuatu had been absolutely honest and courteous.

Even if our ventures only brought us into contact with Christianized Ni Vanuatu we would still be learning about a society that differed from others we have visited. Early on, we learned that when dealing with missionized peoples, it is easy but erroneous to assume that they have abandoned all their tribal ways. Because so many aspects of their material culture have been lost, it may be natural to suppose they have also forsaken their emotional ties and spiritual values. However, frequently this is not the case. Even though they have embraced the basic tenets of the Christian faith, these have been intertwined with their traditional beliefs and superstitions and colored by their own worldview. While we may see these two systems of belief as mutually exclusive, they do not. Surprisingly, in many ways their lifestyle has not changed much for hundreds of years. Their ways of gardening, fishing and cooking food and their basic diet have remained unaltered. Unchanged also are their ideas of kinship, values tied in with communal living, respect for ancestors and concepts of disease etiology and treatment. Essentially, they are still living a Stone Age existence. It's as if time stood still. Their surroundings, the physical environment, have not change. What Western intruders have often failed to grasp is that cultural identity, developed over centuries, is not easily displaced.

One of the great misconceptions held by missionaries and colonial governments was their conviction that people could exchange their habits and values as easily as they could replace their traditional dress with Western clothing. All over the Pacific today it is possible to see first hand the folly and the failure of such misguided policy. America, Britain, Spain, Portugal, the Netherlands and France have all tried to establish an infrastructure, to recreate in their colonies their own forms of government. Over and over we have repeated these same patterns, common to our paternalistic period of instruction and education. We pump in millions to subsidize a replica, almost as if believing it is possible to clone something as amorphous, rich, vital and essential as society. We deceive ourselves into thinking we are helping them learn to be like us. But what happens is really quite different. Each of these island nations has one or maybe two towns that attain some semblance of urbanization. These towns have banks, stores, electricity, telephones, cars and politicians and civil servants. Such places assume the outward appearance of their models, but the underlying essence, the cultural resonance, is lacking. If you come here as a tourist, you see there are certain amenities, a reasonable number of restaurants and some sights and tourists attractions. You probably would not detect that what you are seeing is but a facade without the viscera. But leave these little contrived Meccas, go down the coast a few miles to the villages and to the villages on outlying islands where there are no telephones, no cars, no banks, no restaurants, no hotels. Most of the population is young and there are many infants and children. There are few old people.

Old in these places is in the 50s. There are coconut trees, taro, yams, breadfruit trees, pigs, dogs, and fish in the lagoons. The ancestors are buried beside their dwellings, still very much a part of those in the present. Time appears not to be separated into the present, the past and the future. Sunshine, rain, and the pounding of the surf on the reef are endless, ageless, eternal. That's it. That's paradise.

If we scratch a little deeper, we perceive some other interesting things. What happens to all the millions being pumped in? Is it all concentrated in the little fabricated "cities"? Who is getting educated? Has it really changed the lives of those living in the villages? They are still eating the same diet with occasional canned foods thrown in when the monthly or bimonthly supply ship comes. They may drink coke and beer, when and if they have the money, smoke Western cigarettes, but they also still make their own traditional kava and smoke local stick tobacco rolling it in newspapers or banana leaves. They may have ghetto blasters and outboards. But when the outboards, ghetto blasters, cars and generators quit working there is no one to repair them.

How many of the citizens of that country speak English or French? What is the educational level of the people? Who is going to school? Boys and girls? Mostly boys? What do they learn in school? What industries are being created? What jobs are there for young people receiving an education? What kind of health care is available? How many young people are getting the kind of education needed to become doctors, dentists, lawyers, teachers, or engineers? Just what are the effects of outside influence on these peoples? Too often they have become independent countries in name only, but sadly, not independent and self-actuating. And, basically, the fault lies not with them but with the industrialized nations that have used and abused them, usually for their own ends and justifications.

Schools are teaching reading, writing, history, arithmetic, science, a curriculum modeled after our own. Why not teach them practical skills such as improved agricultural methods, repairing equipment, cars, outboards and generators, things that relate to their everyday life? We have taken people from a third world country, from an essential Stone Age culture, and expected them to make the quantum leap into the twenty-first century! Peace Corps was meant to help teach some practical skills, such as sanitation, agricultural methods; but Peace

Corps is a mere trickle. The only other practical teaching institutions I have seen are a few Catholic training centers here and there, most of which educate only boys. Girls and women are given almost no training and no skills to cope with the "new" society. As has become abundantly clear, until women are educated, societies essentially do not change significantly.

Looking on the other side of the coin, one can wonder about the lack of development from within the culture. One of the questions Joy and I have frequently discussed is why the Pacific Island peoples have not made technological advances beyond a Stone Age level. Is it because they live in "primitive affluence", meaning they do not need to work very hard to feed themselves because with minimal effort they have an abundance of food? Is climate a factor? It is hard to be ambitious in tropical heat and humidity. If you have your basic needs at hand, easily fulfilled, then there is not cause or reason to struggle. What is apparent is that people develop the technology necessary for their own survival. With regard to the Pacific peoples, technological innovation appears to have concerned primarily methods of fishing and certainly canoe building and navigation for times when it became necessary because of overpopulation for some island families to migrate to another island. If we were to compare the types of seagoing crafts constructed by the islanders with the ocean going ships of their Western conquers, we would have to concede that overall the Polynesian, Melanesian and Micronesian vessels were much more stable and suited to these waters than the terrible top heavy rat-infested deathtraps the European explorers sailed.

The reef breaking off Port Sandwich was an inspiring sight. Circling wide, we headed up the broad bay where dense forest slopes down to the water's edge. Leaving the marker of a midchannel reef to port, we gradually rounded a conspicuous sandspit and tucked into a serene cove behind Planters Point. We anchored about 150 feet offshore, south of a jetty that fronted a large building with a tin roof. A few people on shore casually gazed at us, but no one came paddling out, much to our relief. We just wanted to relax.

The town of Lamap was several miles away, but crowing roosters and sleek cows along the shore indicated nearby habitation. Amazingly, there were no other yachts here. Since meeting with our friends in Havannah Harbour, we had seen no other cruisers. Having seen so few Europeans since leaving Vila, we were beginning to feel like the only whites in the world, a strange sensation when you are accustomed to being in the majority!

That afternoon *Anna Rosa*, a 60-ton, 97 year old Norwegian ketch came in and anchored close by. We had met Bart, her Canadian skipper, in Vila and also in Havannah Harbour where he brought a charter group in for one night. The following morning we joined their crew and passengers on shore for a fish barbecue.

On our second day in Port Sandwich the American yacht *Quickstep* with Eva and Jim and their five-month old son, whom we'd also met in Vila, anchored near us. Later, *Incantation*, another American yacht, arrived. Having the company of other cruisers was something we had come to expect, but after leaving Port Sandwich we saw not one cruising boat until Santo, although we did have another meeting with *Anna Rosa*.

The first night at Port Sandwich I came down with some mysterious tropical ailment (probably malaria, even though I was taking prophylaxis). The illness left made me weak and feverish for several days. For this reason, I didn't go ashore with the others when they went to Lamap to buy fresh bread and pick up a few things. Several hours after they had gone, heavy black clouds rolled over the mountains surrounding the bay. Rapidly the gloom closed in as the rain, a solid silvery veil, swept up the bay. Despite my feverishness, I scurried around setting up to catch rainwater, our only fresh water source for drinking, bathing and washing clothes.

The rain blotted out the shore, pelting the water so fiercely it was smoking. Within 30 minutes, I filled a five-gallon jug from our cockpit awning and within an hour all our water tanks and jugs were filled to the brim. For almost three hours, it rained torrents. Before it stopped, the wind started howling. Watching all three yachts thrashing and tugging at their anchors, I became concerned that we and they might drag. During the strongest part of the blow, I turned the engine on so I could power into the wind and keep us from going aground if the anchor broke loose. Fortunately we all held. By myself I would have been unable to do anything for the others.

Midmorning on October 3, we left Port Sandwich in a flat calm, making our way a few miles south to the Maskelynes, a group of islands off the southern tip of Malekula. We entered by way of the northeast pass and found to our amazement a well-marked channel. Inside the basically landlocked area the water was calm except during certain phases of the tide when the current boiled vigorously. We followed the curving channel around to the west side of Sakau Island. Here we anchored near a sandspit in front of the ruins of what had been a coconut plantation. The coconut palms still thrive, but the house and outbuildings of the European owner have long been abandoned.

It took some nosing around to find clear sandy bottom for anchoring amidst the reef. As we were setting the anchor, a young man paddled up and greeted us in English.

As we were almost ready to go ashore to explore the island, an old man and his wife stopped by. They neither spoke nor understood English, but Joy's attempts at Bislama served us well. The only problem is, if you speak a few words of Bislama, most people automatically assume you know it well, so they chatter so fast you can't follow. So eager was the old man to see the boat that he craned his neck at such odd angles, trying to see inside, I thought he would injure himself or fall into the water. He, as is true of many locals, had absolutely no compunction about looking into the ports. On occasion we have even been sitting inside and looked up to see a face framed in the port with big eyes staring at us! But to give them their due, other locals are overly polite. When approaching the boat, they never call out or come alongside until invited or spoken to. To get our attention they whistle softly.

Not wishing to be delayed any longer, we got into our dinghy and headed for shore, having told the old man and woman what we were doing. To our surprise they followed. Ashore the woman disappeared, but the old man dogged our heels, generally being a nuisance. We beach combed, talked with the man and with another old couple who came ashore to speak with us.

About half an hour later the old man's wife returned, a large smile on her face. She was carrying a stick on which she'd strung about a dozen mud crabs. She had bound their legs with strips of palm so they couldn't escape, but their massive fierce claws, which were capable of breaking a finger or crushing a hand, were free. Her husband carefully handed us two crabs, gifts, he said. We were delighted. Two crabs would not be enough for dinner. Could we possibly have more? They came back to the boat and gave us four more. We dug into our bag of clothing, carried expressly for this purpose, and found a shirt for him and a skirt for her. They went off extremely pleased with their gifts while we were extremely pleased with ours.

Again we were anchored in the middle of the freeway, so to speak. During morning and afternoon "rush hour" dozens of canoes glided to and fro from village to garden, each on different islands. Many friendly folk stopped by, offering vegetables and fruits or asking what we might like so they could bring it on the homeward journey. In return we gave clothing -- mainly t-shirts --- fishing gear, matches, tobacco, soap, seeds, simple but useful things. More than once, when we were below, we heard voices calling out, "Good night, *Banshee*!"

On the second afternoon, a very attractive young couple with their two children stopped by. Speaking limited English, the man introduced himself and his family. He was Roveth, one of three chiefs from Avok Island. He asked if we knew Vincent on *Ahimsa*? Yes, we replied, Vincent is our friend. Roveth said Vincent was his very good friend who had invited them to a barbecue and had given nice clothes to everyone in his family.

Roveth invited us to come visit his village, adding that he had many gifts for us when we came. We assured him we had planned to come because it was a good anchorage. Roveth and his family were returning to their village from Lamap where they had gone to watch a soccer match. In his outrigger Roveth had paddled there and back, as did a number of villagers. One way it's over five miles! They think nothing of taking their fragile canoes out into the ocean and traveling long distances in settled weather.

About an hour after we anchored in the bay near Avok Island Roveth came for a visit, bringing his three-year old son and mangoes and fresh corn. We talked for a long while. Before leaving Roveth invited us to his village on Sunday to attend church and a big feast afterwards. If we came early, his wife would show us how to make *laplap*, a specialty of Vanuatu. We assured him we would be there. He told us to come around 7 a.m., as the service began at 8.

As Saturday was a very stormy day, we had fears we would not be able to go to the village. But Sunday dawned clear. Joy and I dressed in wraparound skirts, our usual attire when going to a village, climbed into the dinghy and were off. The distance to the village was about a mile, much of it over reef. Because it was low tide, we proceeded slowly and cautiously. Still a good distance from the village, the water became so shallow it was necessary to get out and pull the dinghy behind us. Walking over reef in a pair of thongs is not my idea of a pleasant pastime. I was apprehensive about either stepping on something poisonous that would sting me or cutting my feet on coral! Of course our skirts were an encumbrance, as they had to be held up with one hand while the other hand was towing the dinghy.

Being early morning, the breeze had not come up to disperse the smoke from village fires. The bluish haze clung to small palm thatch huts that appeared to sprout from the ground. The pungent smoke was saturated with all kinds of village odors. Chickens pecked and scratched at the dirt. Proud roosters, their iridescent feathers shining, their bright red combs and wattles shaking, stretched out their necks to add to the crowing resounding from the hillsides. The children playing along the edge of the water were the first to greet us with gleeful smiles, giggling and yelling, their round, brown eyes sparkling. Standing outside their dwellings, preparing food or talking, adults waved and smiled at us. Carefully we stepped on the slippery, muddy bottom strewn with an assortment of debris. A group of children rushed out into the water to help pull our dinghy onshore. Soon Roveth appeared, looking as though he had just got up. He said perhaps we would like to go to Sunday school. It was starting soon.

His daughter led us to the nearby church, an open sided tin roof structure. Inside benches lined both sides with an aisle down the center. Some children were already seated, the boys on the left, the girls on the right. In the front of the church a man was writing and drawing on a blackboard. His material related to the Trinity. The children were singing, boisterously, in voices so loud and shrill it hurt my ears, but they were singing in perfect harmony. Once a song was finished, some child would start another and after one or two notes the entire group burst into song.

Finally the man turned around and when the current song was over, he spoke to them in Bislama. The older children, who were seated behind the younger ones, were busily writing in their exercise books as the teacher spoke. From the drawings and understanding some of his talk, we could follow his lesson. How boring for the children (and for us as well!). Instead of Bible stories, which children enjoy, the teacher was talking about theology, aspects of the Trinity! Despite the irrelevance of his material to these children, they were perfectly behaved. There was no giggling, no talking. The faces of the little ones looked perfectly blank --- understandably --- and the older ones were totally immersed in their note taking.

It was a great relief when at last I could escape this deadly drone of dismal theology. How much more interesting to walk about the village observing the preparations for the midday feast and conversing with villagers. As we approached one gathering where women sat in a circle on the ground preparing yams, a very young child began to cry and hid behind its mother, intermittently peeking out to stare at us while sobbing shrilly and gasping between sobs. Obviously, it was frightened of our white faces, as we were no doubt the first they had seen. Older children, from five to ten years old, also found us fascinating. They hesitantly approached and cautiously reached out to touch us, perhaps to determine if our skin felt any different or if the white wiped off. Teenagers gathered around to talk with us and ask questions. Most of them spoke passable English. It is taught in school. After walking through the village, we returned to the beach again. Teenagers and some younger children mobbed us wherever we went. By Roveth's house we stood watching and talking with a couple of women making coconut cream to be used for the *laplap*. They were seated on the ground with the pan containing heaps of grated coconut on the ground before them.

Every now and then a canoe filled with people from another village arrived. Friends and relatives came down to the beach to meet and greet them. There was much animated talking and laughter. Then a sailing outrigger with three men tacked up to the beach. They anchored in knee-deep water and walked ashore. After greeting them we expressed surprise and delight at seeing a sailing canoe. One lean man the color of ebony grinned broadly and in perfect English enthusiastically invited us to look at his canoe. He had even made his sail out of canvas, he said, pointing with pride to a fine looking sail. We asked him why more people didn't have sailing canoes. He responded it was difficult to get the proper material to make sails, but also most men don't know how to construct a sailing canoe or how to sail it.

Repeated ringing of a bell announced the beginning of the church service. People dressed in their Sunday best --- men in clean shirts and long pants, women in brightly colored Mother Hubbard dresses trimmed in lace --- barefooted or wearing thongs, walked energetically into the primitive church. Before we entered the church, Roveth handed us a hymnal. There were no musical notes only words, all in Bislama. The men sat together on the left, the women on the right. Rich harmony rang through the air, rising up to blend with shafts of sunlight lightly touching the rustling palm fronds.

The pastor, a stocky man, wore his nicely pressed suit, shirt and tie with a flair. In a sonorous voice, he preached his sermon in Bislama then began one by one the baptism of about 20 infants. The parents with their children were seated at the front of the church. Most of the mothers wore white dresses, but most infants were decked out in colorful clothes. Without exception, every infant squirmed and cried, some more vehemently than others, when placed in the pastor's arms or when his wet finger traced the cross over their faces. Throughout the ceremony, the congregation stifled their giggles as each infant protested. Single mothers were the last ones to be called forward with their babies. Was this treatment intended as non-verbal disapproval of becoming pregnant before marriage, something that is rigorously discouraged in present-day Ni Vanuatu society? This introduced attitude is absolutely foreign to a culture where children were always loved and accepted.

At the end of the service, the pastor asked the parents of the baptized children to exit first. He followed them down the aisle and when opposite us, asked us to exit with him. The parents with their children were lined up outside and we shook hands with each one then got into line ourselves. Thus, as everyone exited, they came down the line shaking hands and then joined the line at the end. In this fashion we got to say a personal greeting and shake hands with everyone who had attended church. The handshakes and greetings were quite individual as were the facial expressions that accompanied them. Some people spoke out and others were shy and hesitant, some squeezed hard and others were limp. At the conclusion of this ceremony, the pastor came to us and introduced himself as Willie Able. During our conversation, we told him about the men on Epi who helped us off the reef. He said Apia was his brother-in-law!

After church the crowd adjourned to the community hall, a long grass hut. Roveth escorted us inside where the entire earthen floor was spread with banana leaves on which sat probably 40 or 50 *laplaps*. Although there were many kinds and varieties, they are all made the same way. Perhaps the best way to describe a *laplap* is to say it resembles a pizza. It is a large circular dish with an assortment of items on it; it is also colorful. Instead of crust, the base is made of mashed tapioca spread out thick, much as a pizza crust would be. Now comes the variation. The next layer may be pumpkin, the next island cabbage, crab, fish, yams, or anything. Coconut cream, made by grating the coconut and squeezing it with a small amount of water, is then liberally spread over the top. The entire thing is tightly wrapped in banana leaves and placed on very hot rocks and left to bake for an hour or so. It was absolutely delicious, but very starchy.

Men and boys were seated on the ground all around the *laplaps*, but there were no women or girls. Periodically, women came in and carried off large pieces that they took outside to share with their girl children. We were invited to sit down and eat right there with the males. As honored guests, they gave us special dispensation, allowing us to eat with the men.

There were no utensils and no plates. The procedure is to pull off a piece with your hands and eat it. Both of us were a bit squeamish about the lack of sanitation, but at this point, the only choice was to join them, be gracious and enjoy the experience.

Once we finished eating, Roveth came over to us and said, "You go have story with women." So out we went, first washing our hands in the sea, as was the custom, then we sauntered over to a group of women and girls seated on mats in the shade. Most of the women were very shy and hesitant to talk even if they knew English. Joy tired Bislama, but the shy ones remained shy. One, though, spoke English quite proficiently and she readily talked with us. She was especially interested that we sail a boat and said that she and three women came together in an outrigger. "We can paddle," she said with animated eyes. Later, at the end of the day, at our invitation they stopped by our boat on their way home for a chat. We presented them with little gifts and took their picture, or tried to. The camera chose that moment, after one picture, to stop functioning.

After lunch we returned to church for a very long session. It included not only a sermon but also a lengthy report on a Presbyterian conference the pastor had just attended in Port Vila and served as a sort of town hall meeting where issues pertinent to the village and to the country were discussed. If we had been fluent in Bislama, no doubt the interactions and topics would have been fascinating. Most of the time, unfortunately, we couldn't follow the discussions. One topic we could follow. The pastor reported that some people wanted to start a business brewing beer. He was opposed to it because he said the women would not want their husbands drinking beer. Of course, imported beer is available in Vanuatu, so it was not really clear what the difference would be, perhaps cheaper and more readily available, if brewed locally

Several days later one young man from Avok brought us some shells. We noticed one of his hands was tied up in a dirty old rag. From the way he favored this hand it was obvious it really pained him. Several days previously he had slipped with a knife and made a deep gash between his first two fingers. We had him unwrap it and saw it was badly infected. To make matters worse he had tied the two fingers together and the rag was filthy. We washed his wound with soap and water then with Betadine. Finally Joy spread antibiotic ointment over it and wrapped his hand with a sterile bandage. We gave him spare ointment and bandages and instructed him how to care for his hand. When we saw him a few days later, the infection was gone and the hand healing nicely.

Both Roveth and his son had a very bad skin problem affecting the entire abdomen of the child and Roveth's arms, chest and abdomen. Roveth asked us for medicine for his son, saying the child had ringworm. We had nothing to treat the condition and advised him to take the child to the hospital at Lamap. We suspected the child and his father had very bad cases of scabies, not ringworm. Roveth and his son had both been to Lamap on the day we met them, attending the soccer game, not visiting the hospital. We stressed that the boy needed to see a doctor as soon as possible, but Roveth was in no hurry and had no concept that disease could become quite serious, if not treated. Typically, Roveth wanted help right at hand, but did not want to make the effort to seek help.

Scabies and head lice are endemic among villagers because standards of personal cleanliness and sanitation are not very high and both are highly communicable diseases. In this situation, the entire village should be treated, otherwise people will quickly become reinfected. Unfortunately, many villagers tend to view Western medicine as a quick cure. They want to pop a pill and have the ailment go away rather than bother with repeated medications that may be required to combat diseases caused and spread by poor hygiene.

With a little effort and not too much money the Ni Vanuatu government could provide programs to teach villages proper hygiene. "Barefoot doctors", for example, could travel from village to village, treating people for the most common health problems, and they could be trained to recognize symptoms of tuberculosis, measles and other infectious diseases still common among South Pacific islanders. An immunization program would be the preferred method to eradicate these devastating diseases.

As we noticed, Avok Village has created a potential health hazard. Both the latrines and the pigpens are situated on the hillside just above the village. All of these contaminants leach down to the water table and to the village below. Another bad practice is that they wash their dishes in the seawater at the shore, the same place where they throw their rubbish.

One day before we left, three teenage boys dropped by in the morning. They were generally bored and looking for a diversion. What did they want to do, we asked? They replied that they had been out fishing on the reef.

"Let's have a picnic," they suggested.

"A picnic," I exclaimed, surprised they knew the word.

"We don't want to fish. That is no fun. A picnic with lots of food would be fun."

Obviously, they had done this before. Some cruiser (Vincent?) had invited them to a picnic. We didn't have time to put together a picnic then, as we were doing a project on the boat and wanted to finish it so we could move on the next day to Ambrym Island. Then Joy came up with a brilliant idea: they could collect some "lobster water" (their name for fresh water shrimp living in the creeks and rivers). If they brought us enough for dinner we would give each of them a t-shirt. They were ecstatic and enthusiastically paddled away, racing each other to the creek on their outriggers. They were gone for hours and we began to think maybe they had changed their minds. About four hours later, three triumphant faces appeared and they gleefully produced a package wrapped up in banana leaves. We opened it up and found almost half a bucketful of shrimps! "Wow, you boys really got a lot of lobster water! You've been working very hard. Thank you very much." They were so proud and couldn't stop smiling, seeing how pleased we were. Joy brought up three t-shirts and three happy boys took them and waved goodbye.

We couldn't believe it when they returned later, with more shrimp! Again, great big smiles. This time we brought out fish hooks, swivels and weights. You would have thought we were giving them gold. Everyone was happy now and after a bit of small talk they left again, this time returning to their village.

Chapter 8

AMBRYM AND BEYOND

On our approach to Ambrym --- Benbow, an active volcano --- cast an ethereal vapor over the island. We anchored at Craig Cove, which was located between a mission and a village and, for the moment was free of volcanic fallout. Evidence of past volcanic activity lay everywhere. When snorkeling, we found underwater lava flows that had left the bottom uneven. Much of the shore was heaped with craggy black formations, which lent an unearthly appearance to the landscape.

For the first time we did not have a constant stream of visitors at this anchorage, possibly because the gardens were located in the village. A few visitors stopped by and one, Raoul, came at least twice a day to chat. He tended the small store on shore directly in front of the anchorage and generously let us bring our laundry ashore to wash at his tap. Raoul was definitely attracted to us, although we did not know whether his attraction also had some undercurrent of sexual interest. But his behavior was always decorous and he was also gentle and helpful. When we came ashore with the laundry, he came down to help us bring the dinghy on shore. He also came down again to help us launch it. Raoul always asked many questions. Unfortunately, our discussions were somewhat hampered by his lack of English and our limited fluency in Bislama.

One day he asked me how much *Banshee* cost. He just couldn't believe that two women could afford to buy a boat. He had already asked if we "borrowed" the vessel. Frequently locals asked us how much the boat cost, but I was never sure how to answer this question. I think a dollar amount would be meaningless to them. Whether I said $10,000 of $100,000, the amount would be a fortune to them. So, I tried to answer Raoul in a way that might be comprehensible. I said Joy and I had worked for about 25 years before we could afford to buy a boat and sail across the ocean.

Raoul's expression was completely incredulous. He asked, "How many years *blong* you?"

"Fifty-one," I responded.

"*Tu mas*," (very many) he replied.

"How many years *blong* you?" I asked.

He said he was 25. Then, for about the third time Raoul asked me, "Why you no marry?"

"I have *tu mas* I do. Go to school, teach, travel by boat! You married, Raoul?"

"No."

"Why not?"

He paused, searching for words, "*Tu mas* expensive!"

"A nice man like you, Raoul, you should marry!"

I asked Raoul if he liked his job at the store. He made a big face and said no. What would he like to do? He said, "make money, but no way to make money". I said to him if I lived in Vanuatu and I wanted to make money I would sell enough copra to buy a cow, let her have a calf and more calves until I had cows to sell. Raoul had never thought of it. He had no capitalistic inclinations and no entrepreneurial spirit.

The second day we were in Craig Cove an old rust bucket supply ship came in and anchored nearby. Joy and I decided we'd like to go aboard to have a look. On deck they were transporting livestock --- two young calves and a goat were munching on leaves and branches. In pens right beside them were two pigs and some chickens. As soon as we came alongside we were invited aboard. We tied *Nessie* to the ship. Two men at the stern grabbed our arms and pulled us aboard.

Immediately we met Tom, the engineer, a very well spoken Ni Vanuatu who offered to take us on a guided tour of the ship. She is a Russian built fishing boat bought from the Solomons and rebuilt as a cargo boat. At Craig Cove they were loading on copra. Twenty-four and soft-spoken, Tom told us a bit about himself. From a small village near Port Vila, he went through the sixth form (most unusual for a Ni Vanuatu) and then on to more years of study and apprenticeship as a diesel mechanic. There are few diesel mechanics in Vanuatu, he said. Tom likes his job because the ship is constantly picking up and delivering cargo to all the islands of Vanuatu. In this way, he learns about navigation around the islands and about the cultural life of various villages. As we said goodbye, we promised to keep an eye out for Tom's ship in other ports. We never saw him again.

Originally, our plan was to move around to the north side of Ambrym and visit Ranon and the nearby village, Fanla, one of the most traditional villages on the island. However, on our third day in Craig Cove a wind shift brought a steady rain of fine black volcanic ash that covered the boat inside and out. We decided to leave Ambrym the following day.

The main reason for wanting to go to Ranon was to see the monumental drums carved here. Standing six feet and higher, these drums are of two types, one with multiple oval faces --- one over the other in totem pole style --- with exaggerated eyes. The second type is with a single head at the top of the drum. Both kinds are carved from logs that have a slit where the drum is hollowed out. These drums thump out rhythm for songs and dances and send messages to villagers around the island and in the lagoon. Tribes on Ambrym also make masks carved from the trunks of tree ferns and bamboo flutes decorated with geometric patterns.

We left Craig Cove with light winds and an overcast, dull sky. Through the day we had winds, calms and scattered showers. By mid-afternoon, as we neared Norsup Island, the wind picked up and gave us a boisterous sail into Port Stanley. Norsup Island sits off a town by the same name located on Malekula. Since the anchorage off the town was completely exposed to the southeasterly trades now blowing about 20 knots, we tucked in behind the little island close to a sandspit. While we were anchoring three teenage boys came out in a canoe and greeted us.

Soon two more canoes came out, one with a man and a boy and another with a woman. Unlike other women we had met in the islands, Mary was extremely gregarious and had a wild sense of humor. She even upstaged the man who sat quietly by listening. Our entire conversation proceeded in Bislama as we bantered back and forth with her. She was a big tease, a born comedienne. She would make statements and proclamations with a very stern face, which then spontaneously erupted into a smile as she let out a loud cackle. Mary wanted to know where our husbands were and then, acting as if she didn't believe there were no men on board, she would ask where we hid them. Once or twice when Joy went below for something, Mary said to me, "She's going to feed her husband" or "she's going to get her husband." Then widening her eyes dramatically she would peek through a port as if to sneak a view of the husband. It was all delightful play. We enjoyed her immensely.

Mary told us there would be a big market in Norsup town the next morning where we could buy fruit and vegetables. We planned to go, but it was rainy and squally in the morning so we stayed on the boat. I looked toward the beach and there stood our friend of the previous evening. Mary was waving furiously and pointing with one arm toward the town. She and a young child were standing under an umbrella. Even after I waved, she didn't go away and continued to motion frantically toward town. Finally I told Joy I would row ashore and speak to her because she seemed so insistent. I went ashore in the drizzle. Mary and a very handsome, honey-skinned boy of about ten came to help me beach the dinghy.

She said to me with her stern look, before breaking into a smile, "*Yufala go Norsup long wanem taem*? (When are you two going to Norsup?)

"*Mifala no go Norsup.*" (We are not going.)

"*From wanem*? (Why not?)

"*Ren i foldaon.*" (It's raining).

"Eh," she made some sound, perhaps of disgust, and shook her head. The expression on her face was almost sad. I thought, why is she so insistent? Then it occurred to me that she probably thought we needed food.

I said, "*Mifala tu mas kakae.*" (We have plenty to eat.)

That must have been it, because she broke into a smile. Now we could talk of other things. The boy with her was her son, the youngest of five children. Her oldest was a daughter attending high school. She was married to a Tongan who was back in Tonga visiting relatives. I tried to find out how she met and married a man from Tonga, but she couldn't understand me. My rudimentary Bislama has great gaps.

The anchorage at Norsup Island was very uncomfortable, especially at high tide when the water covered the sandspit. With no land to break it, the southeasterly swell swept around the island and rolled us violently back and forth. This situation prompted us to leave on the morning of our second day at Norsup. The ripple of bad weather had passed. It was a glorious, bright day. Blue sky. Puffy white clouds.

Toward the north end of Malekula there are three small islands lying close inshore. It is possible to go inside, between them and Malekula. We choose to do this so we could see more of Malekula. The chart showed an anchorage on the second and third islands but not on the first. It was only three and a half miles up the coast to Rano, the first island.

As we approached Rano, a heavily wooded island, we saw a very inviting sandspit projecting into turquoise water that gently lapped onto a tree-shaded beach. A man standing on shore, wearing a blue shirt, not only waved to us but also motioned us to come in and anchor. Well, why not give it a try? It looked perfect. We dropped our sails, headed into shore and anchored on a sand bottom in about 30 feet.

We were graciously invited ashore and accepted, saying we would first have some lunch and then come ashore. From where we anchored we could glimpse no habitation because huge thick trees spread right down to the water's edge. As we learned, there are three villages on this tiny island.

Upon landing we were greeted by several young men, including James, the village chief. They offered to give us a tour. Off we went following the shoreline as it curved beside the village that was cool and shaded. Built of thatch and bamboo, these neat dwellings blended into the surroundings. They sported colorful geometric designs painted on the woven bamboo sides. Many houses were nicely landscaped with rock gardens planted in flowers and spring onions. It was the cleanest and best-kept village we saw in Vanuatu.

It was Sunday. People were relaxing, sitting in the shade talking, or strolling. Everyone smiled and waved. One elderly man gave each of us a mango. He was the father of one of our guides. Our walk took us from the village into jungle where we followed a well-trod path that led to gardens of taro, yams and bananas. After 15 or 20 minutes we came to a church of European design and a very large mango tree. Several of the young men in the lead --- we had an entourage of about eight --- had already collected some mangoes, which they handed to us. We took a break to cool off and to quench our thirst. All of us were eagerly biting into and sucking on the juicy fruit.

When they saw we liked mangoes, they decided to have us sample different kinds. So, off we went again, stopping here and there at the foot of a giant mango tree while everyone picked up a stone to throw up into the tree to dislodge mangoes. Of course people were positioned at various places around the tree, so occasionally someone from the opposite side would send a mango down to the feet of someone else. If it were a soft fruit, it would splatter on the person's legs of feet, always causing much laughter from the others. One such fruit managed to splatter on Joy, which was even funnier to them because it was also a trifle embarrassing! We passed several dwellings in the forest where canoes were being built. In this village they use mango, *nega* (pronounced ninga) and one other type of tree for building canoes. All are carved by hand using three different adzes.

Finally, we came to a house and one of our escorts, a very dark man with a heavy beard, told us to wait. He went inside. We thought it was to get a shell to see if we wanted it, but he returned with a pig tusk. Joy was elated. She had wanted one in Vila, but they were too expensive. She asked him what he wanted for it. Immediately an animated conversation ensued among the men, as if to determine what was a fair price. Then someone said 500 *vatu*. Joy gasped. That was only $5.00! She said she would give him the money.

On our way back to the beach, they picked drinking nuts, mangoes and bananas for us to take back. We invited them to come aboard to see the boat. We found gifts for them, t-shirts for some, a cassette tape, tobacco and seeds. Taking turns playing our guitar, they harmonized and sang away the afternoon.

After our guests left, Joy and I took our rubbish ashore to burn. "Blue shirt" came back and we started talking. I mentioned that we were thinking of going to Vao, a little island at the north end of Malekula. He warned us that there were "rowdies" there and suggested we reconsider.

Before we got up in the morning several canoes were stationed around the boat. Jason was afraid and ran under the table! Ever since our reefing he had shown fear of visitors. Did he think they caused our reefing? Or perhaps it was their loudness. They are spontaneous, often laughing and calling out to each other in a boisterous fashion, despite their gentle nature. Perhaps he objects to their smell. Some are potent with what we called "village scent" --- the odor of smoke mixed with the heavy sweet smell of coconut oil.

Sometimes Joy and I discussed a paradox we perceived between present-day villagers as we knew them and how they were described by earlier voyagers and missionaries who came here. Early visitors described pre-missionized Ni Vanuatu as extremely fierce and warlike. Today, they appear to be very thoughtful and gentle people. Is this a change attributable to being converts to Christianity? Somehow I find such character modification questionable. First, we must consider the source. Usually accounts of their bellicose nature come from European explorers who often were the first to strike a blow. To me it seems highly unlikely that there would be such a drastic change in nature following a change of religion. Also the source itself is questionable. Is such an assertion more than a virtuous self-aggrandizing attitude promoted by missionaries? My assessment of the impact of Christianity is far from praiseworthy. If the missionaries were intolerant, their strictness often contributed to the initial breakdown of village life and customs, and for denuding the islanders' lives of validity. Of course, one could argue that Christianity has done something very positive because it stopped intertribal warfare and wanton slaughter that occurred so regularly in some areas. But consider this: Western criticism of intertribal warfare comes from a society that has developed an excess of nuclear weapons that could wipe out the planet how many times over?

Still, we must consider another important intrinsic difference between European culture and tribal society. Philosophically, Europeans and Americans contend that each individual human life is valuable, whereas among tribal peoples, it is not the individual life but the collective life of the clan, the tribe, which is perpetuated. In general, the communally centered approach appears to foster a more ecologically friendly way of life.

If we ask which is more successful biologically and ecologically, civilized societies or tribal, tribal society has won, hands down. The most serious damage inflicted on our planet by human commerce has occurred during a fraction of the time that Homo sapiens have inhabited the earth ---- all during recent centuries. All serious assaults come from industrialized nations, otherwise referred to as "civilized" peoples. Oil spills, man-made pollution, and inadequate disposal of radioactive substances are only several serious ways that we of the civilized world have been destroying the earth's environment…at a rate that defies its regeneration. In contrast, tribal societies (before tampered with by industrialized countries) lived in balance with nature because they were subject to its laws of life and death and because they were tied to the soil. They also lived under the authority of family ancestors whose power continued to be recognized after death when they were buried in their midst. For some years now tribal societies have become endangered in the same sense that many animal species are endangered. In fact, many tribal peoples have become extinct. I was astounded to read in a 1971 issue of *National Geographic* "…in Brazil alone more than a third of 230 known jungle tribes have become extinct in this century" (20th century). That is more than three decades ago. What are the figures now?

The collision of the two diverse value systems and the devastating effects upon society and people can be witnessed in all the South Pacific islands. The timetable, of course, differs from country to country. Vanuatu lags behind, say, French Polynesia. Presently, Vanuatu is feeling pressure to become a consumer society. We saw signs of the initial stages of this trend, which appears to start with young males. The mature people are acutely aware of this social breakdown. "Blue Shirt" told me he was very contented with his life in the village. He's lived the "city" life in Santo, working with expats, so he knows what European style life is like. He said, "We have plenty to eat, we need little money, but we need no money to eat."

Blue Shirt's reference to "rowdies" is a disturbing sign of the transition that is beginning to take place in Vanuatu. Several other people at Rano warned us about problems in Vao. Commercialism and theft were mentioned by other yachties. Hoffman, the museum curator, told me in Vila that *National Geographic* had established a bad precedent on Vao by paying the people large sums of money for taking pictures. Since that time they have charged anyone who wants to take pictures $10 a photo. One of the big attractions on Vao is their ceremonial grounds. In addition, the inhabitants have a reputation for being good carvers. Now word is getting around that the people of Vao pressure visitors to buy things and to give them gifts. Sometimes they become angry and abusive if visitors refuse to buy something or give a gift.

Regretfully, we had a disturbing experience that may indicate the tide is turning in Rano, too. Typically the disintegration of village life begins with teenage boys who have become restless and dissatisfied with village life. They have seen videos, mostly featuring violence, war and sex, and had contact with European and American tourists. They begin to want things they cannot afford to buy. Often they end up in the city seeking work, but do not find it. Here they become destitute and start stealing just to survive. The whole experience of not having food or a place to live is totally new to them. Having come from a communal setting, they have no survival skills once outside village protection. In the village, everything is shared; no one goes hungry as long as food is available. These disillusioned youths may eventually go back to their villages only to sow more seeds of discontent.

I believe we saw the beginning of this cycle in Rano. The incident happened on the day we were leaving, just when we were taking up anchor. A young man of about 16 --- whom we had not met --- paddled up to the boat and said to me aggressively, "I come for t-shirt." I was so taken aback that I asked him to repeat what he had said. He repeated his demand. I looked him directly in the eyes and said, "We have no t-shirts, all gone, *all finish*." Joy had been on the bow and heard none of the exchange, but she came back to the cockpit and knew by the tone that something was not right. She asked me and I told her what happened. Then the young man turned to her and said, "Give me fishhook!" She too was outraged by the blatant demand and responded. "No. We have no fishhooks for you. We are going now."

It is a pity we were leaving then. What we needed to do was go to the village chief and report what had happened. The young man would have been reprimanded and possibly this would have straightened him out. Perhaps curtailing the tendency in one young man would delay the inevitable, but it would not stop it.

As this incidence shows, attitudes are changing drastically. Nowhere in the South Pacific is it customary for islanders to demand or beg. Typically they come to visitors offering hospitality in various forms. For their part, visitors are obliged to follow certain protocol by reciprocating. To us it may seem like trading, but to the islanders it is an exchange of gifts. There is never any bartering or bargaining.

As much as I hate to acknowledge it, village life seems doomed. Christianity and colonialism started the demise by diminishing the very matrix of their culture. The final blow is the slow spread of a money economy and the introduction of Western mass culture in the form of gas guzzling vehicles, videos and the unsettling need these people feel to live the type of life they perceive as "normal". These perceptions, of course, are derived from media and from tourists (ourselves included).

Today the basic link with their heritage is their working of the land to grow their own food. Now even this tie to their past is threatened by importation of costly western foods and consequently diminishing production of their own foods, and a younger generation who reject their culture as they desperately attempt to catch up with the rest of the world.

I would like to believe that their government and Western governments will find ways to ease the transition, but I am pessimistic. What I have witnessed tells me otherwise. I see no effort being made to shift the population to any kind of sound economic basis, no development of industry, no methods to assist people in becoming independent entrepreneurs, not even sufficient training and education for young people to develop skills needed in a modern society or even opportunities to use the limited skills they have acquired.

But must they become a modern day society, a carbon copy of a society that squanders natural resources and pollutes the earth? Is there no middle ground? Obviously industrialized nations need some alternative directions and a realistic reassessment of how we needlessly consume resources and contribute to global warming. Perhaps the Ni Vanuatu have some lessons for us. Here and there in Vanuatu are pockets of resistance, villages who have firmly rejected Christianity and western ways and cling to their ancient customs and values. Instead of converting them, we should attempt to understand what makes them vital.

Despite these unsettling developments, we had some delightful contacts with some women at Rano. One day an attractive young woman and her six-year old son came to visit. She paddled out in an outrigger painted black with a racy red stripe running the length of the hull. The woman's bright eyes sparkled. At our invitation to come aboard, she extended a line to me with a slender but muscular arm. After her outrigger was tied onto *Banshee*, Joy lifted the boy up onto the boat and the woman followed. She handed us two woven baskets. Being Catholic, Vera spoke French, but happily switched to Bislama when we told her our French was less fluent.

Vera had made the baskets. The larger one was filled with mangoes, the smaller with *nega* nuts that her son had shelled. This local nut, a delicacy, we had first tried on Sakau Island in the Maskelynes. They come in a thick sort of fruity outer covering which has to be removed. The next layer, a woody shell, is harder than a Brazil nut. Under that there is a paper-thin dark brown skin. The nut is white, resembling an almond in shape, except that the meat is softer. They taste delicious, but preparing the nuts for eating is quite tedious and a skill we never became as proficient at as the children!

Vera was not at all shy, probably because she was accustomed to Europeans, having worked in a French household in Port Vila. Greatly taken by her open friendliness and gifts, we presented her and her son with t-shirts. His eyes lit up when he saw his shirt, but what made him even happier was eating a muesli bar!

That same day two more women came out to visit. Ullamula and Evelyn asked if we needed water. As it happened, our water supply was getting low, as it had not rained for some time. They promised to get us some rainwater. Later we took two five-gallon jugs ashore and left them with the women while we went for a walk along the beach. When we came back, they had filled our jugs. Evelyn, who spoke very good English as she had also worked in a European household in Vila, offered to go along the beach with us in search of shells. In no time she had collected quite a number. We learned that it was her husband who sold Joy the pig tusk.

Even though living in the village, both Vera and Evelyn have been to school and no doubt were good students as they would have to be to get jobs with Europeans. This experience apparently was enough to liberate them from the wholly traditional role that usually discourages village women from approaching strangers on their own. The fact that we were women also made us approachable.

Evelyn was from a village on southwest Malekula. In Vanuatu, as among other Melanesian societies, upon marriage women move to their husband's village. This custom puts the woman at a disadvantage, because she has to live with her in-laws. More than that, in Vanuatu it often means going to live with people who speak a totally different language and whose customs may likewise be very different. It also means the children will be closer to the father's family, at least physically and probably also emotionally. This circumstance also seems to have a bearing on how kinship is reckoned. For a while we were confused when someone would say "my other father." Then we learned the brothers of one's father are considered fathers too! This also means that first cousins are considered as siblings, rather than cousins, with the result that one can have an inordinate number of brothers and sisters.

Chapter 9

THE SAIL LOFT

Loganville — commonly called Santo town — on the island Espiritu Santo, is the second largest town in Vanuatu. Located on the southeast corner of the island, Santo was an important U.S. Army base during World War II. In the 1970s, it became the center of an abortive secessionist movement led by NaGriamel chief Jimmy Stevens. By 1980, Stevens had acquired monetary aid, arms and radio transmitting equipment from a right wing American group in exchange for land on which they intended to develop a hotel and create investment properties, turning the area into a capitalist paradise. With the rest of Vanuatu on the verge of declaring independence, this fly-in-the-ointment was creating a big problem. Finally, Vanuatu's Chief Minister, Walter Lini, declared Vanuatu's independence unilaterally and Stevens was arrested and sent to Port Vila for trial. This political development effectively quashed plans for the building of paradise, leaving half constructed resorts to be reclaimed by jungle. Santo settled back into the sleepy little dusty town that it had been, a small economic center dominated by overfilled Chinese stores selling everything from thongs to whiskey and a port handling Vanuatu's major exports of copra, coffee, cocoa beans and peanuts.

Although Santo is a port, it has no decent place for yachts to anchor because the harbor is open to the prevailing southeasterlies. Most yachts planning to spend any time in the area choose to go to Palikulo Bay, an attractive area lying behind Palikulo Peninsula. Just off Tutuba Island, about six miles from Palikulo, while we were surfing down the side of six to eight foot seas, a mahimahi hit the line and Joy had an exciting time reeling in and lifting the 12 pounder into the cockpit. I could offer no assistance, as I needed both hands on the wheel in these lively seas.

Soon we could see the pass into Palikulo Bay through the coral reef, bordered by breaking seas. A wrecked ship on its side ominously warned not to stray too close to the reef. In no time, we had sailed through the pass and turned up into the harbor that stretched a couple of miles before us. Slowly, we threaded our way up to the anchorage where three boats were moored. The water, a gorgeous shade of blue-green, lay off a perfect sand beach. On the beach, stood an open-sided structure, the Santo Nautical Boat Club.

Toward evening, a tall, thick-bearded, well-built man came rushing up to us in a super fast inflatable. He introduced himself as Jay Jarvis from *Blue Jay,* the boat we had anchored beside. An Aussie (by immigration but British by birth) Jay offered any information we might need and a ride into town, mornings about 7:15.

We joined him the next morning to go into town to check mail and do some shopping. With the wheels of his car barely in contact with the unpaved road, we sped past thick jungle that gave way to gently rolling hills uniformly planted in row upon row of tall coconut palms. This area was, Jay said, one of the large, old coconut plantations.

Fifteen or 20 minutes later, we arrived in Santo, a quaint place that hugs the waterfront. Jay gave us a quick tour then dropped us off in the middle of town. Already it was hot and dusty. We headed up a slight hill to a wooden building that announced itself as the Post Office. The clerk handed us a stack of mail and we found several letters for us.

We had been in Palikulo for only a couple of days when it occurred to me that the tables in the boat club would make an excellent place to check over all our sails and make repairs. When we mentioned the possibility to Jay, he replied it would be fine. Furthermore, he would let us use his generator to power our sewing machine. He also had some awning work and other canvas projects for Joy. Jay encouraged Joy to recut some sails for Curtis, another sailor in Santo who had just finished building his boat and was ready to launch it. Thus, in this unexpected fashion, we came to have a sail loft right there in the shade, fanned by tropical breezes, ideal, except for swarms of mosquitoes — especially after rain. The only defense was to coat ourselves liberally with insect repellent when going ashore. Several days after our arrival, three other yachts anchored nearby. One was a Kiwi, another Aussie and the third, Swiss. Suddenly, our community was becoming more international. The Kiwi and Aussie boats stayed only a couple of days, but *Swiss Family* stayed on. We had not met these folks, and never seeing them outside, we were hesitant to go over and introduce ourselves. Finally, one day the mystery was solved. Just after we had returned from town, the young woman from *Swiss Family* was standing in the bow of her dinghy, paddling from the bow as she made her way toward us. It was a very hot, windless day, and she looked tired and bedraggled. I began the conversation in German — eager to have an opportunity to use it again. She came along side and asked if we had some ice she could have for her husband. Peter, she explained, had been having a very high fever for several days and severe headaches. I wondered if he had dengue fever or malaria. She said they were beginning to suspect he might have malaria. We gave her some ice and suggested she take Peter to a doctor. Joy told her about the Ni Vanuatua physician she had recently seen in Santo. When Rosie came back to return our bowl, she said they were going to hitch into town so Peter could visit a doctor.

It was rather ironic. Rosie and Peter never went ashore, if they could help it, and their cockpit was completely enclosed in mosquito netting. To avoid land, as a precaution from getting bitten by mosquitoes, they had only gone ashore in Port Vila, Port Sandwich and now Santo. Despite these excessive precautions, Peter had contracted malaria, *falciparum*, one of the most severe strains because it affects the brain and can be fatal unless treated quickly. *Falciparum* is a resistant strain in Vanuatu; therefore Peter should have been taking Malprim in addition to Chloroquin. Peter was lucky. Because he was young and received timely treatment, he recovered within about ten days. Rosie was even luckier —she escaped malaria altogether.

Joy's medical problem was quite different from Peter's. One Sunday there had been a cookout at the boat club with dinghy races. Joy had noticed a few areas on her forearms and hands that were very itchy and weepy. She thought she had contracted poison oak or something similar. While talking to a couple of expats, she asked if they knew of any plant in Vanuatu that caused a reaction similar to poison oak.

Several of them said there was such a plant. The following day, with the condition spreading and itching intensifying, Joy went to a doctor in Santo. In his bantering manner, Jay had suggested he thought it was something more serious than plant poisoning, perhaps yaws or scabies! It *was* scabies. Probably she had picked it up from one of the children she had been around. Because scabies is a highly contagious disease, the doctor thought I too would be coming down with it. As a matter of fact....I did have a suspicious looking lump on my right hand. With fear and trepidation, I watched in until it disappeared on the third day.

Sometimes the treatment is worse than the disease. The treatment for scabies, a microscopic mite that bores under the skin and lays its eggs, is quite involved and not easy to cope with when one is living aboard. First of all, the infected person must soak in hot water in a tub and then scrub good all over with soap. We, of course, have no tub. The largest container we had was a plastic garbage can, which we used for washing laundry. We heated water on the stove and Joy tired to soak each area of her body in the garbage can. Those areas she couldn't fit into the can, I poured water over. Once washed and dried the next step is to spread a medicated lotion over the entire body, working from the neck down to the feet. For some reason the mites never bother the face of an adult, only children. The lotion must air dry (and it burns) and the body must be kept dry for 24 hours and then washed once again in hot water.

All the clothes and bedding need to be washed in boiling water. This was impossible because we did not have enough fresh water to wash all our upholstery. Instead, we dragged all cushions topside and set them in the sun for most of the day.

If — heaven forbid — the treatment doesn't work, it must be repeated. Fortunately, it worked.

One morning, Jay left very early. He said he was going to help Curtis G. launch his boat. This was the same Curtis for whom Joy had recut sails. After dark, Jay returned. When he stopped by our boat, he was quite agitated, swearing like the proverbial sailor.

"What happened, Jay?" we both asked at once.

"Goddamned bloody Steve! Everybody told him, but he's so damned stubborn. We launched and sunk a boat in the same day!" Jay rambled on in a disjointed fashion.

"You mean the chap who launched his boat also sank it?" Joy asked incredulously.

"No. Bloody hell, no. He didn't sink *his* boat. Steve did. Steve's boat. It's his damn Scot's ego. His girl friend, me and another person told him he was coming too close to the reef. You could see the bloody reef coming right up. Just like he wanted to wreck the bloody thing. It's a total loss. Total loss. It's turned turtle. We're all going over there early in the morning to salvage what we can before the locals get out there and strip everything off." Jay sighed dejectedly.

"We'll go and help," Joy volunteered. "Can we go in your dinghy?"

"Sure. I'll be over at first light." Jay fired up his outboard and screamed off as the bow reared high with the sudden thrust of force.

It wasn't yet light when Jay came over, his mood only slightly improved from the previous night. We loaded in our fins, masks, snorkels and a diving light. In no time we were up to the reef just off the tip of the peninsula. Because it was low tide, we had to land further up the beach. Already we could see about six locals on the beach and this made Jay angry. He jumped out of the dinghy asking us to land and tie it up. Meanwhile, he was dashing off over the dried out coral reef, heading for the beach.

Once we got the dinghy secured, we picked our way over the reef, going more slowly than Jay. It was rough going. Once we reached the beach walking became much easier. Just as we were passing by some rocks, I saw something white tucked up between them. Being suspicious, I went over to check it out. Sure enough — it was a sail! I pointed it out to Joy and said we must remember where this was so someone could recover it.

Soon we could see the boat and several people grouped around it. Some gear had already been pulled up onto the beach and dumped into a pile. There was a wooden mast. Jagged wood and pieces of rigging wire lay in a jumbled heap, tangled and twisted. We made our way out into the water, waist deep to the boat. The bottom bobbed up and down in the surge, looking like a beached whale. Pieces of the boat were half torn away and wire and line hung down into the water. Steve was glum and silent. His girl friend was more hospitable and thanked us for coming. Jay was there, taking charge, telling Steve how we should proceed. Two locals were also standing by, waiting for instructions so they could help. The sight of this mess hurt. I remembered how trim and sleek this little 23-foot vessel had looked as she sat across the water from us on her mooring, contentedly bobbing up and down. I had also watched her depart on the fateful day, pulling a little dinghy behind with Jay's small outboard.

The first problem was to extricate the boom as some of the rigging wire was hooked on the coral, preventing us from righting the craft. We had brought a pair of wire cutters and eventually the boom was freed. But there was another obstacle to righting the boat. Just under her was a massive piece of coral, submerged but high enough to impede our attempts to turn her upright. We were also struggling against wind and current. And, the tide was coming in. Soon it would be too deep for us to stand on the bottom and handle the boat. By now six locals had come out to help. Seeing them made me feel good because Jay's initial fear was that they would be vultures. Instead, they were exhibiting the kind and caring behavior I had come to expect and to respect in Ni Vanuatu people.

Finally, it was decided we could use Steve's Landrover to right the boat. Several of us had gone ashore and pulled a long line out of the rear of the vehicle. It had been recovered from the boat and was hopelessly knotted. Two of us were trying to unsnarl it so one end could be tied to the Landrover, the other to the boat. But while we whites were fussing around trying to use mechanical power to our advantage, the six Ni Vanuatu men righted the craft using their own muscle power! Typical. We turn to mechanical things and they, who are only used to using their own bodies to do everything, did just that!

Once the boat was floating upright, we all gave a loud cheer and the black men, rightly so, were very proud of themselves. An Aussie cruiser had now come up with his dinghy. We tied the sailboat between his dinghy and Jay's and in this way towed the wreck back to the boat club where we hauled it up on shore to await further attention. By 8:30 a. m. we were back aboard *Banshee*, feeling as if we had done a whole day's work. It was time for breakfast; we had worked up quite an appetite.

The rescue occurred on the same day as the barbecue. Seeing others out sailing their dinghies motivated me to rig mine. As I was pulling out the centerboard, the rudder, tiller and sail, I realized I had not sailed the dinghy since Fiji — almost two years! This was the perfect place to sail it, too. We had a fair breeze, but the water was flat. Soon I had it rigged and jumped in and sailed away.

It was smooth and slick and quiet. Jason had never seen anyone sailing our dinghy. Every time I came near the boat he stared and stared, curiously. Finally I said to Joy I thought he wanted to go sailing. She decided to come and bring Jason. He seemed absolutely captivated. For a while he stood up in the bow. What a picture. Then he started to explore. He walked to different areas of the dinghy, sitting for a time in one place and then another. Finally, he just plopped down in the center and looked at the mainsheet in my hand and then up at the sail, as if he had figured out what made the vessel move.

By now we had quite an audience. Other cruisers simply could not believe their eyes. We were requested to sail close to each of them so they could take photos. *Quickstep* had been there for several days. Being animal lovers, they snapped some pictures, too. On one boat they even got out their video camera to record the adventures of the sailing cat. Two kids got so excited they jumped into their sailing dinghy and followed us around until their parents finally called them home. Thus ended another mellow day in Palikulo Bay.

With the scarcity of fresh water, because there was a draught, we were in the habit of jumping over the side to take our baths. Joy named Palikulo our "big blue bathtub." Of course, regular soap does not lather in salt water, but we have found that VO5 Shampoo lathers wonderfully. With it we washed hair and body, then rinsed our hair with two cups of fresh water. I had thought the constant use of salt water would irritate my skin, but to my surprise it didn't.

On one of our last evenings in Palikulo, Steve came by to give Jason a worm treatment. With some distance between him and his terrible reefing, he was more relaxed and talked about his job with the Vanuatu government. As a veterinarian, his major responsibility is to look after the cattle — whose meat is being exported — and other livestock. In all of Vanuatu, there is only Steve and another expat vet, whom we had met in Port Vila, who are qualified to manage the medical aspects of livestock. Steve was leaving the country within a few months and six months later the other vet was also leaving. What then we asked? They have a 17-year old Ni Vanuatu now studying veterinary medicine in Australia. After his additional four or five years of schooling, they hope to plug him into the position. The Vanuatu government is trying to increase their export of beef, but soon they will have no one to inspect their export meat or treat beef cattle unless, of course, they hire a foreigner.

The morning of departure was breathless in Palikulo Bay. There was no relief until we finally started powering a zigzag course down the bay, around the reef and into Segond Channel, past Santo town with its wharf and customs building.

At Jay's suggestion, we decided to sail up the west coast of Santo to Baldwin Cove. He thought we would enjoy meeting Pierre and Leslie, expats who have a farm there. As soon as the Baldwin Cove came into sight, we saw a yacht named *Couscous* rolling back and forth in the swell. What a beautiful little cove with trees hugging the shoreline.

We anchored next to *Couscous*. No sign of anyone onboard, but we saw two people on land watching us. About half an hour later, three people walked over to the land adjacent to us and waved a friendly hello. We dinghied ashore and they helped us land in the surge.

In the shade, we sat with Leslie and Pierre, who are doing some mixed farming and raising cattle, but their major crop will be vanilla beans. They have just started this endeavor. It will be a few years before the plants begin producing beans. Needing to get back to some chores, they left after inviting us to visit them later.

Roger, the owner of the *Couscous*, stayed on to talk with us. As soon as he opened his mouth, we knew he was French. But Roger's boat is documented out of Honolulu, and he quickly told us he was *American*! Born in France, but an American citizen for many years.

He was also a chef who periodically stops in his travels to practice his occupation. Roger loved talking about food as much as he loved preparing it. He and Pierre are old sailing friends and in the month Roger had been visiting he had created a new dish made with fruit bat! When we made faces and probably a disgusted sound or two, Roger just laughed and asked, "You like chicken?"

"Of course," we chimed in chorus.

"Tink about it. Zee chicken eats roaches and you eat chicken wiz delight. Now, you must tink again — zee fruit bat eats fruit — you know, mangoes, pawpaws, so zee flesh of zee bat is very nice, sweet!"

Logically, yes. But it would take me a while to get used to the idea of eating bat!

On November 7, we sailed away from Santo Island with easterly winds of 18 knots. We had contemplated stopping off at Huon lagoon and reef at the north end of New Caledonia on our way to Australia. But the weather was unstable and we decided to continue on toward Chesterfield Reefs.

Chapter 10

CHESTERFIELD REEFS

We were in the Coral Sea, a vast region stretching East from the East coast of Australia almost a thousand miles to New Caledonia and Vanuatu. South, it extends to latitude 30 degrees South with its northern boundary reaching to the Solomon Islands and parts of Papua New Guinea. Literally thousands of reefs lie across this tropical expanse, waiting to be explored or to snare the unfortunate vessel. As the chart reveals, the greatest density of reef is centered around Australia's Great Barrier Reef. Moving away from Great Barrier, the outcroppings thin out, but never disappear entirely. Our course from Santo to Australia took us straight into Bampton Reefs and the Chesterfield Reefs, two of the larger reef systems in the Coral Sea. We could choose to pass above or below these obstructions, or we could stop and explore. Ever since our visit to Mopelia, an uninhabited atoll in French Polynesia about 100 miles west of Bora Bora, Joy and I have been interested in such places which are sanctuaries for fish, birds, sea mammals and turtles.

Having satnav and radar makes us more confident about venturing into hazardous territory than we would feel if we were navigating solely by sextant. To be sure, electronic aids do not eliminate all dangers, but they do minimize them. Not only are the islands, reefs and sunken dangers in the Coral Sea numerous, many are only roughly indicated on a chart because often, exact location and specifics are not known. We would only attempt to enter Chesterfield lagoon if conditions were right.

By the fourth day out of Vanuatu, we were approaching Bampton Reefs. Around 1:30 a.m., as I looked toward the stern, a sudden movement caught my eye. It was a bird attempting to perch on one of the solar panels. The poor thing was struggling to keep itself on the slanted slick panel. It had landed on the lower end of the panel, making tough work for itself. With each roll of the boat, it flapped its wings furiously to maintain its grip. I laughed to myself. It was a noddy, not the bats I had been thinking of earlier. When I came on watch at midnight, the scene brought bats to mind. Towering stacks of clouds scudded around the near full moon, whose light illuminated gossamer wisps of cloud. I half expected to see bats silhouetted against this Gothic scene! Then I thought of fruit bats. When in Tonga, we took a bus from Nuku'alofa out to a village just to see fruit bats. There were hundreds, maybe thousands of them hanging upside down in several very large trees. Some were darting around, flying from tree to tree even though it was daylight. Being large, heavy animals, they are often called flying foxes.

Bats. Bats on the mind. Joy and I had a hilarious (in retrospect) experience with a bat while sailing off the coast of Mexico. We were sailing along on a brilliant morning when suddenly Joy came dancing up into the cockpit, acting a bit weird. In an excited voice she blurted out, "You'd better go look at your pants hanging up in the head."

"Why?"

"Oh, there's something strange. I was trying to fold up your cords and put them away, but I touched something in the back pocket I think, and it felt very soft and squishy!" She was looking at me with a strange expression.

I went below. My pants were lying on the floor where she had dropped them. I picked them up and clinging to the leg was a bat! It was alive. I wasn't about to touch it. It could be rabid. Finally, I thought of what to do. I ran to the galley and grabbed a pair of tongs and ran back to the head and clamped down on the poor creature. I'll never forget what happened. Its lips curved back, no doubt from sheer agony, revealing a mouth full of sharp teeth.

"God, Joy," I yelled, it's a vampire bat!"

"No," she replied emphatically, "there are no vampire bats here."

111

"Sure there are. Wait till you see it." I carried it up to the cockpit, still gripped tightly in the tongs with its evil looking teeth exposed.

She jerked away and screamed. "Get rid of that damn thing right now! Throw it overboard!"

"But what if it flies back?"

"It won't. Just get rid of it, for God's sake. Right now!"

I tossed it over, fully expecting it to fly back into my face to have its revenge. But it would never fly again. I had clamped harder than I realized with the tongs. It was a goner, jeering at me with its awful teeth.

At last, after much scrambling, the noddy hopped up to the high end of the panel and began living in style, if not complete comfort. It preened and gave me only the slightest glance, as I stood next to it to see it better. It had no fear of me, nor did any of the noises from adjusting sails bother it. Jason had been sleeping below, but a noise, a scent or his cat sixth sense alerted him and he came charging up the companionway, eyes fastened on the noddy. I caught Jason in mid-flight. Even the menacing cat brought no fear to this innocent seabird. I eventually confined Jason below. Until sunup the noddy stayed with us, even balancing through a jibe.

Sunrise on the fifth day at sea was spectacular. The eastern sky was flamingo down drifting over dove gray. Hundreds of boobies circling and making kamikaze dives confirmed that the reef we could not yet see was nearby. On the sixth day we approached Chesterfield on a course for Long Island Pass, which is two and a half miles wide. At the northern end of the pass nothing is visible until within about two miles of the reef when the spray and breaking sea come into view. The south side of the entrance, bounded by Long Island, is seen further off at about four miles because the island is 20 feet high. Amazingly, we spotted the island before the radar that has a range of 16 miles!

In the pass several groups of birds — hundreds — were in a feeding frenzy. In such numbers they formed a black cloud, swirling and diving, throwing up water in silvery flashes. We identified masked and brown boobies, terns and noddies. About midway through the pass, just as the overfalls and tide rips were pushing and pulling us around, a tremendous fish hit the line. The large rubber strap that functions as a shock absorber on the block holding the fishing line, stretched over double its length. I shouted out to Joy who was forward dropping the jenny while I was steering. We started the engine and then Joy came back to check the line.

She was cranking in very slowly. This fish had to be gigantic. Our fishing gear, a massive salmon rig from the Pacific Northwest with 300-pound test line, was robust enough to pull in a *whale*. Nonetheless, Joy protested in a flood of profanity that this fish was big and strong. It was actually swimming opposite our direction, carrying the line across our stern! The shock strap continued to stretch, and Joy played the fish, hoping to tire it. Then she said it had to be a shark because its action was not that of a fish.

Shark it was. Joy managed to get it within about 20 feet of our stern and the beast surfaced. It was probably about four or five feet long, endowed with an inordinate amount of strength and absolutely enormous jaws! We both agreed there was no way would land this monster in the cockpit. Nothing to do but cut the line, losing the leader, weight and our favorite bone jig and, unfortunately, leaving the hook in the shark's mouth.

By the time the shark was aborted we were nearing the end of the pass and the seas were calming. With less demand on handling the boat, we could observe our surroundings. Long Island, mostly barren and sandy, arched into a low hump; its white sands glinted blindingly. With the sun near it zenith, contrasting water colors appeared to vibrate. In the right weather Long Island would be a beautiful anchorage, but not in 20 knot southeasterlies that threw up a nasty chop. As the reef lies in a southeasterly direction, it would offer no protection from the fetch until we neared the bottom end of the lagoon. In the distance, sand cays looked like the backbone of some prehistoric dinosaur strewn across the lagoon. Stretching out for miles were rich colors, every shade of green from lightest leaf green to deep emerald mixed with blues in hues from azure to deep marine. The water was crystal clear. Areas of shallow reef, a brownish yellow, signaled danger.

We powered about two hours, finally anchoring in 25 feet of turquoise water abeam a sand cay that became two as the tide ebbed and completely disappeared when it flooded. The spot was still about three miles from the South Elbow where Loop Islet, a small tufted speck of land, rises only 11 feet above sea level. On Loop, the French have built an unattended meteorological station.

The overall scene in the mammoth lagoon was surrealistic. The sky, a soft blue, was filled with fluffy cumulus tinted pale hues, except for the ones whose brilliant green bottoms reflected the color of the lagoon. This procession of clouds marched over a thin ochre strip of sand and reef that curved around the horizon, separating the sky from a dancing blue-green sea flecked with frilly lace. Birds glided and swooped, their forlorn keening a counterpoint to the distant drone of surf. Here was a timeless universe of sand, sea and wind, a cyclic symphony played night and day, in sun and rain, in the midst of life and death.

In the afternoon the wind steadily rose. We changed our minds about visiting the nearby sand cay. The water was too rough. Onboard it was comfortable enough. The fax weather map confirmed there was no bad weather headed our way, just a new high coming across Australia that was pushing the isobars close together. The rising pressure kept the wind up for the next two days. This condition kept us boat bound. It was an eerie feeling to look out. Except for the distant breaking reef and the light colored water under our keel, it looked as if we were anchored in the middle of the ocean. In reality we *were* in the middle of the ocean in a lagoon! Australia was still about 450 miles distant.

By the third day the seas had calmed enough that we had good visibility for moving across the lagoon. Working our way to within about half a mile of Loop Islet, we anchored in ten feet of water the exact color of a swimming pool. Here in the lee of Loop we were getting enough protection to launch *Nessie* and go ashore.

Even in the lee, it was a boisterous ride to the island. Thousands of birds swarmed around the island and thousands more were sitting on shore. In some areas they were so thick we couldn't see any sand! Their calls and squawks, a solid din audible from the boat day and night, became almost deafening as we approached the shore. We hopped ashore in ankle deep water, sinking deep into a thick soft bottom of crushed coral. Boobies were everywhere — flying overhead, gliding close by to inspect us. Onshore others sat protectively on the eggs. No more than two to a nest, which was no more than a slightly excavated place in the sand. Adolescent boobies and fluffy white booby chicks watched curiously from the perches in wispy nests atop chest-high bushes. Terns by the thousands — both bridle terns and sooty terns — rose up in clouds from the beach as we neared or else scooted along in front of us on the ground. From the clouds of circling terns came a piercing screech. This chatter was not the result of our presence; it goes on continuously. I wonder how the boobies and the noddies, which were silent, could stand the constant noise.

Our leisurely paced walk around the island took less than an hour. Every part of the island was utilized by birds. The interior, covered with low, bushy scrub, provided both nesting and resting places. Coming across some strange tracks in the sand that greatly resembled tracks made by oversized dune buggy tires, we momentarily wondered how any vehicle could come ashore here. After a bit of thought, we realized these were turtle tracks! We had seen some turtles swimming offshore, but none on land.

We identified three kinds of boobies (masked, brown and red-footed), bridle and sooty terns (and one or two single terns that may have been fairy terns), common noddies and white capped noddies. Our estimate of the number of birds was somewhere between four to five thousand!

Being curious, we check out the meteorological station, just a small locked building and a few pieces of equipment — one for measuring rainfall and a bank of solar panels covered with bird guano and probably not very effective until the next rain came to wash them clean. We were disturbed to find a pile of about 40 or 50 castoff batteries. Each one was roughly the size of a car battery. They had been used no doubt to store energy derived from the solar panels and then discarded and left in a heap, rather than being carted off by personnel who come periodically to check on the station.

It would have been pleasant to spend more time exploring Chesterfield Reefs. On the eastern side of the lagoon there is a group of islands with the unimaginative name of Anchorage Islets. These islands are larger than Loop and even have established trees. Probably they offer a different type of habitat for future investigation.

By 10:15 the next morning we glided through the softly rippled lagoon with the mainsail all the way out. A moderate breeze pushed us along smoothly at four knots. We edged toward the center of the lagoon into deeper water where most of the coral heads were very deep. We drank in the magical scene, the clear bright colors, the rumbling surf, the curious circling birds, a whole microcosmic world existing in mid-ocean. This time we went out the small pass. The surf pounding on the reef was close by, but other than a slight swell, it was an unremarkable pass, surely better than the larger pass we used to enter. A quite large turtle swam past us, coming into the pass, returning home, perhaps to deposit eggs on Loop Islet.

Chapter 11

BOUND FOR THE SOLOMON ISLANDS

In June 1990, after spending six months in Australia, we attempted to return to Chesterfield Reef. Five days after leaving Australia and 500 miles at sea, *Banshee* was caught in an out-of-season hurricane. We were rolled and dismasted, but miracle of miracles, not only did we survive, so did *Banshee*. Two very kind-hearted Australian fishermen, Bob Bedford and George Collins, went to sea and rescued *Banshee* and returned her to us. It took Joy and me 16 months to rebuild our boat, which had sustained considerable damage, most of it happened when the rescue ship came alongside to take us off. But this is another story, covered in *Banshee's Women Capsized in the Coral Sea*.

Needless to say, after being dry-docked for almost a year and a half, working at a grueling pace, Joy and I were more than ready to resume our seafaring life. During our final days of preparation in Australia, our dear friend Frank Anderson was present, helping us mentally, emotionally and physically. Frank had a knack for appearing at momentous occasions. There were three such occasions: July 1990 when *Banshee*, after being towed 500 nautical miles back to Australia and trucked overland about 800 miles to Lawries Marina in Mooloolaba for rebuilding; November 1990 when *Banshee* was relauched — minus her mast: September 1991 our first test sail. Without any advance knowledge of these occasions, Frank just appeared like a guardian angel.

Now, with the tethers cut, we, in company with Frank on *Swagman*, set off for Brisbane, intending to spend several days sailing and just getting used to being on the water again. As if cooperating with our relaunching, nature provided a perfect October day, a blue sky, flat water and a super downwind sail to Bribie Island where we anchored for the night. For the first time in over a year, I could take a deep breath and feel some of the tension melt away. Slowly the months of difficult work and anxiety of wondering when and *if* we would ever set sail again, began to recede into memory, to be replaced by anticipations of new landfalls and exotic ports of call. In itself, the act of leaving land and taking to the open water was like a fledgling spreading its wings in flight.

No one knew better than Frank the apprehensions Joy and I had about going back to sea. Joy had been having anxiety dreams for months, whereas I had suffered from insomnia. I would lie awake for hours thinking of all the things that still needed to be done to complete the boat, and often I questioned if we could complete the overwhelming task of rebuilding our boat.

I suppose it was natural that we should experience some trepidation about returning to sea. Many people had expressed surprise that after our devastating encounter with a hurricane 500 miles off Australia we would ever consider going to sea again. But I've never been one to give up easily. I had to "get back on the horse." If I didn't, I would never forgive myself.

For Joy's part, she just couldn't imagine living ashore again, not having a boat and not going to sea. Although she felt anxious, I believe the idea of not sailing was more difficult to bear than confronting any lurking fears.

Frank seemed to apprehend these subtler, unspoken and often inexpressible feelings. His presence was a source of great encouragement. He knew we needed to work on being physically fit to make a passage. He got us exercising regularly, daily. But in addition to these early morning walks, Joy and I had been doing aerobics three times a week for several months.

With Frank, our intention was to sail from Bribie across Moreton Bay and anchor off the dunes. But the weather was not cooperative. The winds stayed southeast, making this plan impossible. Instead, we sailed to Newport Waterways for an overnight in a marina. The following day, we left for Brisbane. For me this was a dream come true. Many a time I had wished to sail up the Brisbane River and anchor off the botanical gardens. Now we were doing it.

The wind was perfect. Astern. We entered the channel at the "coffee pots" (channel markers named for their resemblance to coffee pots) and then breezed along briskly with large ships passing us as they plied up- and downstream. The incoming tide assisted us for most of the 14 miles from the mouth up to the town reach. We made the gardens about an hour before sunset with the wind howling 25 knots, against the current. An impossible situation for taking a pile mooring. We decided to anchor along with some other boats just above the mooring. What a mistake that was. Once the anchor was down, we started sailing in circles! One moment the crazy current would swirl us around, and then the wind would whip us in another direction. Like us, Frank was so concerned after anchoring he remained on deck watching. Then as we watched, the current carried him directly down onto another yacht. Someone immediately came out and spoke to him. Soon thereafter two dinghies with people from moored boats came over to talk with Frank. Then they came over to us. They and three of four other men offered to help us tie to the moorings. They would handle Frank first and then us. On the piles, we ended up between Greenpeace's *Vega* and *Swagman*.

In the heart of the city, the anchorage in front of the botanical gardens was unexpectedly beautiful. The contrast between the serene stately gardens and the high-rise glitter of glass was spectacular. At night the city's bright lights and golden sparkle eclipsed the somber shadowed garden. But in the morning the garden's giant flowering trees, alive with birdcalls and sun-shaded paths beckoned.

Almost a week later, trying to get the right weather pattern for going south to Sydney, Frank headed down river one day in advance of us. To avoid a final farewell, he quietly slipped away early in the morning while we slept. The next day we met Customs at the fuel dock to check out. Southeast winds had been forecast, but the wind with a mind of its own went east and then northeast. We cleared Customs, and then headed out through heavy mist and light rain to Mud Island to await favorable conditions for departing. At the mouth of the river, we sailed into a sea awash with bright blue jellyfish. They were everywhere, choking the water, as far as the eye could see, hitting against our wind vane and banging into the rudder with loud thumps.

It took 15 days to sail from Brisbane to Honiara. The first two days of the voyage, over the shallow water off Australia's coast, was the most uncomfortable part of the passage. The lumpy seas and my extensive period as a landlubber made it doubly hard to gain my sea legs. For us and *Banshee,* this was shakedown cruise. We had been pushing so hard to get away from Australia before the cyclone season started that we really had no time for any extended sailing trials prior to leaving for the Solomons. As expected, we developed a few problems underway. Our fifth day out we discovered a leak in the forward lower chain plate on the port side. Breaking seas had been forcing trickles of water into every locker on the port side of the boat through this small leak. All the linens and towels were soaking wet, as were our charts. We altered course off the wind so we could dry the deck and then fill, redrill, screw and seal the leak. In the meantime, we hung all the sheets and towels outside and the charts inside to dry. As the charts dried, we packed them into plastic bags rather than chance their getting soaked again.

With beam seas, boisterous for most of the passage in 20 to 30 knots, the boat was working a lot. One very disconcerting thing was the horrendous cracking and snapping sounds the boat was making. Most of the sounds were coming from the deck beam just forward of the mast. The sound was so horrible that at times we feared some dreadful damage was occurring. Periodically we searched the area very carefully but could find nothing amiss.

Some pleasant things occurred also. The leak repair worked. We caught a yellow fin tuna, exactly what I ordered in the morning when I put out the line! We ate well that evening on sashimi and herb butter tuna, served in the cockpit during the height of a local squall. A few days later we caught a bonito and a barracuda. The latter we threw back into the ocean and the bonito ended up on the table.

On the evening of November 7, we had the nicest sailing of the entire passage. It was magical. The moonlight cast an ethereal glow over the quiet seas and light winds were laden with a sweet perfume from land. While ghosting along, I detected the faint outline and dim light of a fishing boat. I signaled to them by flashlight. They signaled back.

Morning found us heading between Russell Island and Guadalcanal in the Solomons.

By midmorning, we were not far, as the crow flies, from Honiara. But as sailboats sail, when the course is on the wind, we had a long, hard night of tacking ahead of us. By midafternoon the wind had become an easterly gale, requiring us to tack repeatedly to gain any ground toward our destination. In addition, there was a terribly strong opposing current. We spent the entire night tacking between Guadalcanal, Savo Island and Ngele Sule over Iron Bottom Sound — so named for all the World War II relics littering the bottom. By now the seas had become nasty, breaking peaks. To further complicate everything we had two failures that night. The starboard sheet winch froze, forcing us to attempt to use a smaller winch. Because it was inadequate, we eventually brought the sheet across the cockpit and used the port winch on both tacks. The second problem was the wind vane. We could no longer use the two hand lines to adjust it. Laboriously, Joy had to hang out over the stern and hand manipulate it each time we tacked.

Around 2 a.m., the wind diminished dramatically and sailing became quite pleasant. Most memorable was the sweet scent that once again filled the air, as on the previous night. I believe it was frangipani mixed with earth odors. Repeatedly in the Solomons this exquisite aroma hung heavy in the dark tropical air. By sunrise, the wind died altogether and we powered the final five miles into the crowded anchorage in front of the Honiara Yacht Club. This expansive two-story, open-sided building of native design is the city's most attractive landmark.

We were elated to have completed this passage, which laid to rest some of the ghosts that had been haunting us. But before we could begin cruising the islands we had some repairs to do. After careful examination, we determined there was no structural damage to the deck beam. Together with others who inspected the mast, we agreed that the wedges shipbuilder Peter Crease had inserted around the new mast in Australia, after it was stepped in Mooloolaba, needed to be removed. We had not had wedges with the old mast, so why have them with the new one? As it turned out, having the wedges caused the pressure from the mast to be transmitted to the deck beam. Had we continued to sail with them, I believe we would in time have caused structural damage to the boat. Once the wedges were out, Joy filled the space around the mast with silicone seal. There were no further problems and no horrendous noises and cracks when sailing even in the worst weather.

In most respects, Honiara was a disappointment. It has little of the charm of other South Pacific ports we have visited. For the most part it is a dusty, dirty, crowded town with a limited supply and selection of highly priced imported foods. The best buys were at the public market where there was the usual assortment of coconuts, bananas, taro, yams and sometimes green peppers, eggplant, tomatoes, green beans, cucumbers and watermelons. Best of all were huge juicy, very sweet pineapples, selling for 50 or 75 cents.

Unlike Vanuatu, which promotes tourism, the Solomons have not encouraged visitors, nor has the government made any substantial outreach to develop ties with other countries. It is hard to understand this kind of insularity or the reason for it. From all appearances, during the previous ten years the Solomon Islands had steadily been going downhill, losing whatever gains they may have made economically or otherwise. As late as the mid-1980s, the Solomons enjoyed a fairly healthy economy, based on the export of palm oil, rice, fish and lumber. But something has happened to erode these industries and devalue their money. The Solomon dollar was down to three to one US dollar when we were there in the early nineties. There were never many resort hotels in these islands, but most of them had folded, leaving Honiara as practically the only place with hotel accommodations for visitors. Other than people who come through on yachts, almost no visitors frequent these islands.

The Solomons are comprised of many small islands and six large ones: San Cristobal, Guadalcanal, Malaita, Santa Isabel, New Georgia and Choiseul. Although the inhabitants are Melanesian, the people vary considerably in skin color from very light to very dark and hair color ranges from blond to black. Language and customs differ considerably from island to island. In addition to the Melanesians, there are Polynesians on the outlying islands of Rennell, Bellona, Ontong Java, Sikaiana, Tikpia and Anuate and some Micronesians from the Gilbert Islands who have been resettled near Honiara and in some of the western islands.

The earliest of the Europeans to visit the Solomons was Don Alvaro de Mendaña. What brought the Spanish *conquistadors* to the Solomons were old Incan legends that told of the Incan hero Yupanqui who voyaged west of Peru about 600 leagues where he found two very rich islands. From these he brought back gold and silver, a copper throne and black slaves and the skin of an animal resembling a horse. Always eager to find new wealth, the Spanish sent Mendaña from Callao, Peru, in November 1567. He fetched up at Santa Isabel on February 7, 1568. Mendaña found no riches, but there occurred an episode that suggested the Spanish began hostilities, which were then reciprocated by the natives. Mendaña had sent out a nine-man party in search of water. The commander of this party reputedly initiated violence, which resulted in every man of the party being killed. The natives had a very effective way of expressing their dissatisfaction with the intruders. A fleet of war canoes paddled up to Mendaña's ship and presented him with a quarter of a man garnished with taro roots! Although Mendaña found no riches here, he named the islands the Solomons, as if to confirm they were the source of King Solomon's wealth.

Mendaña made a return trip to the Solomons in 1595, but no other Europeans came until two centuries later. By the nineteenth century, unscrupulous traders began kidnapping workers for the sugar cane fields of Australia and Fiji. Some of these treacherous traders even disguised themselves as priests so they could land peacefully. Such practices ignited strong anti-European feelings and distrust, which sometimes resulted in the murder of many innocent traders and missionaries.

The colonial period, beginning toward the conclusion of the nineteenth century, ended the blatant practice of economic slavery. The British declared a protectorate over Guadalcanal, San Cristobal, Malaita and the New Georgia group in 1893. The Santa Cruz group, Rennel and Bellona were added in 1898 and 1899. Germany, who had held power in the Shortlands, Choiseul, Santa Isabel and Ontong Java, handed these islands over to the British in 1900.

Certainly there was no coherent government in the Solomons until the British stepped in, and when they did, they decreed that the colony must be self-supporting. Until just prior to their independence on July 7, 1978, almost nothing was done for the islanders. The government's responsibility covered primarily tax collection and punishment. Education and medical care were left to the missionaries.

To be sure, World War II left some deep impressions on the Solomons. Americans brought in military forces and equipment to overthrow the Japanese invaders. Abandoned artillery shells, tanks, guns, bullets, sunken ships and aircraft still turn up today. Many of the present roads, airfields and wharves were built during the war.

As usual, we didn't want to spend a lot of time in the city. Just as soon as we could make our repairs and do a bit of provisioning, we were ready to explore the islands. In the meantime, our Canadian friends Peter and Joyce on their catamaran *Canowie*, had come in about four days after us. We were planning to do some cruising together. *Canowie* got a head start. About two weeks after our arrival in Honiara, we left for the Florida group, a trip requiring two to three hours, and a rendezvous with *Canowie*.

Tulaghi, the pre-war capital of the Solomons, is located in the Florida islands. Today Tulaghi is the homeport of the Japanese tuna fishing fleet and also boasts several shipyards and a small village with a few Chinese stores. We joined Peter and Joyce in Port Purvis. This bay, wide at the entrance, narrows at the northern extreme to a slit, which separates two islands. We anchored roughly midway at an area we dubbed the "waterhole." During the war, the U.S. installed water pipes to carry water from a limestone cave down to the bay so Allied warships could anchor in this bay of refuge and fill with water. Only a few posts of the wharf that was built here remain today, but the water pipe continues to dump gallons of water into the bay nonstop. Villagers come here to collect water and it has become a favorite stop for yachts as we seldom find a place with unlimited fresh water.

Canowie was anchored off the bow with a stern line tied to the mangroves. We anchored further offshore in 56 feet. What a spectacular area, a high wall of jungle, exquisite birds in flight, soaring above the trees, exotic calls and colorful butterflies as big as your hand. But it was oppressively hot, humid and still, almost breathless. Peter and son Paul managed to rig a hose from the pipe onto their boat which made it easy to fill all our jugs and take a long, cold shower.

It was here we met Gabriel, the gardener. As we came back to this spot on several occasions, we got to know Gabriel rather well and learned that he is an avid gardener. He brought us a large variety of fruits and vegetables, usually the best that we found in the entire country. But the biggest surprise was the day he brought out a large basket filled with huge straw mushrooms! We had not seen fresh mushrooms since leaving Australia. What a treat that was. Later, when we returned, we brought Gabriel many different kinds of seeds. He was elated. He had never had corn kernels before and he was eager to plant them.

Several days after arriving, we moved from the "waterhole" to Makambo, a small island facing Tulaghi. This area was close enough to dinghy over to Tulaghi for fresh bread from the bakery, fresh vegetables and fish from the vendors who sat on the roadside and to mail letters at a very tiny post office. The big attraction at Makambo was the reef where we were anchored. Joy and I snorkeled and discovered a gorgeous underwater scene of huge elephant ears, each of slightly different pale color, measuring perhaps three to five feet across, brain corals and thick fields of staghorn with glowing blue tips.

The above water scene was also impressive. Stretching away on every side were layered hills, each a mass of green. Some planes were sun-drenched while others receded into a bluish haze. I felt privileged to be in the midst of such grandeur and serenity. It made the mad race for progress removed and trivial. I contemplated how easily we lose our sensitivity to such natural grandness if all our energy is spent in pursuit of material possessions.

One morning Moses, a muscular middle-aged man with a broad smile, canoed over and hailed us with a friendly greeting. We launched into an interesting and lengthy conversation. Because of their latitude, the Solomons are rarely hit by cyclones, but the rare ones that hit are especially menacing. I asked Moses about his experience with cyclones. He told me about the devastating hurricane that hit the Solomons in 1972, killing over 100 people on Guadalcanal. In the Florida group, whole villages were totally destroyed by 85-knot winds. Moses pointed to the trees on the mountains and said the trees stood, but were stripped of their leaves. The grasses and vines had been blown away, leaving a denuded hillside. Their gardens were ruined and many palm trees blown down. How did they live, I asked? They ate coconuts. The government sent in crackers for three weeks, but after that the people were on their own. It was six months before their gardens were growing and producing again, so they ate coconuts and more coconuts. What about water? The water was dirty and had to be boiled. They had to rebuild all their houses. Now, almost 20 years later, the land has recovered and the reef, too. Of course, when the reef is destroyed, often pounded to bits by the raging seas, the marine life that inhabits these reefs is also destroyed. Unfortunately, it takes many years for a reef to become reestablished.

Moses is the caretaker of Gavutu Island. I told him we planned to go there and he said to enjoy it. He told me he is the *kastomu* (custom) man in his village. I asked him what that meant. For example, he said, if there is a problem, perhaps someone steals something, the custom man must tell the thief what amount of money he must pay to the victim, in addition to returning the stolen goods. If the thief fails to do as bid, then Moses reports him to the police in Tulaghi. They arrest the thief and put him in prison. This incident shows how traditional law and Western law have been combined.

This was the first time I realized that many Solomon Islanders have no concept of their age and in fact often do not know the day, month or year of their birth. Moses told me he was getting old, near 60! I was truly surprised because he is a trim man and doesn't even look 40! Then he said he was born two years after the war started, in 1945. I explained, "Moses, if you were born in 1945, you're not even 50! You're 44!" A little more confusion occurred when he said he married young, at 21, and now his oldest child, a son, is 30. He also has three daughter, one 22, one 17 and one 13. While Moses was confused about numbers and dates —something not important in his society — it was evident by his bearing and manner that he is a man of wisdom.

Gavutu Island is a miniature, uninhabited paradise. Except for the remains of a large concrete wharf built by the American forces, Gavutu resembles other small South Pacific islands. Although some sections of the wharf have fallen away, much of it is still functional and is used frequently by local fishermen and by visiting yachts. When the Allied Forces were here, officers' barracks were located on a small nearby island connected to Gavutu by a causeway. The wreckage of an airplane lies on the wharf where it came down years ago.

Our anchorage at the wharf was so well protected that few breezes could penetrate. Consequently, it was stifling. On a later visit here we sat out some bad weather created by a budding cyclone for several days. On this first occasion, two memorable things occurred. The Australian yacht *Race the Wind* with Eve, her daughter Kate and husband George came in and tied up at the wharf. This was the beginning of a very comfortable friendship which continued as we cruised together for close to five months until finally they had to turn East and we had to go West. The second event was that I spent three days here very sick. It wasn't until almost a month later that I found out I had had an attack of malaria.

Chapter 12

MALAITA

The Malaitans, reputed to be the most aggressive of the Solomon Islanders, are also the most distinctive physically. Many have ginger to blond hair, sometimes strikingly combined with very dark skin, but often with very light skin. Some have black hair, which may be kinky or curly or straight. Most of the politicians in the Solomons are Malaitans. In other endeavors, the Malaitans have proved themselves to be the most enterprising and the most highly motivated of their citizenry. That's a lot of superlatives, but none of them is exaggerated.

During the twelve days we stayed in Malaita, we divided our time between Auki, the administrative center of the island, and the Langa Langa Lagoon. Malaita, a large, high island, is populated along the coast as well as in its interior. We saw roughly one eighth of the island's coastal region and nothing of its interior, much of which is inaccessible because of intense conflicts between the official government and the *kastomu* or pagan (the term they use) peoples dwelling in the interior. The cause of these conflicts, we were told, date from some years back when the Solomon government attempted to place a head tax on the hill dwellers. More recently, when some government officials ventured into the interior to take a census count, they were killed. Later, while visiting the Marists' school at Vanga Point in the Western district of the Solomons, we heard from the Catholic Brothers who run the school that in the past several years two Peace Corps successfully walked into the interior and began to interact with the inhabitants. Their entrée was gained through the medicine they brought in to treat problems in newborn infants and pregnant women. From many comments made by the coastal Malaitans, I detected considerable mistrust still exists between the coastal and hill peoples as it has for centuries.

Our first view of a Malaitan village occurred as we came through Auki pass on a rare windy day under full sail. A dramatically picturesque view of legendary South Sea island beauty spread before us: a village of stilt houses built out on the sea's edge in the lagoon. This village, with the musical name of Lilisiana, lies on a sandy point of the main island. Poised on the opposite side of the pass is a round shaped piece of land, an artificial island that was built several hundred years ago. In Langa Langa Lagoon we would see many such artificial islands, the only distinctive feature from natural islands being their sides constructed of coral rock. Indeed, we would be told the history of such islands many times. Several hundred years ago (no one is really certain of the date) the coastal dwellers, tired of being raided by the hill tribes, decided to make themselves more secure by building artificial islands approximately one quarter to a half mile offshore where they could live. This innovative move apparently afforded them two advantages: without boats, the hill people could no longer raid them nor could mosquitoes. Fresh water on the mainland provided excellent breeding grounds for the malaria-carrying *Anopheles* mosquito. As the artificial islands had no water, the Malaitan sea dwellers continued to cultivate their gardens on the large island during the day and retreat by night to their island fortresses.

Auki may be the administrative center, but in fact it is little more than a primitive settlement with several tiny stores, a depot selling diesel, gasoline and kerosene, a dilapidated wharf where local supply ships tie up to load and unload cargo, a small post office, a bank, a bakery and a police station. Adjoining the wharf, a fenced area with a few stalls serves as the local market where villagers bring their produce to sell. Most of the vendors sit on mats on the ground, gossiping with their neighbors. We quickly learned if we wanted anything other than coconuts, taro, slippery cabbage (not any better tasting that it sounds), betel nuts or stick tobacco, we'd better get there no later than sunrise. If we were lucky, we might find at least one special thing. Once it was watercress. The poor lady bringing it to market was instantly beleaguered by eager buyers before she could even unload her bundles of spicy green watercress. Another time, it was tomatoes or green peppers or sometimes green beans. For the most part, such vegetables were in short supply but high demand.

Another early morning activity, occurring on the water between Lilisiana village and the wharf, was fishing. This area was dotted with canoes, one man in each jigging a line with a shell hook up and down. The favored place for this activity was around the wharf where numerous colorful small reef fish darted through the cool aqua water. The other type of fishing we saw only here was done with a very large fishing net supported by four hoped branches and controlled by a long pole. The fisherman handles the fishing net with one hand while standing in his canoe and poling into position with his other hand. Amazingly, this pose is maintained motionless as a statue, sometimes for several hours.

Since the Solomons lie in an almost windless latitude, we were having to use our engine excessively. With no wind, our wind generator, which generally does a super job keeping our batteries charged, was almost useless. In order to make electricity we were going through a lot of diesel fuel. Fortunately, Auki had fuel, so we emptied our jerry jugs into the tank and went ashore to fill the jugs. It took two trips to shore, walking a block to the fuel depot and carrying the jugs back to our dinghy tied to the wharf.

Another serious problem here was water. Due to El Niño, a weather system that among other things makes dry places wet and vice versa, the Solomons were experiencing a severe drought of many months duration. Finding drinking water was almost as difficult as finding gold. In villages with spring water it wasn't a problem, but in those where water catchment was the only source of fresh water, we felt asking for water would be an imposition as they barely had enough for their own use. We had been told that water was available in Auki at the wharf, but because of the drought, none was to be had there. We asked a policeman in Auki where we could obtain water. He said the water was now coming from a nearby village spring (piped in), but it would only be tuned on from 4 to 6 p. m. in Auki and in the early morning. He showed us a spigot at the local market and said to come back in the afternoon at four.

Joy went back with two jugs, but with others also waiting, she was disappointed when the water did not come on. It was here she met

Theresa Taloga who, seeing Joy's difficulty, walked over to her and said she would be happy to bring us water from her village. Joy brought Theresa back to the dinghy by the wharf where I was waiting. We gave Theresa a ride to her village and left all our jugs, which hold 15 gallons of water, with her.

Around 6:30, Theresa returned with our full jugs. With her were two of her girls, Brenda and Mary, ages seven and four. Theresa said the water never came on in town so she took our jugs up the river and filled them. As we found out later, when we went up the river ourselves for water, it was a distance of about two miles each way. Theresa paddled both ways to get our water, an exceedingly kind act. It was Theresa's overture to friendship.

She spoke reasonably good English and was eager to tell us about her life, her family, her village, and her culture. But also contact with us meant an opportunity for her to get some clothing and a bit of money. She was quite ingenious in achieving her ends. Bringing us water obligated us to return the favor. Then she brought coconuts, pineapples and bananas. With each act she would say something like, "My daughter needs a t-shirt, or my son would like a pair of shorts." One day Theresa brought us some shell money necklaces. They were for sale. For cash. Naturally we bought one.

Despite Theresa's plotting and planning, all her dealings with us were pleasant. Unlike some islanders, whose approach was entirely mercenary, her actions were always conducted in a friendly way because she knew how to extend herself in friendship. Before marrying she had taught school, so she had had a few years of high school education. She invited us on a walk to see a large inland lake. It was a long walk through her mother's village, over raised walkways built of coral, constructed, as Theresa informed us, for convenience of getting around the village during the wet season. The neatly built "leaf" houses gave the village a prosperous appearance. The frame of these houses is of solid wood. Woven coconut palm or pandanus mats cover the wooden frame while the roof is constructed of palm thatch. From the village we passed into Lilisiana, Theresa's village, and here we saw close up the stilt houses we had seen when entering Auki. Soon we passed out of the village following a dirt road that ran parallel to the lagoon. Much of the road was shaded by coconut palms and other trees, but some patches were in full sunlight. Along the way we passed the brick making house and also a graveyard where Theresa asked me to take a picture of everyone standing behind her grandmother's grave.

At last, we came to an area where Theresa led us from the road into the jungle. Here the earth, very black, oozing mud, was strewn with palm fronds and cut pandanas. Our thongs offered little protection against the saw-toothed pandanas, which cut our legs and feet. Theresa and her two girls were blithely walking over this razor sharp cover in bare feet! Eventually, Theresa ended up carrying the younger child who was tired. After bogging down several times in the mud, we finally arrived at the lake. The edge was covered in water lilies. Brenda immediately set about picking a bouquet. This looked like perfect crocodile territory to me. I asked Theresa about it. She said formerly many crocs lived here until the priest blessed the lake. Now, no more crocs! (This same day, an old man told us they used to worship crocodiles here, much as they do sharks in Langa Langa Lagoon.)

We had a pleasant walk back, meeting along the roadside on our way from the lake, the same mother and three daughters who had earlier been collecting and chopping firewood. Now, they were loading it onto their heads, first putting a stack of leaves underneath to cushion the load. They balanced this hefty stack of wood on their heads with no hands. We wondered why they still persist in this laborious method of collecting wood when they could cooperatively use a truck to haul wood to the village. Why have they never imported and used work animals or a wheeled vehicle that could be hand pushed? We felt perplexed that these people adhere so religiously to custom, doing things the way they have been done for centuries. We did notice one change. They use nails in building houses instead of lashings.

Once back in the village, I was able to examine closely one of the suspended fishing nets used by the statuesque fishermen. These nets, handmade from very find fishing line, must require a lot of time and patience to make. Characteristically in traditional societies, work is not measured by how long a task takes, probably because so many tasks —being essentially repetitive — are accomplished without any conscious thought or effort. Usually the women's weaving, for example, is done while they talk among themselves and watch their young children and infants. Likewise, the men building a house or canoe talk or even sing as they work.

After almost a week in Auki, we knew it was time to move down through Langa Langa Lagoon. What an attractive scene with the reef breaking on one side, the solid green forested mountains on the opposite side and the blue and green studded lagoon in between. Most of the passage through the lagoon was well marked, but we did come to a place that abruptly wound through a narrow channel which was up to 70 feet deep but only about 30 feet wide and came up to a depth of one or two feet on the reef on both sides! All along the lagoon we saw artificial islands, some with only one hut and a few banana trees and palms. Finally, we came to a very wide place in the lagoon where we anchored off Talakali village, a Seventh Day Adventist's (SDA) settlement. There are about four villages in the general area.

In less than 30 minutes after we anchored, an older man stopped to talk with us. He introduced himself as Harry, a captain on one of the cargo ships; he is from Talakali and invited us to come for a visit. In this immediate area a number of wooden ships are being built, each in its own shed on an artificial finger built of coral rock. We told Harry we would very much like to see the ships they were building here. We followed Harry's directions, coming ashore at a "wharf" which was another artificially made projection built of coral rock. When we landed, we were met by a young man named Clifton. He took us to Harry's house and then gave us a tour of several boats under construction, answering our questions and generally telling us a lot about the boat building industry. These massive boats built from local hard woods range in size from 40 to 100 feet. This is the only place in the Solomons where these cargo/fishing boats are being made. The boat sheds are a unique extension of the artificial island. The shed is placed on an artificial peninsula made of coral. Obviously, they have not lost their centuries-old technique for such construction, but have modified it by extending its use.

We thought it a bit strange that Clifton never looked directly at us, but assumed it was his shyness. Later, he told us that his vision is very poor. His story is a sad one. About three years before, someone had given him and two other men mentholated alcohol to drink, telling them it was a drink like beer. The other two men died from drinking it. Clifton, very sick, was taken to the hospital where he remained unconscious for two or three days. He survived but sustained permanent damage to his vision.

We told Clifton that on our first evening here we had been visited by Peter, the chief from the custom village, Lalasi. Peter said we could visit Lalasi, but it would cost us $15 each to come. Clifton volunteered to be our guide, as he did not think it would be a good idea for us to go there alone. Clifton said he had an uncle in the village who was an old man.

Anchored in front of Talakali, we had many visitors, both children and adults. Some came wanting to trade vegetables or fruits for money or clothing; many brought shells and shell money necklaces for Langa Langa Lagoon is the only place in the Solomons where shell money is made today. Not that many years ago it was the currency used in Malaita. Today, its use has survived primarily as the bride price. Brides are still purchased in Malaita, regardless of the religion one practices, be it Church of England, Catholic or SDA.

Albert, a man from Koalia, another custom village on an island near Lalasi, came to sell shell money necklaces and shells. He wanted us to come to Koalia. It would cost us $30 each plus $10. I bought two shell necklaces from him and one map cowrie, but I told him we had already made arrangements with Peter to visit Lalasi. Albert kept telling me that what Peter was doing was wrong. We should not go to Lalasi because we would be overcharged (even though Albert's price was over twice as much!). Albert, a very fat, slovenly man with a mouth stained red from betel net and big drool patches of red at the corners of his mouth, did not inspire confidence. He had a terrible scar on one arm. He said it was from a shark bit. Albert was an operator, a high-pressure salesman. In Los Angeles, he would have been working at the sleaziest used car lot! As he talked, the price for the village visit kept rising. I expected him to add tax any minute!

Later, when we returned to Auki and told Theresa about our adventures, we mentioned Albert. She knew him and told an interesting story about his scar. She recounted that Albert had been in a fight with another man who was a witch doctor. The witch doctor sent the shark after Albert and it attacked him.

On the day after we visited Lalasi, Albert appeared very early in the morning, angry that we had not come to his village as he had made preparations for us, he said. Uninvited, he hefted his obscenely obese body right onto our boat at the same time putting on deck his anchor, an indistinguishable lump of rust. I asked him to get off the boat, but he repeated his litany once again. I remained calm and apologized for the misunderstanding, but I refused to be intimidated by his blustery, demanding manner. He then stuck his ugly, disgusting betel nut-stained face right up to mine and yelled that I had lied to him! I told him again to get off my boat immediately, but he was enraged and continued to yell at me in a threatening manner while his eyes blazed. Joy was on the ham radio and apparently oblivious to what was happening on deck. I went below, hoping Albert would leave. But he didn't. He kept yelling that we must come to his village, that Clifton had no right to take us to Lalasi. Finally, Joy went out with me and told him to get off the boat. She came back below. He left. None too soon.

Shortly afterwards, a young man, who must have been hovering nearby in his canoe during all the hullabaloo, stopped by and asked what the problem was. He understood English, said little, but laughed when we said we did not like Albert, his prices or his push ways. Once he heard our story, the young man left.

Some years ago Lalasi Island suffered severe hurricane damage which washed away much of the island. Today, it is a crowded, backward village. Primitive grass huts — not as well constructed as those we saw in Christian villages — sit on sand with just three or four feet between them. This village was such a contrast to the SDA and Catholic villages we had visited. As non-Christians, the villagers receive no education and as far as we could determine, Peter was the only one who spoke a little English. The biggest part of the village, and probably the nicest, is the men's area, which is taboo to women. Like most primitive Melanesian societies, Lalasi is largely divided by gender. The women have their taboo area too — a place now in tatters. This is the area where women are to go during their menstrual cycle or during childbirth. But the astounding thing is that the place is totally open for all to view, even though it is off limits to males. By contrast, the men's area is totally secluded, sequestered in the trees and hidden behind a coral rock wall. The entire village, which is on an artificial island, is surrounded by a waist high coral rock wall intended to keep the sea out. One fenced area, set apart by coral rock, is a pig pen for the animals sacrificed at the shark ceremony.

At Lalasi, a group of young boys led by two boys of 13 or 14 did several dances for us. The youngest dancers were no more than four or five years old and they wore no clothes. Music for the dance was sung and clapped by the adults.

All in all, it was a very poor village with no water and no place for gardens. Villagers must paddle across the lagoon to the mainland for everything. Peter seemed sad when he admitted to us that all the young people are leaving Lalasi, and indeed, there were no teenagers and no young men. Peter and a few adults are desperately trying to continue the old customs, but it seems the young people are uninterested.

One of the ways Lalasi makes money is by putting on the shark calling ceremony for tourists. In times past, native priests performed this ritual regularly as a form of shark worship, but now the ceremony is conducted only once a year or specially for tourists at a rate of $5,000 a performance. We were told the sharks are now called by name and fed pig meat, a substitute for human flesh. Those who worship the sharks say they can swim among them and will not be attacked. Clifton told us he has seen the shark calling, that the sharks responded to their names and came from smallest to largest. Even though he is an avowed Seventh Day Adventist, some of the old ways still linger in his thoughts. As we were coming back across the lagoon from Lalasi, he said if he fell overboard at sea, the sharks would rescue him and bring him back to land. He would then be obligated to pay them back with pig meat. If he failed to give it to them, they would kill him.

Clifton had a keyboard. When he learned I could play, he eagerly asked me to play it. For this purpose we came to his house on a Sunday afternoon. His nephew, a very shy young man, was finally persuaded to play the instrument. Although totally self taught, he had a nice style. Clifton also played, a little more hesitantly and not as well as his nephew. Clifton's forte was singing, harmonizing. I played some sing-along tunes and some church hymns, including some Negro spirituals which a number of people sang and harmonized beautifully. Like his nephew, Clifton plays by ear. They would love to learn more about playing the keyboard. Over and over I encountered Solomon Islanders who wanted to learn more about playing the keyboard and the guitar.

The Solomon Islanders' love for music manifests at a very young age. It was quite common to hear children in their canoes, often not even close to each other begin singing in harmony. Adults, too, would spontaneously sing alone or in harmony in their canoes. One night in Auki a number of men were out fishing. For hours their voices crooned some haunting tunes. For all their apparent problems, these people must feel some kind of joy when they vocalize.

Often the children, very young ones of four to six, would paddle out in their canoes and just hang around the boat, giggling when we spoke to them, but in no way bothering us. One day they started singing in English, "My Bonny Lies over the Ocean." After they sang it several times and started again, I went into the cockpit and started singing along. They were so astounded and amused that they stopped singing and listened to me, smiling sweetly.

Several days before we left, we gave Clifton a spare pair of sunglasses that we had. He had once said that the sun hurt his eyes. He was so thankful and pleased. From then on he always had his sunglasses on when outside.

Our plan had been to sail to Hanesavo, an island at the northwest of the Florida group, when leaving Auki. Our plans changed when we developed two problems. First, our alternator had been acting up. On the power back to Auki, it stopped altogether. Joy slapped in a spare that we carried, but it does not put out as much voltage. We needed to get it repaired. Secondly, the refrigerator stopped cycling. Since it was running constantly, we had to turn it off. The only place to have a chance of finding parts for the refrigerator or having them sent in was Honiara. Possibly we could find someone there who could repair the alternator. From Auki we returned to the "waterhole."

Three boats were anchored there. *Ariel, Sea Smoke,* and *Aku Ankka.* That evening, having drinks on *Aku Ankka,* we learned that all of these people had been afflicted with malaria. They and other cruisers had had blood tests in Honiara. About 90 percent had tested positive for malaria and were treated. Joy and I decided to return to Honiara so we too could have the blood test.

There were three places in Honiara to have the tests, but everyone was recommending the Malarial Research Clinic where you could see your own slide. Since it was only a few days before Christmas, few staff were at the clinic. A young Solomon Island university student offered to test us. He was home from Papua New Guinea where he had been attending school until the university was closed down as a result of political problems set off by difficulties in Bougainville. Although Bougainville is populated by Solomon Islanders, it belongs to Papua New Guinea. It had recently been the scene of riot and revolution.

We watched the student make the slides and then stain them. All three of us looked at our slides under the microscope. The student had already showed us pictures of what to look for. Joy's blood was normal, but mine showed some broken up parasites. The student identified them as *Plasmodium vivax*, the type of malaria that recurs.

From the clinic we went to the Honiara Hospital, a rundown place, perhaps best described as a pest hole. I must admit that I felt just entering the place was to invite some lethal disease. Nonetheless, we entered the dirty, dim place filled with people. From the waiting area we could see lethargic patients in their beds. Also waiting to see a doctor were our friends Pam and Jim from *Dream Maker* from Boston. Pam was sure she had hepatitis. She was jaundiced and extremely tired.

Finally, the nurse, sitting at a small table cluttered with papers, called me over. I sat on a bench opposite her and handed her my slip of paper, which designated that I had malaria, PV, stage 1. The nurse handed me a thermometer and indicated I should hold it under my armpit. She spoke very softly, so that I had to ask her to repeat what she said. She told me that in the Solomons nurses take care of patients with malaria. She wrote out a prescription for me and directed me to the pharmacy, a separate building just down from the hospital. I went there only to learn that as I was not employed, I was not entitled to medication from there. I would have to go to one of the pharmacies in town.

At the pharmacy I bought 12 Chloroquin tablets. I was to take four each day for the next three days. On Christmas Day, I took my last dose.

Peter was not so lucky as I. Just shortly after we arrived in Honiara *Canowie* powered back in from Morovo Lagoon. When Peter came down with a very high fever, nausea and vomiting, his family powered back, night and day, as quickly as they could to Honiara. By the time they arrived Peter was just barely conscious. A blood test showed that he had *Plasmodium falciparum*, stage 4. Very serious. It was only two days before Christmas and there were no doctors to be found. Joyce went to a pharmacist who gave the proper medication and later came to the hotel where Peter was staying, bringing a doctor. For the next week, Peter lay in bed, often unconscious while taking the cure, which made him feel as bad or worse than the disease.

Fortunately, *Race the Wind* returned to Honiara and George quickly fixed our alternator. Joy replaced the thermostat in the refrigerator and it worked once again. It was time to escape the city and begin exploring again. With *Race the Wind* a couple of hours behind us, we left for Gavutu. We had intended to go directly to Hanesavo, but a low on the weather map prompted us to seek a more secure anchorage. En route, *Race the Wind* passed us. They tied to Gavutu wharf and we rafted up next to them, none too soon. A huge downpour overtook us and filled all our tanks and every jug in no time and washed down the boat as well.

Chapter 13

HEADHUNTING AND
BLACKBIRDING

Almost two weeks of bad weather, spawned by a cyclone in the making, kept us holed up at the Gavutu wharf with *Race the Wind*. Seldom do these weather systems become a full-blown hurricane in the Solomons, but this time we were concerned that it might. During this cyclone watch, other boats came into Gavutu for protection. Joining us were *Dream Maker* with Pam and Jim and *Ariel* with Glen and Erja. On our last night at Gavutu we got together for a potluck and barbecue on the wharf with a large bonfire to discourage the mosquitoes.

The next day, January 12, we left Gavutu in company with *Race the Wind* headed for Morovo Lagoon in the New Georgia group. Cloud cover was 100 percent, but the wind had calmed down. From the protection of Gavutu we couldn't anticipate what the swell would be or how much wind we would have. Clear of Gavutu, we found a large southwesterly cross swell, resulting from cyclone "Betsy" that ran counter to the NNW wind. It was light enough to carry a full main and full jenny. By midafternoon, the fresh sailing breeze stopped and we turned on the diesel. Then about sunset an incredible squall swept down upon us. Its center was located about two miles off our port stern. We monitored its movement on the radar and were surprised to see it was two miles wide and ten miles long. It caused us no particular problems, but shortly after it passed, another squall full of wind and torrential rain got us. Then once again, no wind. We powered through the night. Sunrise found us surrounded by squalls. About two miles ahead of us, *Race the Wind* got clobbered by a giant squall. It passed us by but left a confused sea. Like an army, the squalls marched over us. Our entrance into Morovo Lagoon seemed iffy as continual squalls wiped out sight of land and visibility for determining the depth of the water. *Race the Wind*, two or three miles ahead of us, got through the pass and reported on the VHF that they were waiting for us. We decided to continue on to Mbatuna as there was no place that looked secure enough to anchor at Mbili. Also, the wood carvers gave us no peace as hoards of them in canoes hovered around our vessels as we tried to navigate through the lagoon.

What a view greeted us: high mountains and hundreds of heavily wooded little islands. Clouds and mist clung to the scene that periodically disappeared entirely as black squalls whipped through with furious winds and blinding rain. The lagoon peaked with white caps. We plowed into the froth, sometimes barely making headway. We were hugging *Race the Wind's* stern as we could not see the color of the water to judge where shallows, reefs or shoals lay. Her steel hull was our insurance against running onto a reef.

Naturally, as soon as we anchored, the weather cleared. There's some perverse law at work here — almost as predictable as the tides — which any deep-water sailor can confirm. Of course we were exhausted, but precocious Solomon wood carvers were not going to miss an opportunity to display their wares. Within minutes, a swarm of canoes loaded with carvings had surrounded our two boats. It wasn't long before as many as eight men at a time had scrambled aboard and laid out a fantastic assortment of masks, *nguzu-nguzus* and other carvings, most of them beautifully inlaid with mother-of-pearl from the nautilus shell. Of all the Pacific peoples, the Solomon Islanders are the most aggressive traders. They were interested in anything — silverware, plates, pots and pans, sheets, towels, clothing, fishing line, lures, batteries, radios and tape decks. The following morning more hopeful carvers arrived with their wares, and once again the feverish trading began. Much of their pleasure seems to derive from the bargaining itself. They wanted to see the entire selection of trading goods and try various combinations of items before striking a final agreement.

Of all the Solomon Island carvings, the *nguzu-nguze* is the most symbolic. In earlier times, when setting out on an expedition, headhunters placed the human-like *nguzu-nguzu* figures on the prows of their canoes. It was believed these figures would protect them from *kesoko*, spirits who lurked at sea. With its open eyes, the *nguzu-nguzu* could prevent the *kesoko* from warning the intended victims that headhunters were coming on a raid.

Not only were heads taken in battle. Heads were taken when human sacrifices were required as part of many kinds of ceremonies. The building of a house or the launching of a canoe demanded a human sacrifice. Afterwards human heads were hung in the village canoe house on display.

The introduction of iron axes resulted in building more houses and canoes in a shorter period of time, activities which required human sacrifices, so headhunting reached an almost fevered pitch in the final decades of the nineteenth century, according to Romano Kokonge who wrote about these practices in *Ples Blong Iumi: Solomon Islands, the Past Four Thousand Years.*

One day later we powered to Telina Island to join *Canowie.* Even though arriving at 5:15 in the evening, we were besieged by wood carvers. Many consider the carvers in this area to be the best in the country. The most renown of these is John Wayne. A medium sized affable man, John enjoys taking visitors on a tour into his rain forest. Not only was this privately guided tour breathtakingly beautiful, John's discussion of the history of the conversion of Solomon Islanders was in itself worth the trip. He took us to what had once been the sanctuary of his last pagan ancestor. Inside a little chamber built of stones was a stack of skulls. He also pointed to a much larger stone structure that was totally enclosed. According to John, this one too was filled with skulls of his great grandfather's victims. Rather wryly, John remarked that this ancestor was noted for his fierceness. His popular name translates to something like "the man you never defy." John mentioned that his great-grandfather fought against the missionaries as he refused to be converted. The colonial impact on the Solomons accounts for some of the darkest moments in human history.

Some of the most severe traumatic change occurred in the Western Pacific during the last third of the nineteenth century. Earlier in the century the British had become the world's largest producer of cotton cloth. One of the major reasons for expanding the British Empire had been to acquire more raw materials, cotton being one of them. After 1860, Britain gained possessions in Melanesia, and British Australia began to take a lively interest in the economic development of Fiji and the Solomons. But in order to develop these enterprises in Australia and Fiji, the colonials needed unskilled labor to work the cotton and later sugar cane fields. The native Australian Aboriginals would not work on these plantations nor would the native Fijians. To find laborers the colonials turned to the Solomon Islands and parts of Vanuatu. Between 1863 and 1914 about 100,000 Pacific Islanders went as indentured laborers to Queensland (Australia), Fiji, Samoa and New Caledonia. About one third of these came from the Solomons, according to Matthew Cooper. When not enough workers could be secured through normal recruitment efforts, people were kidnapped or tricked, a practice referred to as "blackbirding." About 10,000 Solomon Islanders were transported to Fiji between 1870 and 1911. By 1914, only 4,061 had returned. Between 1871 and 1904, 18,735 went to Queensland. Of these, 14,105 returned home. By the 1880s, most of the recruits came from the interior, especially on the islands of Guadacanal and Malaita in the Solomons. The coastal people profited from their exchanges of provisions for recruits — people they had captured from the interior. As well as raiding the interiors of their own island, some Solomon Islanders made a practice of raiding other islands and taking prisoners whom they exchanged for trade goods. Perhaps it was this very practice, which caused the animosity between coastal dwellers and bushmen, which lingers today in a less intense form. No doubt raids of this type would have triggered revenge attacks, which may explain the excessive number of skulls John Wayne's ancestor accumulated.

Labor recruiting intensified in the 1890s. Most of the recruits were unmarried men in their teens or twenties. Women formed only about 7.5 percent of the laborers. When the Queensland trade began to taper off, colonists cultivated about 36,500 hectares of coconuts in New Georgia, Guadalcanal and the Russell Islands. Approximately 1200 islanders, many with previous experience in Queensland or Fiji, were employed on these plantations in 1907. Expansion, in fact, continued until World War I.

Of course, the colonial labor trade had many other profound effects on Pacific Islanders. Solomon Islanders received payment for recruits through trade goods such as pipes, mirrors, and axes. In turn such trade goods altered the material culture of the islanders. The most important trade items, however, were firearms. Muskets and rifles were introduced to Malaita on a large scale prior to 1884, when British vessels from Fiji and Australia were prohibited from carrying guns aboard. After that date arms were still smuggled ashore or openly traded by German and French recruiters who were not subject to the British ban on firearms. When weapons were recalled in 1927, 1070 rifles were surrendered in just one district of Malaita.

The introduction of firearms upset traditional customs and values on Malaita and elsewhere. The possession of guns stimulated domestic hostilities in unprecedented numbers and increased casualties. A missionary named Ivens described a "thirty years war" on Malaita as resulting from the possession of firearms. During this time killing became more casually motivated.

Labor recruiting became extremely dangerous to all concerned. Not uncommonly, ship's crews were murdered and vessels plundered. Above all other Solomon Islanders, the Malaitans earned the reputation as being the most ferocious and volatile.

Probably the most complete record of events we have for the labor recruitment comes from Malaita, which also seems to have been the center for such activities. Anthropologist Roger M. Keesing has spent more than three decades studying the Kwaio people's struggle against European cultural aggrandizement and conversion to Christianity. His book, *Custom and Confrontation: The Kwaio Struggle for Cultural Autonomy,* provides a lucid account of some major conflicts — many of them preserved through oral narrative forms — occurring in the last 120 years among these bushmen of Malaita. Keesing's analysis, based on oral accounts of witnesses and participants in some of the most violent confrontations not only between Europeans and Solomon Islanders but also between Solomon Islanders themselves, reveals the nature of these conflicts to be complexly multifaceted issues embedded in cultural values that have been blatantly ignored and often maliciously derailed. A case in point is the first known recruiting vessel, the *Carl*, which came to the east coast of the Kwaio in 1871. A ship based in Fiji, it gained its reputation for kidnapping islanders and transporting them in sub-human conditions. The kidnapping set the scene for revenge, but a further problem it also initiated was that of blood feud. Families of young men who did not return might assume that the young men had been killed. In Kwaio society murder was cause for blood feud. Whoever avenged the wrong would be rewarded with pigs and shell wealth. Blood feud could involve many killings and be carried on for three or four generations. If a family put up a blood bounty for lost relatives, the killing of *any* European would satisfy this bounty. Further incentives for attacking these labor-recruitment ships and killing of the entire crew was, of course, the plunder the warriors gained from these ships.

The fact is, the warriors gained power and prestige and goods from plunder while at the same time fulfilling "kinship obligation." Yet, the bottom line is that Europeans were intruders and their invasion threatened Kwaio power and disrupted the normal functioning of their culture.

Clearly the European intrusion resulted in increased violence. The physical factors of violence, the introduction of firearms, revenge and plunder, are easily pinpointed and explained, but what is far more allusive is the extreme psychological and spiritual havoc that prevailed in the wake of colonialism. One passage Keesing quotes from a young plantation worker who had been missionized in Queensland in 1886 gives us some glimpse of the trauma experienced on a personal level. The young plantation worker said he didn't want to become a Christian because he would be unable to fight, which meant someone would kill him immediately when he got back to the islands.

Since the Second World War, many of the Pacific island groups have gained their "independence", a word that is truly a misnomer because most often these peoples, as I have already described, have had no control over their destinies. Nonetheless, throughout the entire process of Westernization and Christianization, the Kwaio of Malaita, some 2,000 tribes people, have managed to embrace their traditional lives tenaciously. But for them it has been an ongoing battle to live as they chose to live. For almost a century, they have resisted Christian evangelism and fought against the government to retain their sovereignty. They steadfastly want to follow their customary law rather than submit to British law. These differences have brought assassination of missionaries and government agents who relentlessly press on. As Kessing wrote: "In the postcolonial period, continuing demands for a substantial degree of cultural autonomy — the freedom to follow customary law and the defense of ancestral shrines and taboos against Christian invasion and defilement — has led to sustained confrontation with the governments of Province and nation" (p. 4).

We enjoyed out stay at Telina. Each day Ruben, a fisherman, stopped to ask if we wanted fish or lobster. He caught lobster at night and would bring it to us around midnight or later. If we wanted fish, he would come by late afternoon with several large fish and let us chose. He asked for $2 or $3 Solomon — about $1 US — for a fish or lobster. For fruit and vegetables we traded with islanders or paid cash, whichever they preferred.

John Wayne came to the boat for a visit, bringing his guitar. He wanted to play my keyboard. Of course, he is a self-taught, natural musician. He plays guitar very well, and we spent several hours making music together on the guitar and keyboard. He would have traded any number of his fine carvings for my keyboard, but I simply couldn't part with it much as I would have liked for him to have a keyboard.

On January 22, we said our farewells to Telina villagers. With us were *Race the Wind* and *Dream Maker*. We spent the night in the Mindeminde Islands tucked up in a bay just north of Chuchulu. The following day, in a flat calm, we powered through Njai Pass past the picturesque villages of Patutiva Point and Seghe. Further down the lagoon, we caught a 2-½ foot wahoo. The exciting part of this transit was crossing Hele Bar. The water varied in depth from 20 to 11 feet, deep enough, but so clear the coral looked as if we would crash right into it. About 2:30 p.m., we reached Viru Harbor, a deep bay that winds back into steep, thickly wooded mountains. They were draped with charcoal black rain clouds, which emitted cool breezes. That evening *Race the Wind* came over for a tempura dinner.

We left Viru under power at 9 the next morning. Runoff, caused by heavy rains the previous night, had colored the bay opaque brown. The sea, though glassy, carried an uncomfortable swell from the Southwest, refraction off New Georgia. We had one false try when searching for

Rendova Harbor. When at last we found Rendova, it was a lovely deep bay with cuts going off around scattered islands. Disappointingly, this was no place to swim. Discouraging such ideas, one local told us there was a resident crocodile.

By 7 a. m. on January 25, we were underway for Gizo where we needed to go to check out of Customs from the Solomons to begin our long voyage northward to Pohnpei, one of the Federated States of Micronesia. There was absolutely no wind but a terrible swell, which prompted us to raise the mainsail for stability. En route we had another heart racing experience when we crossed over two bars with coral heads. The least depth we picked up was 17 feet. We anchored in Gizo Harbor around 2:30 in the afternoon with many other boats. But there were only two we knew: *Shiraz* and *Gypsy Rover*. We had no intention of remaining in Gizo so long, but in the end we were there for just over a week. We needed fuel and in order to purchase it we had to make an appointment at the fuel dock. After we were presented with the bill, we knew something was amiss. It was for about two times as much fuel as we could hold. So, we went to speak to the manager, an American. Prior to this incident Mike had been talkative and amiable enough, so we anticipated no problems. He originally came from Iowa to the Solomons with the Peace Corps. Instead of returning home, he had married a local woman and had been there for 11 years. We explained our fuel capacity to him. Mike said no sweat they would run a test because frequently the calibration was off.

While we had been off talking to Mike, Kate from *Race the Wind* had stayed on board to keep Jason there. When we got back to the dock, she was beaming. She said the test had proved they pumped 200 liters into a drum; both gages confirmed it. But now, Mike, who had followed us down, was not prepared to accept the proof of his own test! I refused to pay for 376 liters when we had taken only 222. Mike yelled profanities and stalked off in a huff. Joy and I discussed the situation. He could always pump the fuel from our tanks; that would prove it. After about 30 minutes, Joy went back to speak with him again. He said he would split the difference with us. I agreed to think about it overnight, but I was not inclined to pay for fuel that I did not receive.

By now all the yachties in the harbor knew what had happened. We talked to *Canowie* on the VHF and Peter said he would come pick me up in his fast boat, *Magic Carpet*, so we so we could go to the police station. This offer was in response to what Mike had told Joy — that he had called the police and reported that we refused to pay the bill.

About six policemen sat there listening attentively to my story. By now it was closing time and Mike had left for the day. I asked the police what I should do. Stay on the dock or leave. They advised me to stay there overnight unless Mike came back and asked us to leave. If that happened, they wanted me to anchor in front of the police station.

It was an uncomfortable night at the dock. Not only was it noisy, there was no breeze whatsoever. Morning was overcast and it rained. Opening time came and went, but Mike did not appear. Joy went to see him. He wanted to know how much we would pay for. She told him 222 liters. He then said he would charge us $1.20 a liter, though the original price had been $1.05 because we took more than 100 liters.

The previous evening Peter had photocopied his bill of sale. He had been at the fuel dock in the morning just before us at 11:00. We came at 1:30, but there was no one between us. He paid for 154 liters — the difference between 376 and 222! Obviously there was a bookkeeping error. Still, when presented with the evidence, Mike refused to listen to reason. Peter and I went back to the police. We showed the Peter's receipt and told them what we thought had happened. They agreed. Sergeant Richards said he would go speak with Mike. First Richards came down to talk with us on the boat. We showed him our full tanks and jugs. Then he went off to speak with Mike. When Sergeant Richards returned, he said Mike had agreed to accept payment for 222 liters at $1.05 per liter! We paid. Mike never once apologized for his behavior of the inconvenience he had caused us.

We were further detained by an infection I developed in my right leg, sustained when I slipped in some spilled diesel fuel and skidded into the stainless bracket for the winch cleat. It was only a tiny blood blister type bump on my shin, nothing serious I thought. My mistake was in not washing it and disinfecting it. Twenty-four hours later my leg was swelling and I could hardly put weight on it. Joy was convinced I had a bone infection. We consulted with Diana, a nurse on *Sea Smoke*. We concurred I should begin taking antibiotics, Fluxloxacylin, which we had in our medical kit.

The day before we left, Joy and I went to the hospital for a malaria test. There was no sign on the hospital, but we knew what it was by the crowd of people waiting outside. The hospital itself is a series of ramshackle, timber buildings resting on concrete stilts. It is painted bright green and in terrible need of repair. We walked up the concrete steps onto an open porch like area thronged with people sitting on wooden benches. We were the only whites. A sign in Pidgin told us to go into room 2 to see a nurse. It was a small room, dimly lit, and crowded with just one long table at which two nurses and one patient were seated. A young man, also a nurse, asked what we wanted and proceeded to prepare a slide then extracted blood from Joy's finger and mine. After smearing them and name tagging them, he handed each of us our slide and escorted us through a hospital room with several beds and two patients, down a hallway, finally outside and down the back steps of the building to a separate little shack with a tin roof. On the wall was a sign: URGENT BLOOD SLIDE. Underneath the directions told us to put our slides through the small window and wait. At least 10 others were waiting, about half of them children. One by one their names were called as the results were known. Finally the man called us. The results were negative. We went back to inform our nurse and to pay 20 cents each for a card, which he filled out, showing we had tested negative. We hoped this test would ease our way into Pohnpei where they have recently expressed concern about people arriving from malarial areas. They have begun spraying the boats and keeping them on a quarantine buoy for 24 hours. The spraying of boats is basically a joke. The only purpose it would serve would be to kill any mosquitoes that may have hitched a ride aboard, which is highly unlikely. A far greater danger lies in the possibility that an infected person coming into Pohnpei would be bit by a local *Anopheles* mosquito, which in turn would then start the cycle in Pohnpei.

Although we had officially checked out of the Solomons from Gizo, we still needed to fill our water tanks. Because of the drought, drinking water was not readily available in Gizo. It had only rained once while we were there and not enough to fill up. We were making a long passage, about 1800 miles. Although we planned stops at several places along the way, it was not likely these places would have water. We knew there was an abundance of spring water at Vanga Point where there is a Catholic

School for boys, and the Brothers like yachts to visit. One of our last minute purchases in Gizo was eggs. Everyone had been checking for days, but no eggs had come in. The day before we left word was passed along by yachties that the eggs had come. We bought two dozen, paying $9.50 a dozen -- $3.50 more than in Honiara. Maybe that was the special price to us, but I don't think so. I wondered how the islanders could afford them.

On February 4, we left Gizo at 2 p.m. It was only about a two-hour power to Vanga Point on Kolombangara Island. We arrived at 4:30, too late to check out the wharf to see if it was suitable for us to tie to. As it turns out, it would have been a mistake for us to tie to. The wharf would not accommodate our small craft. Our water tanks were dry the next morning, so we began the arduous task of jugging water by dinghy. We would load up all four jugs, take them back and empty them into our water tanks and return for more water.

Actually Vanga Point turned out to be one of our favorite places in the Solomons, and we were only able to spend two days there. The school, run by the Australian Marists Brothers, trains boys in mechanical and agricultural skills along with the more usual curriculum. Paul is the school principal. Sevard, a 70-year old who uncannily resembles a saint, keeps the bees and makes mead, and Max teaches the boys mechanics and the basics of electricity. Danny, a 17-year old student who has been at the school for 8 years, gave Joy and me a wonderful tour of the agricultural activities at the school. He very aptly explained how they do terrace farming to save soil. He picked some pineapples and avocadoes and dug some ginger and turmeric roots for us. Danny also showed us the crocodiles they are raising — all sizes from tiny to large. They sell them for the hides and meat. We saw the goats they raise but not the cows. Unfortunately, they had no chickens as their fowls had recently contracted some kind of virus and had to be killed. We purchased some of the freshly butchered steak and mince, which was tender and tasty. They also gave us fresh bush limes and huge grapefruit and we bought some mead and honey. The mead had a wonderfully delicate flavor, like a fine white wine. Brother Sevard took us into his beehives, saying the bees would not bother us and they did not. Several times we enjoyed tea with the Brothers and their delightful conversation. Joining them to teach at the school are two Peace Corps workers, a husband and wife.

We left with *Race the Wind* at 6 p.m. to make an overnight passage to the Arnavon Islands in Manning Strait. *Canowie*, having left Gizo that day, would be rendezvousing with us. Through the night, we maintained radio contact with each other. It was a calm, starlit night. No squalls. We ran the engine continuously as it was glassy calm. Sunrise was bland and gray. At first light Raverave Island was four miles off our beam. About 8 a.m., Jim on *Dream Maker* called us on the radio. He was eagerly awaiting our arrival as we were bringing fresh bread, veggies and fruit for them. Just before passing over a bar, we hit some turbulence and tagged a barracuda. We were forced to land it in the cockpit and remove the hook with a pair of pliers. We made a dramatic entrance. After the barracuda incident, Joy had gone aloft to the mast spreaders so she could see and guide me in. It was then another fish hit the line. Joy scrambled down and hauled in a beautiful wahoo.

Chapter 14

CROSSING THE EQUATOR

Our three days in the Arnavons passed pleasantly. We explored some of the small, uninhabited islands that were little more than sand spits, although they supported a rather thick growth of palm trees and the usual scrub and shrub found throughout the Pacific. We continued to monitor the weather pattern in the northern hemisphere, as we had been doing for several months in order to track of typhoons that were menacing Pohnpei, Kosrae, Chuuk (Truk) or Guam. By February, it seemed certain that the typhoon season had passed. The northeast trades had set in strongly, definitely a good sign. Yet, the reinforced trades — hauling at 30 to 35 knots — would make for a rowdy sail. Since basically our course was due North, the northeasterlies would pretty much put us on our ear. We kept hoping things would calm down a bit.

On the way to shore one day we stopped by to chat with Glen and Erja. Hanging on to their boat, we stood up in our dinghy and chatted with them for perhaps ten minutes. When we were ready to leave, I sat down and was just about to put my hand on the outboard to steady it while I cranked. My hand was perhaps two inches above the outboard when something out of the corner of my eye made me freeze. I looked. It was a black and white banded sea snake that had draped itself over the stern of the dinghy and the outboard! I had almost put my hand directly on it! I must have levitated because somehow the next thing I knew I was standing on Glen and Erja's boat. Simultaneously, I said to Joy, "Get out of the boat!" She had no concept about what was happening, but when she saw my hasty abandonment of the dinghy, she followed suit. Everyone was puzzled and looking at me strangely. "Look," I pointed, "a sea snake!"

It probably would not have bitten me, but I have an innate dislike of snakes. The reputation of sea snakes is that though poisonous they are non-aggressive and that their mouths are too small to inflict a bite except between the *fingers*, toes or earlobes. I had come too close to challenging the lore for my peace of mind.

Canowie and *Race the Wind* were also sailing with us to Pohnpei. Along the way we would stop at Roncadore Reef and then Ontong Java. For several years, I had been interested in sailing to Kapingamarangi and Ontong Java. Both are Polynesian outliers though politically they belong to different ethnic groups. Kaping is part of the Federated States of Micronesia, which is Micronesian, and Ontong Java belongs to the Solomons, which is Melanesian. Originally, we had been leaning toward Kaping, but we talked on the ham radio to cruisers who said the FSM (Federated States of Micronesia) government was not allowing boats from malarial areas into Kaping until they received some spray for the purposed of killing any lurking "mozzies." Thus a trip to Kaping would have been for naught since we were coming from a malarial area. However, I was elated with the prospect of visiting Ontong Java. Probably because of their size and location, both of these places are seldom visited. In fact, Kaping wasn't known to Europeans until first sighted in 1809.

Ontong Java, however, may have been discovered much earlier. Some historians think Mandaña stumbled upon Ontong Java on his first exploratory trip through the Pacific sometime in February 1568, shortly after leaving Santa Isabel in the Solomons. He reported sighting a group of low atolls at a latitude of about 5 ¼ degrees South, which he referred to as Baxos de las Candellaria. The name Ontong Java was bestowed upon this coral atoll by Abel Jaszoon Tasman, the Dutch explorer who sighted the island on March 22, 1643. His crew counted about thirty islands surrounded by reef. Tasman figured the latitude to be just less than 5 degrees South. He did not stop, but a group of islanders bearing bows and arrows came out in their canoes. No one seems to have paid much attention to Ontong Java until the early part of the twentieth century. H. I. Hogbin lived in Ontong Java for nine months in 1927-28 while he studied the customs and language of these peoples. His most comprehensive study of Ontong Java appears in *Law and Order in Polynesia*. Hogbin gives Ontong Java's correct location as about latitude 5 degrees 30 minutes South and longitude 160 degrees East. It lies 160 miles northeast of Santa Isabel.

We left the Arnevons on February 10 at 10 a. m., and powered out the pass across Manning Strait to Kologilo passage. *Canowie* and *Race the Wind* had left the previous day for Roncador Reef. The route we chose knocked off about 30 miles to Roncador. Fortunately, the current was with us through the strait and visibility was good. We passed over a shoal with a least depth of 22 feet. Large swells rocked us, but otherwise it was completely calm. By 4 p. m., a light rain dotted the softly rippled water. An hour later the wind picked up enough for us to ghost along at 2 knots under sail. Gradually, during the night, the wind rose and we made 3 to 4 knots. Several light rains came in the night, but no squalls.

In the morning the wind dropped again. In order to keep a respectable speed so as to make Roncador in the daylight — which was essential — we powered for the next hour and a half. Then again, when the wind came back, we went under sail, making 4.5 knots. A large squall appeared off the starboard and straight ahead as well. The wind held at about 10 knots and the sea presented three-foot swells.

At 11 a. m., we entered the squall area and by noon heavy rain streamed down while the wind disappeared. We furled the jenny and hove to in order to wait out the squall. We were only about 6 to 7 miles off Roncador and in the squall, the radar was useless as the squall blocked out everything. We spoke to *Canowie*, anchored in Roncador. They were also in the midst of a rainsquall. By afternoon, the sky cleared. Peter and Joyce's son Paul watched our approach on the radar to give us a course for the pass. Since Roncador is a sunken reef that surrounds a very large, mostly clear area of water, there is no land to orient oneself, and finding a pass is not especially easy. Since *Canowie* was navigating with a GPS and had a continuous readout of their position, they had easily located the pass. Eventually as we drew nearer, Paul came out in *Magic Carpet* to lead us in. We came through the pass and anchored by 2:24. Shortly after our arrival we went on *Magic Carpet* with Paul, Lorraine and Kate to explore. Paul and Kate snorkeled. The water was wonderfully clear and filled with huge fish. In no time at all, Paul easily speared enough fish to supply everyone with dinner. The sudden approach of a squall drove us all back aboard to close the ports and hatches before the deluge hit.

All three boats planned to leave in the early evening and sail overnight to Ontong Java. We were uncertain what our reception would be there. Since we had already checked out of the Solomons, it would be up to the chief or the headman to decide whether we could stay for a while and visit.

The evening weather map brought bad news. A low had moved in just south of us. It was generating the squalls we had been experiencing. Conditions probably would deteriorate even more, meaning we would have to cut short our stay at Roncador because this place did not offer a secure or protected anchorage in high winds.

The next morning, February 12, I sat in the cockpit and looked at the scene around me. Except for a fringe of light green and yellow brown water from the reef and an occasional projection of a massive piece of coral above the water, we seemed to be sitting in the middle of the ocean. The reef was virtually invisible, especially under cloudy sky. Clouds of grays and silver pressed up against each other, threatening more rain. Earlier in the morning we had had a drenching rain, which would have filled our water tanks, but they were already full from the previous day's downpour at noon.

Dream Maker called on the radio. They had left the day after us and were planning to stop at Roncador even though we were all leaving that evening. We decided to make a pot of chili in advance so dinner would be easy once we were underway.

At 5 p. m., with *Canowie* and *Race the Wind* we raised anchor and made our way toward the pass. It was squally. Radar showed a continuous big squall extending eight miles in front of us. But for the present it was only sprinkling. Once outside the pass, we hoisted the full main and had a nice smooth sail while in the lee of the atoll. The genny was only half unfurled. We only had 50 miles to go, so we needed to keep our speed down. Once away from the protection of the atoll, a heavy northwesterly swell socked into us.

As the night progressed, the winds continued to rise to gale force. It was becoming more and more uncomfortable and a lot of work, reefing for squalls and letting sails out when the squall had passed. The worst squall lasted over an hour, blasting us at 35 to 40 knots with gusts higher. What a miserable night, but we were thankful not to be at Roncador where we would have spent the night being concerned for our safety. In the open sea there were no present dangers. When we talked to Jim and Pam the next morning on the radio, they reported that they had 40 knots and six-foot seas at Roncador. Their anchor snubber of ¾" nylon had parted. Fortunately their anchor held, but they had spent an anxious night.

By sunrise, the worst of the squalls was over, and by 9 a. m., the winds had abated to the point that we let all furled and reefed sail out. Our speed continued to drop until we were creeping along at only two knots. To continue under sail to the pass at Ontong Java meant we would have to tack and it would take all day to get there. Being tired and wanting to arrive before dark, we chose to crank up the engine.

Canowie and *Race the Wind,* who had powered all night on course while we were tacking, were at the pass at daybreak. By 10 a. m., they were in and anchored in front of the village on Luangiua, the largest island in the atoll. Larger boats have the advantage of being faster than small boats, and they can, if they want, power into the teeth of a gale, whereas a 34-footer like *Banshee* can't really push into those kinds of seas.

The atoll, made up of a hundred small islands, surrounds a lagoon that is 40 miles long and 20 miles wide. This chain of coral islands rises only a few feet above sea level. Luangiua is about 4.5 miles long and 300 to 400 yards at the widest point. Fresh water is available from wells. The only mammals inhabiting these islands are rats and fruit bats (flying foxes), but there are numerous birds. As for the history of this atoll, Germany gained control of it in 1893, but in 1900, she relinquished it to Britain along with the islands of Choiseul and Santa Isabel in exchange for British rights in Samoa, which is how Ontong Java came to be part of the Solomons. In 1907, the population was estimated to be just over 5,000, but in 1928 Hogbin said there were less than 700 inhabitants. He predicted that in a few years there would be no people living there. Obviously his prediction did not come true.

What a pass! It was wide and visibility was excellent. The pass itself was a deep marine blue standing out against streaks of turquoise, yellow, and white. Palm trees waved gently above the landscape. We had sailed into a picture postcard of South Pacific Paradise. At 1:30, we anchored close to the other two yachts. They had been to see the chief, David, who said we were all welcome to stay upon presenting our clearance papers from Gizo. We went in for a visit and to meet the chief.

That night the squalls came out of the northwest, putting us on a lee shore. All night we bounced boisterously up and down as the fetch came the length of the lagoon and we worried about our safety. The next morning we went ashore for another visit. Just as we landed, a bad squall hit. Anxiously, we watched our anchored boats tugging fiercely at their anchors. But soon the rain cleared and we made our way through the village amidst a throng of children vying to hold the hands of each of us. The orderly village with large, rectangular shaped dwellings of pandanus leaf thatch, was snuggly set among a luxurious grove of coconut palms. Amazingly, the scene today looks no different from the picture of the village in Hogbin's book.

The headmaster gave us permission to visit the school, five rooms sheltered by tin roofs but open sided. Once we reached the school, children streamed out of their classrooms. Trying to take photos was an exercise in madness. Hands were frantically waving and heads bobbing, children giggling and scrambling to be the foremost body in the photo. My desire to take pictures of the school became an impossible dream. Stretching before me was a sea of waving, jostling children, many of them scraping to get close enough to touch me.

Such beautiful children. Most of them had the light brown, smooth skin of Polynesians and jet-black hair, ranging from straight to curly. Intermingled in the crowd were a number of Malaitans --- who stuck out almost as much as we whites — with their ginger hair, dark skin and broad Melanesian facial features.

We chatted with the teachers who spoke excellent English, but most of the children would do no more than giggle when we spoke to them, a response which does not mean they don't understand or speak English, but rather that they are too shy.

We explained to Chief David that for safety we needed to move our boats into a more protected place. He gave us permission to anchor at

Peiako Island, which is protected in northwesterlies. When we returned to the boat at 11 a. m., Joy and I discovered how close to disaster we were. Our anchor snubber had almost chaffed through. But even more dangerous was that in the steady thrashing up and down our chain had fed out almost completely! In a very short time it could have pulled loose entirely. Without an anchor, the wind would have pushed us onto the reef that lay astern.

George and Eva had returned to the village to drop off some gifts before leaving. By the time they returned, *Canowie* was already underway for the new anchorage. *Race the Wind* was quickly behind them, but Joy and I were still struggling to pull in the anchor chain. The situation became even more difficult when a squall roared in and sat on us. The squall intensified and stayed with us as we crossed the lagoon. Heavy rain and winds up to about 35 knots slowed our progress considerably. It took us two and a half hours to go seven miles to Peiako Island. This island joins to another smaller one by a reef. Therefore, in northwesterly winds we were fairly well protected from fetch, but the wind itself over the next few days became quite fierce and the low land offered little protection from it. As we learned on February 16, a tropical depression south of us had formed into a cyclone. We were getting rain and at times very heavy squalls. Why all the bad weather? It was the cyclone season in the Southern hemisphere, the monsoons.

We moved to Peiako on February 14th. On February 16, we had a double dose of bad news. About midday a strong squall hit. A gust in excess of 50 knots dislodged our anchor and *Race the Wind's*. For the next half hour, Joy and I were on deck in the cold drenching rain and howling wind, powering the boat into the wind to keep the strain off the anchor. Once the squall played itself out, we were in only 13 feet of water. In all the motion and swinging, the chain had wrapped itself smartly around a huge coral head. It took some doing to disentangle it.

Shortly after the squall we noticed the satnav was not working. In troubleshooting, we found a blown fuse, but after replacing it, it blew again. George came over to help. He and Joy decided to bypass the log and compass interface. But once again the new fuse blew. They had at least determined the problem was inside the satnav, not with the wiring. That meant we were back to basics — navigating by sextant. How long had it been since Joy or I had taken shots with a sextant? More than ten years! Well, we knew we had to brush up over the next few days and an atoll was not a bad place to practice sun shots. However, it was mostly cloudy and overcast, giving us little opportunity. Whenever the sun did peek out momentarily, we would run outside and try to take some sights. I felt good that I was able to take the first sight so quickly. Recalling the entire procedure of reducing the sight and plotting, however, took more effort. One problem was that we didn't have a current *Nautical Almanac.* They were not yet out when we left Australia, so we didn't have one for 1992. The 1991 *Almanac* told how to make a correction so as to use the 1991 edition for 1992, but as with most of these kinds of things, the instructions were confusing. Then, we remembered we had a navigation program for the computer, but we had no instructions for using this program. I worked and worked with the program, but I could not get it to give us a correct position, nor was it always off the same distance, which would have indicated it was my error. The randomness of the response led me to believe it was something about the program that was messed up. After hours of trying to determine why it wouldn't give a correct position, I asked Eve to take a look at it. She was more computer literate than I, but she too could not discover any way to make it work. I had to settle with the idea that it would only give us an LOP (line of position). With two LOPs taken three or four hours apart, we could advance the earlier one on our track for the distance traveled and derive a position.

Just about the time we were becoming more confident in our ability to use the sextant, we discovered another problem. Fresh water was leaking into number one cylinder of the diesel engine. Normally a discovery of this kind at Ontong Java, miles from any kind of diesel mechanic would have been devastating. But, only several hundred feet away was George, a master mechanic! His cursory examination led him to conclude it was probably the head gasket. Hesitantly, he asked if we had a spare. To his amazement, we chimed in unison that yes we did! We had been carrying it around for seven years. But, poor George, when we dug out the gasket, his eyes rolled up into his head in despair. He said, "Cross your fingers. This gasket is pretty beaten up!"

George is a genius. And Lady Luck was smiling, at least on one side of her mouth. In several hours he had pulled the engine head and replaced the gasket. He was still a bit dubious that the gasket was the problem as the old one had only a tiny piece broken out. However, here at Ontong Java there was no way to check the head for a crack. Once everything was back together, we fired the engine and ran it for a short while. George said he would not know anything until the morning when we could see if there was water in the air intake, which would mean the problem had not been solved.

For the rest of our waking hours on this night, we considered what it would be like to sail all the way to Pohnpei — about 1,000 nautical miles — with no engine, which meant very little battery power, perhaps not even enough to run our running lights at night or the radio. No refrigeration, of course. And we would be navigating by sextant, a first for me.

Morning came. Finally it was time for the engine trial. No water in the air intake, and the engine started! We took a three-hour break to celebrate. Since our arrival here, we had only worked. We went to the neighboring island to have a look. Joy and George each went in a dinghy, but Eve and I took the long way round. We walked over by the reef. It was quite long but an enjoyable walk.

We weren't the only ones having difficulties. George had to help Peter repair his outboard, and *Canowie* was also having problems with the alternator. Their generator was also shot. As Joyce said, "What happened to those carefree cruising days?"

Shortly after our arrival at Peiako, all of us had gone ashore to meet the family living there and to explain that Chief David had given us permission to anchor here so we could do some repairs and wait for better weather to begin our passage to Pohnpei. An extended family, three generations, lived here in a nicely constructed thatch house. They were gracious, inviting us to come ashore any time we wished. Unfortunately, the almost continuous foul weather, boat work and practice navigation kept us boat bound for most of the week we stayed. We told them a couple of days in advance that we would be leaving. The afternoon before our departure the family — the parents and two of their children — came for a short visit. They brought husked coconuts that were neatly tied together by strips of the outer husks, which were still attached so the coconuts could be hung up in a cluster. They said they knew for a long sea voyage we would need green drinking nuts.

With some trepidation about navigation by sextant, we left our secure little cove at Peiako on February 21 at 10 a.m. George and Eve had planned to stay close by us for the first day or so, which would allow us to check our position against theirs. It was a way to assure us that our navigation was working. Joy had already determined during our sextant practice that the Plath sextant (the Mercedes of sextants) was too heavy for her to use. Peter loaned us a spare plastic sextant, but as we soon discovered, it was so warped that readings were several degrees off. Since each degree represents 60 nautical miles, the error was too great for us to use this sextant.

Joy and I devised a procedure we would follow when taking sights. She would come outside with me and hold my watch, which gave us Universal Coordinated Time (formerly known as Greenwich Mean Time). When I got the sun — that is when I managed to make the sun appear to rest on the horizon — I would say "mark" and she would record the time. Next to the time she would then write the degrees and minutes the sextant measured, which indicated the distance the sun was above the horizon. This angle then was one part of the spherical triangle used to resolve LOP. Within about five minutes, I would take four or five such shots. All of them were recorded. In this way it was immediately possible to see if one of the shots was off. Next, I would go into the computer program and input the time and the sextant reading, using only one of the good shots. What the computer program did was bypass the necessity of referring to the *Nautical Almanac* for specific data, which in turn would then give figures one would use to enter another set of tables. These tables obviated the need to use spherical trigonometry to solve the problem. But the computer program did this computing in a fraction of a second, giving an LOP which then could be plotted.

Normally one plots on the chart, but an ocean sailing chart simply is too small scale for this purpose because of having to advance and retard LOPs to find a position. So as a kind of worksheet I made up plotting sheets for Joy. They are available commercially, but we didn't have any.

When navigating by sextant, sailors like to get a meridian transit, that is, a sun shot when the sun is directly over the local meridian, when it is local noon. This shot will give your position, which no other single sun shot will do. Well, then, why mess around with morning and evening sun shots and advancing and LOP to get a position? Because the meridian transit can be difficult to obtain. Sometimes, of course, you have cloud cover at local noon; also it requires a series of shots before and after the transit in order to determine exactly when the sun passed your meridian. Another difficulty with the meridian transit is that with the sun at its zenith, the degrees can be 80+ and the higher the arc the more difficult it is to get a reliable reading. During this entire passage, I was only able to get two or three meridian transits. One of these was the third day out. Because it worked so well and was so easy, I had a false sense of how easy it would be. However, when it works, it is magic. You know when it's working because once the sun reaches the zenith, it hovers momentarily. Seeing this phenomenon is rather incredible. Today's sailors using exclusively GPS miss this magical moment.

Never voluntarily had I used the sextant to navigate, simply because it was easier to take the fixes from the satnav every few hours and to plot them on the chart. Once forced into using the sextant, I was thrilled with the experience. Somehow, something almost mystical happened each time I brought the sun into the sextant's mirror and, as if controlling it, moved it down to float on the horizon. I felt close to the sun, as if I had merged with the universe, as if pulled into the vortex of some enormous power. This sensation returns each time I think about sun shots.

Race the Wind stayed just a few miles ahead of us, usually within sight. The second night out, just after we had finished dinner, we heard a strange, recurring noise from the exhaust. We finally concluded it must mean there was a restriction in the raw water intake hose. To correct the situation, we needed an elbow, but we didn't have one. George did, so he turned around and powered back to us. We had turned off the engine and were just drifting at half a knot when they approached. George maneuvered *Race the Wind* close and Kate tossed a line into which had been tied the elbow and a float. It was good that we had the float because it landed in the water, but Joy was able to retrieve it with a boat hook. About an hour later, Joy had made the repair and we resumed our course under power.

Around 4 a.m., on Joy's watch, a light westerly came up so she got us undersail and turned off the engine. What a relief after two days of powering. Now it was serenely quiet with only the light rippling sound of the water flowing past the hull. It was too little wind for *Race the Wind* who continued under power. At sunrise, we saw the last of their stern light as it dipped below the horizon. We would not see them again until we made Pohnpei 15 days later. We spoke to Eve on the VHF for a morning chat and set up a schedule on the ham radio for three times a day.

By 11 a.m., the wind had risen to 15 knots, just about ideal for us. We put a single reef in the main and pulled in a little on the genny. We retired Ruth (the autopilot) from steering and rigged up Mildred, the windvane steering. The wind went northerly, forcing us to go on a course of 050 degrees true, which was okay because conversation with people who had made this passage earlier confirmed that they should have done more easting. Once they got to the Northern hemisphere they hit a strong westing current and reinforced NE trades, which meant they had difficulty laying Pohnpei.

On February 24, I got another noon fix. Navigation was taking up a lot of our time. The entire day was planned around morning, noon and late afternoon sun shots. When I could not get a noon fix, I could still use the shots for a running fix.

Sometimes the ocean can be an eerie place. On February 25, very fierce squalls came in the early evening, but two hours later the wind was little more than a zephyr. On this day I didn't have a noon fix, but I thought I did. Apparently, I chose the wrong shot as the transit, and I failed to check the time of the meridian passage from the computer. So, even with the help of modern technology, I still made a human error.

I had no luck trying to get shorts of stars and planets, which can also be a good way to get a position. Just three different heavenly bodies, shot one after the other, gives a position. But there are some limitations and disadvantages here. These shots can only be taken at morning or evening twilight, the only time the horizon is visible along with these bodies. On February 27, I got up in time to get morning stars and the moon, but clouds obscured Jupiter before I could get it and by then the others had disappeared because it was too light for the stars. I got several moon shots, but they were all off. In its waning phase, it was difficult to tell when the lower limb reaches the horizon and the horizon line itself was not clear. We got a running fix of 00° 35' S, 163° 54' E. We were only 35 miles south of the Equator!

We had sailed across the Equator seven years earlier. This would be our first time back into the northern hemisphere, and we decided to celebrate by dropping a bottle overboard at the Equator with a message and an address to respond to. But on February 28, we were not able to get a fix, so we didn't know when to launch the bottle. 1992 was a leap year, so we had a February 29. I tried to get three LOPs on this day and a noon fix. Two morning shots were perfect, but the noon shots were no good. I had trouble seeing the horizon because the seas were so big. When I finally got myself positioned, standing on the highest part of the boat, I had difficulty balancing and hanging on as the motion was quite lively. Just as I was ready to begin shooting, a bank of clouds swept over the sun during the transit. Fortunately, the 2 p. m. sights were good. Our position was 01° 35' N. 163° 45' E. Sometime during the early morning hours we had crossed the Equator and missed it! We were now making good time as a NW current of about one knot was assisting us. We picked up the 15 to 30 knot trades at 01° N. We were sailing hard on the wind and pretty much on our ear.

On March 1, when I presented my LOP to Joy to plot, she did not believe it. She said there was something wrong with my sight because the intercept was 85 miles. But all of my sights were consistent, so I thought there was not a problem there. We had been making so much easting that we thought it would be all right to go onto the starboard tack a NW course. As we thought everything through, it became obvious what must have happened. If there were a strong westerly current of about three knots running, that would explain the large intercept. Our fix on March 2 supported this argument. We had paid dearly by tacking. Now we had to make sure we stayed moving easterly to counteract the current.

On the night of March 4, we battled continuous squalls. The weather of the previous day had also been frustrating. Changeable winds went from 0 to 20. It kept us busy furling and unfurling the genny, running under power in the calms and sailing when it blew. Such a pattern is typical of the weather near the Equator. About midnight, we just turned on the engine and powered due North as it seemed the only way we could get North. The strong westing current was still running, giving us a push of about 72 miles west every 24 hours. Our noon fix put us about 60 miles south and west of where we thought we were.

On March 5, we were not able to obtain a sight. We were in the middle of the convergence with heavy rains and squalls of varied intensity. The worst squall hit in the afternoon and laid the boat over in 50 knots. It also dumped gallons of water. We hove to in the worst of it. For 30 hours we had been without a sight. We were pleased the next morning to see the sun and finally get an LOP. At noon we got a fix, which put us at 03° 51' N, 158° 38.4' E. We talked with Eve and Jim on the radio. Both took the information on our sights to reduce and plot them to see if they came up with the same position as we. They did.

On March 8, morning greeted us with multiple squalls. At 9:40, between squalls, Joy let out a loud whoop. She had just spotted the dark shadow of Pohnpei, looming on the horizon. It lay exactly where it should — according to our navigation — just off our port bow. Once we got to 03° N, the westing current stopped and we started getting an easterly current which was assisting us. Seeing Pohnpei was proof that celestial navigation worked, or more precisely that *our* celestial navigation worked.

We were unable to make the harbor during the day, so we had to stand off for the night. With reef everywhere, we did not rest well that night. Early morning brought squalls again. Twice we had to turn back from the pass as blinding squalls overtook us and obliterated everything. Finally Paul and James came out in *Magic Carpet* to escort us in. It was blowing a good 25 knots as we entered the pass with rollers slamming into the reef on both sides of us. Finally, we raised Port Control on channel 16 just as we were almost into the harbor. They told us we must turn back and anchor at beacon #5. This procedure was different as previously yachts had been entering the harbor and anchoring off the wharf until they were sprayed for mosquitoes. After that, the officials boarded them. We checked our chart and found the depth at beacon #5 was 35 fathoms! No way we could anchor there with only 300 feet of anchor rode. We reported the problem to Port Control. They responded that if we came in and anchored off the wharf — as Joy was suggesting — they would confiscate our vessel. Joy was talking to them on the radio. I suggested she tell them we would not put ourselves or our vessel in danger and that we had very little fuel. For these reasons, I, the captain, would not proceed to beacon #5! Upon learning we had very little fuel, they backed down. The regulation concerning beacon #5 was new, just enforced when our friends on *Gypsy Rover*, Theata and Dick, arrived with Dick who had been incapacitated with a malaria attack for days. He had to be carried off the yacht and transported to the hospital, but they would not let Theata, his wife, accompany him, as she had to remain aboard for clearance procedures. Such is bureaucracy. We were suddenly in the thick of it after years of relatively little contact with this curse of the modern world. Welcome back to America! As a member of the Federated States of Micronesia, Pohnpei is not really American, but under the compact agreement, it receives American money and has been influenced by American culture and language for the last century.

Chapter 15

POHNPEI

We entered Pohnpei at Jamestown Harbor, which today is a large commercial port. We anchored at the southern end of the bay alongside other visiting yachts. Sokehs lies to the west and Net and the town of Kolonia to the east. Whenever we went ashore, it was but a short dinghy ride to a rock retaining wall at the base of a steep hill. The owners of a lovely house located here were kind enough to allow yachties to tie their boats on the wall and walk through their property up a steep dirt road to reach a paved road that goes into town. Snugly built into the jungle bordering the winding steep hill were thatch guesthouses belonging to the hotel perched at the top of the hill. From these houses one had a panoramic view of the bay, where the fleet of cruising boats bobbed at anchor. Once having reached the paved road, we had several choices. It was possible to take a taxi into town from the hotel, but generally we walked for the exercise. Either direction took us to town. The choice was usually determined by where we needed to go in town. To the right, the road leads through Kapinga village where the setting was the same as on some remote island. Polynesian adults, most clad in lavalavas, would be sitting or strolling leisurely through the village and children played and chased each other. In one area of the village, the Kapinga gathered to work on weavings and carvings. Greetings were exchanged as we went along, sometimes a friendly wave, sometimes a vocal acknowledgement. This road eventually took us past the town library and to the largest supermarket where we normally did our shopping. Fresh vegetables and fruits, almost all imported, were prized items. Occasionally, we might see some shriveled potatoes or a rotting onion in the store, but otherwise, until the ship came in, there was no fresh produce. After that it would be sold out and there wouldn't be any more until another week or so when the ship returned. Frozen meat and canned goods were readily available in many stores. A number of mom and pop stores stocked jam, candy, junk food, sodas, beer, liquor and a limited assortment of canned goods. Ambros, another large supermarket at the other end of town, would sometimes have things one could not find anywhere else. Cat food was not readily available, so when we did find some, we stocked up.

One night at a party we met Rita, a librarian at the Community College. She encouraged me to visit and use the library. It has a small but prized collection of publications pertaining to the Pacific region. I spent some pleasant hours there doing research. Rita took Eve, George, Joy and me on a tour of the island. One of the highlights of this tour was eating at the Village, a hotel and restaurant built on the eastern side of the island overlooking the lagoon.

Shortly after arriving in Kolonia, we faxed a marine store in the States to have a GPS (global positioning system) air freighted, which should only take several days -- ten at the most. Joy and I wanted to sail to many more islands and atolls in the Carolines, but in these reef-strewn areas we didn't want to be dependent on sextant navigation. GPS, which had just recently become available, was still quite expensive, but even so $1,000 was cheap insurance for the safety of *Banshee.*

The place of most interest in Pohnpei is Nan Madol, the ruins of an ancient city built on 34 islets. With friends, we hired a motorboat to take us for a visit. Our arrival and departure had to be coordinated with the tide so we could approach through the canals. James O'Connell, who visited Nan Madol and wrote about it in the 1830s, called it the "Venice of the Pacific." For decades archaeologists have been interested in the history of Nan Madol and Lelu on Kosrae, which has similarly constructed massive stonewalls and platforms. The Pohnpeian structure, begun around A.D. 1200 to 1300, is the larger and older of the two. The basalt columns used in the construction of Nan Madol had to be transported for considerable distance from the quarry sites. Our guide told us a legend, which attributes the transport of the columns through the air to magic. These two sites represent the only clear cases in Micronesia where a large island was ruled by one political authority. The layout also suggests a complex social and political structure. Other stone platforms of similar construction survive in Kiti and at Sapwtakai, which may have been the seat of the government when the building of Nan Madol was begun. Indeed, the mystery surrounding Nan Madol's origin is greatly enhanced by the imposing vision of the basalt prisms that are stacked up like logs, making these structures truly impressive.

After our tour of Nan Madol, cut too short because of the falling tide, we stopped by an uninhabited island for a picnic lunch and snorkeling in crystal water. From there our guide sped over the smooth lagoon, much of it shallow, until he landed us on the main island where we paid the owners a nominal fee to hike over their land to a waterfall where again we cooled off, rinsing the salt from ourselves in the cool, fresh pool and showering under the falls.

This seems to be a good place to depart momentarily from my travel narrative and cue in some overview of the history of Microneasia and the U. S. involvement in this region. Until Ferdinand Magellan "discovered" Guam on March 6, 1521, the Micronesians had lived a secluded life for hundreds of years on scattered islands and atolls. Except for Guam, most island groups in Micronesia would remain unknown to Europeans for several hundred years. The Micronesians had had a lengthy period living unmolested in the Pacific. Archaeological findings suggest that as early as 3,000 B.C. voyagers from the Philippines or Indonesia sailed to Guam, Yap and Palau, all high volcanic islands in western Micronesia. With them they brought basic food crops and some animals, perhaps the chicken and dog. About 2,000 years later, a second wave of seafarers moved from Vanuatu up to the Gilberts and Marshalls, first settling these areas and then moving westward to the Caroline Islands — Kosrae, Pohnpei, Chuuk (Truk) and hundreds of small atolls.

The first European to lay eyes on Pohnpei was Pedro Ferdinand de Quiros, the chief pilot for Alvaro de Mendaña when he made his second Pacific voyage in 1595. On this disastrous voyage, Mendaña died of a fever in the Solomons where he had tried to establish a colony. His death propelled Quiros into the position of command. Eventually, under Quiros, the group abandoned their effort at colonizing because the Solomon Islanders, first friendly, had become inhospitable, no doubt a result of the Spaniards' abusive behavior. To save the colonists -- plagued with illness and starvation as well as the escalating hostilities with the locals -- Quiros knew he needed to sail to the Philippines for assistance from the Spaniards settled there. Sailing northward, Quiros by chance came to Pohnpei on December 23, 1595. In fact, he almost went up on the reef. Although natives signaled to him to come ashore, he hastened to get away from what he perceived to be lurking dangers. His discovery appears on early maps as "Quirosa." But it was 230 years before another European would land on Pohnpei. In 1827, a Russian, Fedor Lütke, made an expedition through the Pacific that took him westward from Kosrae through the Carolines. He rediscovered Pohnpei, which had only been sighted once since Quiros' hasty sojourn in 1595. Although Lütke saw Pohnpei in 1828, the island was almost as free from foreign intrusion as Kosrae had been in 1824.

When the American brig *Spy*, diving for bêche-de-mer (sea cucumber) came to Pohnpei in November 1833, the crew found a few white men living on the island. Within just a few years since Lütke's visit, Pohnpei had become a kind of hub, visited frequently by whalers out of Sydney and merchant vessels running between Australia and China. Often they carried crew who were convicts from the Australian penal colonies. Some of these convicts jumped ship in Pohnpei to escape. One such character was James O'Connell, an Irishman from Australia who reached Pohnpei about 1830. He "married" a chief's daughter or rather fathered two children by her. O'Connell is probably Pohnpei's best known beachcomber because he wrote a book, *A residence of Eleven Years in New Holland and the Caroline Islands*. One of the merits of his book is his detailed description of life and customs among the Pohnpeians.

O'Connell was of no mind to remain in Pohnpei. He approached Captain Knights of the *Spy* to take himself and his friend George Kennan away on the *Spy*. Captain Knights agreed and the *Spy* departed rather hastily after a short stay because trouble was brewing. Word had it that several beachcombers, all British subjects, planned to seize the *Spy*. Perhaps O'Connell concocted the story of the planned seizure because once at sea he was insubordinate and was attempting to gain control of the ship. Captain Knights managed to prevail and turned O'Connell and Keenan over to the authorities upon arrival in Manila. When the *Spy* left Pohnpei, almost 30 whites were living on the island.

As Francis X. Hezel, S. J. reasons in *The First Taint of Civilization: A History of the Caroline and Marshall Islands in Pre-Colonial Days, 1521-1885*, the presence of whites was a mixed blessing. They served as necessary intermediaries in trade with visiting ships, but their rowdy behavior, lack of respect for local customs and abusiveness led many locals to believe they should be killed. In fact, a plan was afoot to do this, but one important chief refused to follow through. By 1835, some Pohnpeians wanted to get rid of all whites and not allow any foreign ships into their harbors.

It wasn't long before the Catholics tried to move onto Pohnpei. In 1837, two missionaries who had been evicted from Hawaii boarded the schooner, *Notre Dame de Paix,* bound for Pohnpei to found the first mission. One of the priests died before the ship arrived. The remaining priest only stayed on the island for about six months. Less than two decades later in August 1852, Protestant missionaries serving an interdenominational mission agency out of Boston arrived. The *nahnken* (chief) of Kiti, one the districts of Pohnpei, helped establish the mission. The older *nahnmwarki* of Kiti, who was senior in rank, did not share the younger man's enthusiastic response to the missionaries or to Europeans in general. But the chief had enormous power and popularity. He guaranteed the missionaries' protection. The major issues that concerned the missionaries were prostitution and the drinking of alcohol, both situations that developed because of the European presence. Pohnpeian men soon learned they would be given money or alcohol by the sailors if they brought their wives, sisters, and female children aboard.

In 1854, the whale ship *Delta* brought in smallpox, which quickly swept through the island, killing many. The missionaries, with a very limited supply of vaccine, could do little to stem the tragedy. The disease killed between two and three thousand Pohnpeians. Many who died were chiefs for whom there were often no suitable successors. Consequently, social upheaval contributed even more turmoil to the lives of the villagers. With nearly half of the native population dead from the smallpox epidemic, the missionaries began to despair that they might have to abandon the mission. In the entire district of Kiti there were only seven births in three years. Albert Sturges, one of the original missionaries on Pohnpei, said that first the islanders had to survive the white beachcombers, next the whalers and then the trading companies. His fear was that the newly established commercial enterprises would encourage the new Christians to throw away their religion for riches.

A brief look at the history of colonial rule in the Caroline Islands, Kosrae, Pohnpei, Chuuk, Yap, Palau and numerous smaller islands, demonstrates the rapid social and political changes affecting these islanders. Originally, from the sixteenth century until the latter part of the nineteenth century, the Spanish assumed these islands as their possessions. Basically they had become more involved in the western Carolines while Britain, Germany and the United States had centered most of their activities in the eastern Carolines. In 1874, Spain pressed its claims to the Carolines and a kind of tug-of-war developed between Spain and Germany who had some business interests in these islands. While America's whaling industry and Christian missions had firmly established themselves in the eastern Carolines, the U.S., like Britain, did not wish to colonize these islands. Initially, Germany had not desired Pacific colonies, but by 1884 her attitude was changing. Very astutely, Bismarck worked out an agreement sanctioned by the Vatican in 1885 that Germany was free to establish coaling depots and naval stations in the islands though Spain retained sovereignty. Likewise, European powers granted American missionaries freedom to continue their work. However, in 1898, the Germans assumed control from Spain. Their position of power was short lived, however. Japan seized the islands in 1914, only to lose them after their defeat in World War II when the United States gained control and established the U.S. Trust Territory and later worked with Chuuk, Yap, Pohnpei and Kosrae to ratify the Constitution of the Federated States of Micronesia. Finally in 1986, the U.S. negotiated a Compact of Free Association with these states. When it was the U.S. Trust Territory of the Pacific Islands, the budget was U.S. $6 million in 1960, but by 1979 the figure had risen to $96 million.

It is one thing to visit a foreign culture and appreciate it for its uniqueness and its intrinsic value. But the Europeans and Americans did not come as passive observers. Each group had its set agenda. While we can point to many kind-hearted and well-intentioned acts performed by the intruders, the question we must ask is, at what cost to the islanders? What did the Micronesians gain compared with what they lost? Did they not have a free, well functioning society that had been intact for several thousand years? After European intrusion, their population dwindled alarmingly, disease brought untold suffering, religion in the name of the Christian God destroyed their sacred shrines and taught them their beliefs and culture were inferior to those of the foreigners. To assess the extent of the impact is not easy. Not only are there many complex issues involved, but also the impact continues today and the local people still do not have freedom or self-determination.

Many see one of the most positive contributions of Europeans and Americans as being education. After all, the first missionaries to Pohnpei formed schools where they taught their pupils singing, reading, writing, arithmetic, spelling and English. Unfortunately, during the smallpox epidemic, schooling ceased. The schools were finally reopened in 1855 by the missionary wives and an interesting thing happened: now students spent most of their time learning to read in their own language from texts written out in long hand! Nonetheless, the missionaries' idea was to prepare students for the day when the Bible would be translated into Pohnpeian. So education was viewed as a necessary tool for religious conversion.

In addition to the social disruptions engendered by economic development, which usually entailed exploitation of the local population and the negative impact of colonial rule — in this case a succession of colonial rulers — there was the virtual robbing of people's identity. This loss of identity may well be the most damaging experience of all. What happens to people when their souls are wrenched from them in so many insidious ways? Most outsiders don't know enough about the islanders' culture to perceive the depth of the loss.

What of Pohnpei and Pohnpeians today? Many Pohnpeians as well as some outislanders such as the Kapinga, Sapwuahfikese, Chuukese, Mokilese, Pingelapese and Mortlockese live on Pohnpei. The capital, Kolonia, is a commercial and residential center. It is a densely packed town with docks, shops, restaurants, hotels, hospital, Catholic and Protestant churches, schools and a community college. Formerly, the government was also located in Kolonia, but today the Congress of the FSM is located at Palikir, Sokehs, one of the five polities — Net U., Madolenihmw, Kiti and Sokehs. Each of the polities has its own leaders, two chiefs: the *nahnmwarki* (highest chief) and the *nahnken* (talking chief). Many of the outislanders were brought here during the Japanese rule, either as laborers or to alleviate some of the crowding on the small islands. Today, many still come to Pohnpei hoping to find jobs and make a better life. The passing of time has not resulted in a "melting pot" of these different ethnic groups. Kapinga (from Kapingamarangi), as well as other islanders, live in enclaves. Each group has maintained its own language and all know English with varying degrees of competence. The FSM government is a kind of bicultural arrangement with its basic structure modeled on the U.S. form, but it also allows the traditional forms of power and control to be maintained in a small, more cohesive social unit, which was the system in force when the Europeans arrived. Some might conceive of this arrangement as a convenient compromise. As a whole, the society is a kind of hybrid, albeit one still in transition. In many respects, the islanders are attempting to live a life consistent with that of a U.S. mainlander. They attend school, they study the subjects *we* deem essential, including U.S. history, and study to become literate in English but often remain illiterate in their native language. Some of the more adept academic students aspire to a university education. Some have been my students at the University of Guam. But the bulk of the population remains stranded, one foot in Pohnpeian culture and the other tentatively trying to gain access to an urbanized U.S. lifestyle. The colonial attempt to educate out of them their "heathen" and "primitive" ways has led down a road that does not, for the most part, prepare them for life on their island or for living an enriched and rewarding life. Drug and alcohol abuse, crime and suicide rates are high. These behaviors appear to be the result of being a disturbed, unsatisfied, unfulfilled and rootless people.

What is at the bottom of this rat's nest? Partly it is economics. Once islanders are introduced to Western ways, they desire to become consumers. But how do they acquire sufficient money? What can the island produce that will bring enough capital to support all the islanders and at the same time provide the infrastructure to enable this lifestyle? These are logical questions, but what has happened on Pacific islands has nothing to do with logic. Colonial governments never intended to take care of the local people. Instead, their agenda attempted to use the local people to achieve their own aims: acquiring wealth. The Christianization of Pacific Islanders was perceived as a convenient way to contain and control the native peoples and to oil the skids for financial plunder. By claiming to do good deeds by saving the "heathens," the West could appear to legitimize European and American hegemony.

We have been looking primarily at the physical process of colonialism, the taking over of land and the establishment of a foreign government with complete power to usurp the indigenous power and attempt to control these islanders, displacing local society. Let's look at the process that legitimized colonial exploitation of Other people. In 1978, Edward Said articulated this process in his book *Orientalism*. Orientalism, according to Said is a discourse "by which European culture was able to manage — and even produce — the Orient politically, sociologically, militarily, ideologically, scientifically, and imaginatively" (Said, 3). Discourse is a way of projecting meaning on the world. Discourse theory is a means of analyzing the strategies of power and subjection, inclusion and exclusion. As Michel Foucault pointed out, discourse is a way of organizing power. Western discourse intensified with the development of Western capitalism. Over time this discourse became Knowledge (with a capital K), perceived as a neutral authority concerning the histories of Other people. As Said makes clear, this perception holds that European texts about the Orient are more objective than contact with the Orient itself. In this discourse, the West is upheld as the norm, as rational, developed, mature, superior, while colonized peoples (non-whites) are constructed as undeveloped, inferior, savage, unpredictable, and therefore needing to be controlled.

Meanwhile, jump to the present. Time is rapidly running out for the inhabitants of FSM. Beginning in 1987 with its Compact of Free Association, the U.S. gave the FSM $60 million U.S. annually until 1992. In 1993 the amount was decreased to $51 million U.S. and in 1997, it dropped to $40 million U.S. The Compact terminated in 2001 and a new agreement had to be negotiated. Nearly 75 percent of the nation's revenue is derived from Compact monies. The stated goal has been to establish an infrastructure and work toward generating their own economy. Yet, in the fist decade of the twenty-first century, these goals are far from being achieved. An article in the *Pacific Daily News* (July, 2000) provides an update of the Bank of Hawaii's report on the FSM. According to this report "the FSM economy experienced growth and prosperity" from 1989 to 1993, but for the last half decade the economy has "stagnat[ed]." What did FSM "pay" for this aid, amounting to $826 million by expiration of the Compact? It gave the United States "exclusive" strategic access to the FSM's waterways.

This report leaves out many details about the Compact agreement and how it has operated. Elsewhere some of the criticisms that have surfaced have to do with the irresponsible handling of money by the local FSM governments. Some of the accusations state that graft and corruption by those in power have subverted large sums of money from the intended purpose into the pockets of government officials. There may be some truth to this accusation, after all the U.S. mainland experiences much of the same kind of corruption, white-collar crime, whose perpetrators more often than not seem to slip through the justice system unscathed. However, I see another problem which appears to go unnoticed. In essence, the U.S. has been throwing money at the problem. Such an approach is totally naïve. People who have had no experience managing large sums of money do not suddenly acquire this wisdom out of the blue. Where are the training programs? No one in private business would just pull someone off the street without any expertise in money management to run a multimillion-dollar enterprise. Yet, essentially that is what has happened in the Compact Agreement. Think of the impact of a country essentially going from zero dollars annually to $60 million. It must appear to be an inexhaustible fund! And these millions are promised for 15 years.

What kind of a population are we talking about? The 1990 census placed the population of FSM at 100.000. However, the birth rate is high. As of 2010, the combined population of Kosrae, Pohnpei, Chuuk and Yap is 149,000. A long time resident and writer from Pohnpei, Gene Ashby, maintains that the most serious problem is the lack of infrastructure — things like expanding and improving airfields and roads. But perhaps the most serious neglect of all is the lack of adequate dock facilities and shore facilities which would enable the FSM to earn money from their fisheries, the single most promising local resource. But once again, the fisheries have not been developed because of a lack of knowledgeable people to establish, manage and run such an enterprise. There is enough population of working age — 50 percent is 15 to 64 years old — but of these too few have enough training and skills. For the most part, skilled and semi-skilled labor is imported, a pattern that goes back to when these states were part of the U.S. Trust Territory. Usually the two percent of the population that does become well educated leaves FSM and migrates to Guam, Hawaii or the U.S. mainland. These are some of the major dilemmas that occur regularly across the Pacific with minor variations.

On March 22, we dined on *Race the Wind*. Almost immediately upon coming back to the boat, I experienced terrible pains extending from my neck on the right side all the way to my right calf. Shortly thereafter, I began having chills and body spasms. These were followed about half an hour later by a fever. An hour or so later, with the fever gradually rising, I downed four Chloroquin tablets, knowing I was having a malaria attack. The Chloroquin took effect. Soon the fever began to subside and the headache lessened but did not cease.

I knew I had to go to the hospital the next morning. Dick, our friend who had arrived on Pohnpei with malaria, told me that he had been treated by Dr. Kapeteni when he was brought to him almost unconscious. Dick's malaria had progressed to the stage where he had what is called blackwater fever, a condition where blood is excreted in the urine, resulting from chronic *falciparum* malaria. I knew it was Dr. Kapi (as everyone called him) I needed to see.

Hard as it was, in the heat and in my weakened, feverish state, I had to climb up that steep hill to the hotel. From there we took a cab to the hospital. A nurse weighed me and gave me a form to fill out. She asked my complaint. When I told her malaria, she looked incredulous. She didn't believe me. I repeated that I knew I had malaria. I had had it before and I was just coming from the Solomons. I asked to see Dr. Kapi. She said that he had no openings for over a week. I knew that most American trained doctors know nothing about malaria. Dr. Kapi's specialty is tropical medicine. Not only that, he told Dick he knew how to cure malaria. I pleaded with her, saying it was urgent I see Dr. Kapi. We had gotten to the hospital around 8:30, but by noon I was still waiting. I was feverish and weak. From 12 to 1 the doctors went to lunch and saw no patients. By now Joy was becoming concerned about me. She talked to the nurse and finally persuaded her to send me in as soon as the doctors returned from lunch.

The nurse kept her promise. I no longer remember the name of the doctor they sent me to. We walked in — Joy accompanied me — and immediately I told him I had malaria and needed to see Dr. Kapi. He agreed with me and escorted us to another part of the hospital. He left us in Dr. Kapi's office and went off in search of him.

After about ten minutes Dr. Kapi, who'd been making rounds in the hospital, entered. He was a tall, solidly built African. He exuded warmth, confidence and caring. He looked at me and said, "You look very sick. We'll take some blood. I'll read the slide myself because I can't trust anyone here." On the phone he ordered what he wanted. Soon a young man arrived with a large syringe. Kapi was visibly irritated. "That's not what I asked for!" He repeated his instructions. Finally the young man returned with the correct things: a sharp pricker and a tiny glass pipette. Kapi pricked my finger and squeezed several drops of blood into the pipette. Off and on he had been telling us about the horrors of malaria, that it kills more people than any other disease. He said that people who have chronic malaria would eventually have every organ invaded by the protozoan parasites.

Dr. Kapi went off to make the slide and analyze it. When he returned, he asked me how I was able to walk into the hospital. He said ten percent of my red blood cells were involved. Only six percent of Dick's had been and he was almost comatose. Kapi told me I was infected by *Plasmodium falciparum*. After physically examining me, he said my liver and spleen were enlarged. He cautioned that the cure was extreme as it required heavy drugs for a prolong period. This is the treatment he prescribed and I took: for two days every eight hours 600 mg of quinine and 500 mg of tetracycline. For two days the same amounts of each drug every 12 hours. For the next three days, two doses of quinine and two doses of tetracycline once a day. Then I saw Dr. Kapi again. The spleen and liver were no longer enlarged. He said I had had a very severe case and I was very strong and had good resistance. This treatment was followed by 15 days of Malaprim. At the end of the treatment, Dr. Kapi saw me again. He took another blood test and pronounced me cured. Eighteen years later I have had no episodes of malaria, which encourages me to believe I have been cured, rare as that may be.

Joy, fortunately, felt no symptoms, but Dr. Kapi recommended that she take heavy doses of Chloroquin for three days because he felt certain she had probably been bitten by a infected mosquito. It was the same treatment I had taken in Honiara, as prescribed by the nurse at the hospital.

Chapter 16

WESTWARD THROUGH MICRONESIA

Repeatedly, the parts of equipment most desperately needed are the very ones that go astray in the mail. Our order for the GPS was no different. The end of April was rapidly approaching, and although we had ordered the GPS almost six weeks earlier, it had not come. In desperation we had faxed the marine company several times (fortunately there was a telecommunications center in Pohnpei) and they assured us they had sent it by air. Residents on Pohnpei, when hearing of our plight, always had some horror story to tell us about the mail — all mail from the States comes through Hawaii. In most such stories, Hawaii was the "black hole" where mail was said to pile up for months on end, or worse still, was swallowed up, never to be seen again.

Normally, the only thing that really makes us hurry along is the weather. If the season is changing, we may need to move on for safety. In this instance the pressure to leave was work. We needed to get to Guam so we could find employment and replenish our dwindling coffers. Since both of us intended to find a teaching position, June seemed like a good time to arrive. If we waited much beyond June we felt our chances of finding a job for fall semester would lessen.

Originally, we planned to spend at least two months cruising FSM, but sadly our time was being wasted waiting for the GPS that either had gone by ship or gone astray somewhere en route. We couldn't afford to pay the company to send us another GPS. We decided that without the GPS or the satnav, we would have to give up island hopping, as it was too dangerous without either of these electronic navigational devices. That meant sailing directly to Guam. Then, unexpectedly, Lady Fate stepped in. One day as we were walking in a different area of Pohnpei on our way to a store to buy some fishing lures, we passed a TV repair shop. Joy wanted to talk to the technician. Perhaps he could fix the satnav. We went into the shop and met the owner, a Filipino. After we explained what it was we wanted him to look at, he said he didn't know anything about satnavs. But Joy explained that she thought it was simply an electrical problem. He dubiously relented and said he would look at it. When we brought it in the next day and he opened it up, he immediately spotted the problem. One of the connections was fried. It must have happened as a result of the electrical surge from the wind generator that day the fierce squall got us in Ontong Java. It was a simple thing for him to resolder the connection, which we could have done too, had we known what we were looking for. We could hardly wait to get back to the boat to see if it worked. We plugged it in and reprogrammed the satnav. It stayed on and when a satellite passed, it locked on and we got a position! It didn't blow a fuse either. We were ecstatic. Now, with about five or six weeks left, we could cruise some islands.

Almost a month earlier, we had said a sad farewell to *Race the Wind* on their way back to Australia via the Gilberts and Fiji. Other friends had made the short sail to Ant Atoll just a few miles south of Pohnpei. Reports were that this deserted atoll was stunningly beautiful. The island is privately owned by a Pohnpeian who lives in Kolonia, so we asked permission to visit and remain for a week or two on Ant. Permission was granted.

In order to leave Pohnpei, we had to check out by going to the wharf which was fully occupied by ships, but a Taiwanese fishing boat let us tie to them. We stayed there overnight, as the officials wouldn't see us until the next morning. The Taiwanese didn't speak a word of English and we not a word of Chinese, but sign language took care of all the essential communication. It was amusing to watch the shock on their faces when they saw Jason because he was so large.

The next morning, April 24, an official from Port Control boarded us and issued a clearance. One down, two to go. About half an hour later, along came Customs. More papers to fill out and another clearance! No fee from Customs but Port Control charged $15. Finally Immigration arrived and stamped our passports and visas. Soon we slipped our lines, hoisted the main and made our way down the channel, easing quietly past Sokehs Rock — the most obvious landmark on Pohnpei. It was 10:15, a bright sunny morning. Halfway down the pass, we hoisted the genny and moved along smoothly on a beam reach. Once outside the pass, the boat moved evenly until we entered the channel between Pohnpei and Ant where the seaway became erratic. To assist us through the confused seaway, we cranked up the engine for half an hour until the seas became more regular.

We tried to gage our speed in route in order to arrive at Ant Pass at slack water. However, we arrived at 3:30, about 15 minutes early as the tide was still ebbing. Since the pass was well marked, we entered under power and steamed against the tidal flow. Once through the pass, we no longer needed the engine and easily tacked across the lagoon to anchor just behind *Dream Maker*. We joined Pam and Jim for evening drinks and delivered their package we had picked up in Pohnpei plus fresh bread and oranges.

A few days later, Pam and Jim returned to Pohnpei and we had the lagoon to ourselves except for an occasional boat bringing tourists in for a look or fishermen stopping to lunch and rest ashore for a few hours. We explored one island where the remains of a resort had collapsed into a heap, struck down by a rare typhoon that had blown through a few years earlier. But the best exploring was underwater. We found an especially beautiful reef off the island where we had anchored. Its gigantic coral formations of 15 or 20 feet tall looked like rounded hedges that had been neatly groomed. These structures provide a home for hundreds of fish of many varieties. Their bright colors flashed through the water. We spent hours on several days swimming through the paths between these coral heads, watching the underwater drama.

One day, we took the dinghy all the way back to the pass where we had entered Ant Atoll. We arrived just shortly before the incoming tide. When it turned, we jumped into the water with snorkel and fins and tied the dinghy to one of us. We drifted on the incoming tide the length of the pass just following along the wall so we could see the wonderful array of shallow water and deep water fish and sharks which swam below us in the depths. This pass was the most gorgeous area we had snorkeled in the entire Pacific. Hordes of fish swam in their quiet world, eons removed from the sand and palms. Swept along by the strong tidal flow, we glided above the underwater ballet.

By May 3, we knew it was time to inch our way further west. It was an overnight passage to Ngatik (pronounced without the "g"), also called Sapwuahfik, as the atoll was originally named by its inhabitants. Ngatik refers to the large island where nearly 600 inhabitants live. Nine small islands enclose the nine-mile long lagoon. We left at three in the afternoon so as to arrive in the daylight. Out of Ant, we rode the outgoing tide. The sky was gloomy gray, still overcast from the heavy squall that had swept over just prior to our departure. Outside the pass, a strong wind hit, and we rolled in the lumpy seas. It was so bouncy neither of us felt like staying below to cook, so dinner was crackers and cheese. Jason got sick and went without his dinner. After several hours, the seas settled down into a more rhythmical trade wind motion. With 20 to 25 knots, we roller reefed the genny to a small bit of Dacron and still made 3.5 knots. We slowed ourselves down because we didn't want to arrive at Sapwuahfik before noon, at slack water.

The next morning, just before Sapwuahfik appeared on the horizon, a huge squall trampled us. We hurriedly rolled up the genny and took down the cockpit awning as 40 knots laid us over and torrential rain pounded the decks. It was so severe, we thought it might be a weather front moving in, but eventually it cleared and the islands popped up. We arrived at the pass at 3:30, late, having missed slack water, but fortunately it was an incoming tide. Upon entering, we were violently pushed and pulled by whirlpools and slicks, but I was able to steer out of the hazardous forces. Just then, another squall struck. This one packed a lot of wind but little rain, which was lucky because rain could have blotted out our visibility, not good when negotiating a pass.

It was a wide and deep pass. About a mile long. We anchored at a small island indicated as Bigen Kelang on our chart. What a beautiful spot! We had a view of the breakers on the reef, a sandspit, multicolored waters of the lagoon and the pristine little island crowded with palms and other tropical vegetation. Soon two young men in an outrigger came alongside, introducing themselves as Castro and Aruit. We gave them some stick tobacco and paper for rolling cigarettes for which they promised to bring us lobsters in the morning. A bit later the head man, David, from Wat, the neighboring island, came by in his "cowboy" boat. We had first seen these large, open fiberglass boats in Pohnpei, always powered by huge outboards (hence their nickname since they bucked across the lagoon). David wanted to check our papers and asked if we had a ham radio. He explained that he wanted to bring the chief from Ngatik — the big island at the other end of the lagoon — on the following day so the chief could contact their senator on Pohnpei. The village radio had been out for some time and the *Micro Glory*, the small ship that brings supplies and passengers from Pohnpei to the outer islands, had not been at Sapwuahfik for weeks. They needed supplies. We told David we knew the *Micro Glory* was hauling water to Chuuk and other atolls because of the drought.

The next day the chief came and we reached the senator on the radio. The senator confirmed what we had already told them, that the ship had to abandon her normal schedule in order to provide water from Pohnpei to other islands. Even while we were in Pohnpei, the city water supply was only running from 6 to 8 mornings and evenings to conserve water. For us to get water meant a long dinghy ride up to the commercial wharf with our water jugs.

Around midnight on May 5, a 40-knot squall out of the southeast tore through. We started dragging. It was a fire drill in pitch black, trying to reanchor. Since there was no protection from southeasterlies where we had anchored, we decided in daylight we would reanchor by Wat Island, which did offer protection. David had already invited us to anchor there. He came by every morning and brought us fried banana and breadfruit chips from his wife. On days he took his boat fishing, he stopped by to deliver some of his catch to us. David explained that seven families live on Wat and because he is the only one with an outboard, he supplies fish to all of the families. Now, he said jokingly, we were part of these families to whom he was obligated. He told us his four boys were on the mainland (Pohnpei) attending school, and his daughter, the youngest child, lived on Wat. We asked if it wasn't expensive to have four children going to school on Pohnpei. He agreed and explained that he raises pigs to earn money and has found it to be quite profitable. He sells them to Pohnpei where pigs are always in demand for obligatory social occasions. We had seen plenty of pigs being fattened up on Pohnpei. They were huge beasts, crammed into tiny pens with just enough room to stand up and lie down. They could not even turn around in their cages. Apparently the owners wanted to ensure the pigs didn't expend any unnecessary energy, as they were not willing to risk even minimal weight loss. Perhaps Pohnpeians have some cultural value for largeness because the men grow yams in secret places and enter them in a contest after they are harvested where they are judged by size. The winning yams are too large to be picked up by one person!

One day David recounted the story of the Sapwuahfik massacre, which took place in 1837. To the people of this atoll, this event holds prominence as if it had only happened yesterday. Like most incidents of extreme violence, this event underscores the kind of wanton cruelty some Westerners inflicted on local people. During this time, there was rampant misunderstanding between Europeans and Pohnpeians, so relations were uneasy at best. It was also before the Protestants or Catholics had established a mission on Pohnpei. Of the few Europeans who were in Pohnpei, most were either whalers or beachcombers. About a year before the massacre, Charles "Bloody" Hart had discovered that the people of Ngatik had a good supply of turtle shell. Wanting to secure it for trade, Hart and his crew had gone ashore to negotiate with the inhabitants. Although the initial reception was friendly enough, a large band of armed men eventually attacked the Europeans. Even though they managed to escape with no loss of life, Hart, an Australian, was bent on building a wealthy trading empire, and he habitually used force to get what he wanted. In addition to tortoise shell he now wanted revenge.

Less than a year later, Hart returned to Ngatik, loaded for bear. In Pohnpei he had picked up more Europeans and 20 Pohnpeians, all armed with muskets. He brought along two native canoes and a whaleboat. Of course, when the Ngatikese saw the *Lambton* lying offshore, they rightly guessed foul play. Concealed, the warriors with native clubs and slings waited. On the following two days, the *Lambton* crew landed and shot everyone they could find. They killed every grown man on the island, about 50 or 60. Only a few males, who took to the sea in their canoes escaped, never to return to the atoll. Many of the Ngatikese women killed themselves and their children and of those still alive after the killing, Hart's crew spared. Ironically, Hart found little tortoise shell despite the all out war and chaos he had spawned. Intent on establishing a community, which could supply him with tortoise shell in the future, he left an Irishman, Paddy Gorman, gone native, to be in charge. To help Gorman, a few Europeans and the 20 Pohnpeians were left as well. So the Ngatikese women and children who survived the massacre now had to live with the very men who had killed their husbands, fathers, brothers and sons. No doubt rape, seen as the appropriate spoils of war, ensued without any sense of guilt or wrongdoing. As David explained, to get new husbands for the women — in addition to the men who stayed — men came from other islands, mainly from the Gilberts and the Mortlocks to settle down with the women. Yet today, according to anthropologist Lin Poyer in *Cultural Identity and Ethnicity in the Pacific*, the Sapwuahfik people identify themselves as a single cultural community.

Hart did not confine his violence to the Ngatikese. He was also involved in attacks on Pohnpeians of Madolenihmw. In fact, the *nahnawa* (chief) was captured and taken to Hart's ship. Onboard, the young chief was tried and sentenced to be hanged from the yardarm. The execution turned into a grotesque affair with the crew pantomiming hanging in front of the chief for several hours. The hangmen, two black men, were dressed in long red gowns with their faces painted red, apparently to make the occasion as hideously frightening as possible.

Several times we saw a local outrigger sailing around the lagoon. One day I looked up to see a small outrigger making its way toward Bigen Kelang. After grabbing our cameras, Joy and I jumped into the dinghy and powered after the outrigger. Sailing it was an old man who had a young boy with him. We told him we liked his outrigger and wondered if we could take some pictures of him sailing it. I don't know how much English he understood because he responded with nods and smiles. He proudly began sailing again, this time demonstrating what the outrigger could do by making various maneuvers. Amazingly with our little two and a half horse outboard we could not keep up with him. The most versatile feature of these craft is that rather than tacking or jibbing around, the sailor simply turns the sail around so that the bow becomes the stern and vice versa.

On another day there were outrigger races across the lagoon from Ngatik Island to Wat. We snapped pictures as they hauled by before landing on Wat. What a thrill to see these vessels as they have evolved after hundreds of years, still being used here.

A good indication that Micronesia, more than Melanesia or Polynesia, has better preserved its culture, is that even until the present, some Micronesians are still building and sailing ocean going outriggers. Moreover, the art of Pacific navigation is still alive in some areas of Micronesia, but less known in Polynesia and Melanesia. In his classic study, *We the Navigators*, David Lewis reported on the extensive knowledge he gained about traditional navigation of Pacific Islanders who used no instruments whatsoever and regularly made open sea passages of between 300 and 500 miles and less frequently, longer voyages. Two primary navigators, who taught Lewis their ways of navigation, were Hipour from Puluwat (Carolines) and Tevake, a Polynesian from Pileni Atoll, one of the Santa Cruz Reef Islands. Under the tutelage of these two navigators, Lewis sailed hundreds of miles. Lewis also interviewed navigators from Tikopia, Sikaiana and Tonga in Polynesia; Puluwat and the Gilberts in Micronesia; and, several Melanesians from Ninigo Island in Papua, New Guinea. His research revealed beyond a doubt that in earlier times, Pacific Islanders made many intended two way voyages, and that navigators had a rigorous training, beginning in boyhood. Thus Lewis's significant study demonstrated that parts of sea lore have been preserved in some pockets of the Pacific. The broader picture he exposes, based on his personal investigations and research of the literature — especially several early European accounts — is that the ancient voyagers frequently made open sea voyages and that the basic principles of navigation were probably fairly uniform from culture to culture. The star paths of the sailing directions were memorized. As well, the navigator had to know how to read the swells for steering in the open sea. Since ocean currents and wind direction are subject to change, the navigators also used techniques to expand the target of landfall. Thus, rather than just aiming for one small island or atoll, the navigators looked for signs that indicated a zone which expanded the target substantially. For example, the navigator used the whole archipelago for a target rather than an individual island. The signs he looked for were homing birds, clouds and wave patterns. Using these signs, the navigator could spot even very low-lying land.

Writing in the late 1960s, David Lewis expressed concern that the people with boat building and navigation knowledge are aging. Younger males no longer show any interest in learning these skills, so soon this knowledge will be lost to us as well as many answers to questions about Pacific migrations. Early Europeans paid little attention to Pacific navigation. Of course, initially the language barrier would have hindered interpretation. The one exception was Tupaia, a high chief, priest and navigator whom Captain Cook encountered and questioned at great length. Tupaia's geographic knowledge was astounding. He knew every major Polynesian island group (he was from Raiatea, one of the Society Islands) except Hawaii and New Zealand, in all an area of 2600 miles.

With the decline in voyaging came a decline in general navigational knowledge and boat building. Typically, colonial governments discouraged or even forbade voyaging. The amount of information navigators needed to memorize was considerable. Navigators recited the location of islands correlated with star courses. As W. H. Alkire reported, based on his studies at Woleai Atoll, the navigator memorized courses from 18 islands, some 270 items of information. Another researcher, W. H. Goodenough, reported that a navigator from Puluwat gave him several pages of sailing directions, which encompassed every known place to every other known place. Obviously committing to memory this kind of information without the opportunity to make voyages and use it would be sheer tedium. At one time, traditional canoes were the only means of transport across the ocean, but for most of this century, islanders could take an interisland ship, which is easier than learning how to build outriggers, sail and navigate them.

Often Joy and I discussed many such topics with David. One day he said to us that he would like to make his "cowboy" boat into a sailboat. He would still use the outboard, but his concern was that if he was outside the reef and his outboard quit and the wind or current was going away from the atoll, he would be condemned to drift. This is a fate that befalls many native fishermen today. As a matter of fact, in June 1995, Joy and I met four Gilbertese men who had been adrift for 60 days. They were finally picked up by a Korean fishing boat and brought to Guam. Actually they looked quite healthy and fit. They were fortunate in that they had plenty of rain and were able to catch enough fish — by hand — to survive, as they did not have any provisions with them and were in an open boat, an outrigger. They had both sail and outboard, but after a series of squalls pushed them out of sight of land, they didn't know how to get back to their island. They had no navigational knowledge whatsoever. Incidentally, they told an interesting account of a dolphin that assisted them in getting fish. They said the dolphin chased fish toward their vessel, enabling them to catch the fish by hand.

In response to David's request, we drew up a plan, complete with measurements, for converting his powerboat into sail in an emergency. Actually, it would not be as expensive as buying a second outboard, but it would require careful work on David's part to install the necessary rigging.

On May 9, in the morning, we left Sapwuahfik. The day started fine with 15 knots and the landing of a small yellow fin tuna just off the atoll. Then gray clouds closed in and released torrential rains. It looked as if the drought had finally ended. Our passage to Chuuk Lagoon was plagued with changeable conditions — winds from every direction — that kept us awake for most of the night. Finally, by early morning on May 10, we turned on the engine to keep moving. This calm lasted about five hours. By afternoon, the wind returned and then shifted from NW to NE. Skies remained cloudy with occasional showers and wind squalls. With the wind astern, sailing under a reefed main was quite comfortable. Just after dawn on May 12, it went to a flat calm. The engine droned on, pushing us toward our destination. Around noon we entered the NE pass to Chuuk Lagoon. Half an hour later, a fishing boat with two men was speeding toward us. We wondered why they seemed so determined to reach us. They came along side to say hello and then handed us a beautiful fish! What a fine welcome to Chuuk.

From the lagoon entrance to the wharf is ten and a half miles, which took us until 2 p. m. At the small, crowded wharf, we tied up next to a fishing boat to await the officials. Two came immediately and quickly filled out the appropriate forms. It was 4:30 before Customs and Immigration arrived. Meanwhile, we chatted with men on the fishing boat from the western islands. Most talkative among them was Remy, from Puluwat. He smiled proudly when we complemented him on his English. He had gone to the university in the States he told us. After finally completing all the entry papers, we powered down to the southern end of Moen island and anchored off the Continental Hotel. We had been informed that this was the only place we should come to anchor without an invitation. Because Chuuk Lagoon is considered a world-class diving area, there are regulations preventing people from diving on their own. The fear, of course, is that divers would take away trophies from World War II wrecks, which are the main attraction for divers. Divers must hire a guide, even if they have their own boat. Snorkeling is also not permitted without a guide.

Joining us at Moen were *Canowie* and *Ambler* with Tom and Jan. Joy and Peter hired a guide and went on several diving expeditions. I went on a shallow wreck to snorkel. The underwater scenery was spectacular. The most outstanding sight to me were the soft corals that had lodged themselves everywhere on the vessel. It looked as if these life forms had done their best to decorate the wreck, turning an eyesore into a fantasyland. On the set were brilliantly colored ballet dancers. Strangely, all appeared to be fish of one kind or another! Everything swooped and swirled in that kind of slow motion that operates in the subterranean world.

Paulos, Joy and Peter's guide, invited us to come and visit his family on Fefan Island. On May 18, we left Moen, heading across the lagoon to Fefan, which was only a few miles away. As we neared Fefan, a "cowboy" boat zoomed toward us, almost running us down. The single man on board was drinking and was, in fact, drunk. He started yelling at us, telling us we could not go to Fefan. He rudely insisted we needed the mayor's permission and *he* was he mayor's assistant. He demanded money. We tried to ignore him when we realized he was a troublemaker. But it was impossible. When we dropped the anchor, he ran his boat into *Banshee* and did it several more times, despite our angry protests to leave us alone. Meanwhile, he was asking us a lot of questions and repeating that we could not anchor here. Fortunately, a canoe that was passing by came up when they saw he was maligning us. The driver spoke to him and whatever he said made the troublemaker leave. The man driving the canoe was Carlos. With him were his mother and another man named Benny. Carlos told us the man who had been hassling us was Joseph Kametaria. Later we learned that Joseph doesn't live on Fefan. He is from the other side of the island. He had also bothered *Mischief* when they came here to anchor. Tom and Jan told us about Joseph over the radio and suggested that we notify Senator Mikki on the main island (Moen). We never contacted Senator Mikki, but we did tell Paulos and he talked with the senator. Chuuk has, at least among cruisers, gotten a bad reputation because of rowdies like Joseph who pester foreigners. More specifically whites. Alcohol abuse is a major problem on many islands. When islanders have over imbibed, many of them become belligerent and abusive. Of course, this behavior concerns those Chuukese who are working in the tourist industry because they know it can have a negative impact on their livelihood. And beyond this concern, they want to be cordial to visitors and go out of their way to be kind and helpful.

Once everything settled down, we took the dinghy ashore and two youths offered to lead us to Paulos' place. It was quite an uphill hike through thick jungle. Periodically we passed a dwelling, a leaf hut. The immediate area around the dwelling was planted with ornamental plants and food crops. Finally, close to the top, we came to Paulos' hut. His family was preparing breadfruit, which is their main food staple. He explained to us the entire process for making this dish. First, many breadfruits are peeled and placed in a very large cast iron pot in which they are cooked. When done, each breadfruit is placed on a rock and pounded with another rock. This part is demanding and was being done by Paulos' son and a nephew. When the boys had finished pounding, which made the breadfruit pulpy and pliable, it was shaped into round loaves, which looked exactly like loaves of bread. Then each loaf was carefully wrapped in banana leaves and stacked in a pile. I asked Paulos how long the supply would last — it looked like a month's supply to me. He said about three days. What happens is that the breadfruit, because it is not refrigerated, starts fermenting. So, as each day passes, it becomes more fermented, and the Chuukese say, tastier. We tried some just after it was pounded. I have to admit that it did not taste any better to me than any breadfruit I have ever eaten. It was very starchy and even just a small bite made my stomach feel like an enormous mass had lodged itself there.

Two days later we left Fefan about midmorning. With overcast skies and scattered showers, we powered to Dublon, a nearby island, where we anchored near the ice plant. We took the dinghy to the wharf for fresh water. It was quite a drop from the wharf into the dinghy, so some kind Chuukese helped us lower the water jugs into the dinghy. Each 20-liter jug weighs about 40 pounds when filled with water. After filling our tanks we made our way back to our original anchorage at Moen with caution through the pass because visibility was poor.

On May 22, around 2 p. m., we left Chuuk. To exit the lagoon, we set our course for the pass lying between Dublon and Fefan. Even doing five knots it took three hours to make the South Pass. No breaking water indicated where the pass was. Fortunately, we could distinguish the pass by the color of the water. The pass itself is quite deep. The depth sounder never showed less than 117 feet. We talked on the radio with Peter and Joyce who were anchored at a small island on the outside of the reef. For miles, their anchor light beamed a pinpoint of light. Just before dark a large pod of spouting whales headed straight for us and soon surrounded us, still spouting. We turned on the depth sounder as we had been told this keeps whales from approaching the boat. I don't know if that's what happened, but they disappeared right after we turned it on. By now we had a perfect sailing breeze, which carried us over the water almost silently.

We set our course for Puluwat, a tiny atoll 157 miles from Chuuk. With any luck we'd be able to meet the famous navigator, Hipour. Although he had been on Moen when we were, our attempts to meet with him were not successful. From 2:30 a. m. until 5:30 a. m., the wind lightened considerably, so we used the engine to keep us moving. By daylight, the wind picked up and we went once more under sail. Around 4 p. m., the wind lightened and suddenly shifted SW, causing the poled out genny to backwind. This occurred just as *Canowie*, who had been behind us since 1:00, caught up to us.

The next morning at 7:00 the engine overheated. Joy talked with Peter who said if we couldn't fix it, he would come back for us with *Magic Carpet*. Meanwhile, I got the boat sailing, as much as possible in virtually no wind. We were making less than 2 knots. Giving the engine time to cool down before inspecting it, Joy fixed breakfast. Afterwards she removed the thermostat and we tested it in a pan of hot water on the stove. Sure enough, it was malfunctioning. Not having a spare thermostat, we opted to operate the engine without it, which meant it would run cooler, actually below maximum temperature for a diesel engine. The engine gage held at a steady 130 degrees. By noon we made the Puluwat pass and zigzagged our way through the twisting pass into a beautiful, well protected lagoon. Already anchored were *Dream Maker, Ambler* and *Canowie*.

During the six days we remained at Puluwat, we spent a lot of time ashore talking with villagers. They proudly showed us their elegant canoe house. Inside was an ocean going canoe and hanks of neatly coiled line made from coconut fiber. One man sat at the side making the rope by rolling the fibers on his thigh. We inquired about Hipour and learned he was coming back on the interisland boat, which was expected that week. We told his son they were both invited to visit *Banshee*.

One of the things that intrigued me was the brightly colored loom woven strip of cloth the Puluwatese wear on ceremonial occasions. I asked many people about the looms and how they learned to weave on them, but no one seemed to know the history. I made the faulty assumption that some missionary had introduced this skill. As I have since learned, loom weaving is known in a line extending from Ontong Java to Papua New Guinea and the Carolines. In fact, the loom design is almost identical to one used in the eastern islands of Indonesia, suggesting that it was known to very early immigrants who brought it with them as they fanned across the western Pacific. Today, Carolinians still weave using banana fibers, but many weavers prefer thread not only because it requires less work but also because of the variety of bright colors available in thread. When using banana fiber, they dye them with vegetable dyes, so the hues are more subdued than with the commercial threads.

Hipour returned from Moen. One morning, he and his son were standing on the shore, waving to us. I went over in the dinghy and Hipour's son asked if they could come for a visit. They got into the dinghy with me. Hipour was dressed in his bright blue loincloth. I recognized him immediately from the photo in Lewis's book. His square, solid body did not seem to have aged much in the intervening years. And his distinctive tattoo somehow imbued him with a regal air. How proud his bearing, which conveyed a man of wisdom. His son translated, but

I realized how much is communicated nonverbally, even down to the character of another person. Hipour projects a great presence, a man of patience and calmness. Good characteristics for a navigator and sailor, I thought. We told Hipour that since reading David Lewis's book, we had wanted to meet him. We expressed our interest in traditional navigation and our great respect for Pacific sailing canoes and navigators. Hipour nodded and smiled and seemed genuinely pleased to have a chance to talk with two women navigators. It was his first time to meet women who could navigate. We asked his son if Hipour knew about satnav navigation. He did not, but he wanted to know how it worked. So we explained. His eyes glowed with interest and excitement as he learned about another method. He knew, of course, something about compasses and sextant navigation. We asked if we could take his picture and he assented. His son told us he, himself, did not know how to navigate. He has too many other interests he told us. Getting his education was important, so he didn't have time to devote to navigation. What a pity. Maybe one day he will reconsider.

Chapter 17

GUAM

I never really considered going to Guam. Originally — before the dismasting off the coast of Australia in 1990 — our plans had been to return to Chesterfield Reefs and Vanuatu, cruise the Solomons, then head south again, stopping off in Papua New Guinea on our way back to Australia. After another season cruising Australia and the Great Barrier Reef, we would go around the top to Darwin and then to Indonesia.

But the dismasting changed all that. The unscheduled sixteen-month rebuild of *Banshee* in Australia had left our funds greatly depleted. We needed to find employment — the sooner the better. Basically we had three options: go back to New Zealand for work; return to the States, or go to Guam. Although the first option appeared to be the most desirable, it was the least lucrative. Because of the exchange rate, we would essentially be earning only about half of what we could in the States or in Guam, a U.S. Territory, and the cost of living in New Zealand is high. Going back to the U.S. mainland was unappealing for several reasons. First, it's a difficult sail back to the U.S. from the South Pacific. Also, once back, re-entry did not hold much promise as being pleasant, and it would be expensive. Additionally, it would mean backtracking all those sea miles. Would we have the energy to begin again? That left the third option, Guam.

We had been talking on the ham radio with friends in Guam who encouraged us to come. They felt certain we could both obtain good paying jobs. I thought perhaps I would be able to teach at the University of Guam. Still, the preconceived, negative images persisted. Most were vague, no more than impressions. From where these notions stemmed, I don't know. The two major expectations I had about Guam were that it would be hot and muggy. At latitude 13 degrees North, I suspected it would be unbearably hot. Guam also has a reputation as "typhoon alley," being lashed frequently by typhoons and, occasionally, super typhoons. I didn't want to be in such a place with a boat in a typhoon. But friends on Guam assured us there was a secure typhoon shelter for *Banshee.* I also thought of Guam as a U.S. military dominated place, an atmosphere not inviting to me. In reality, though, I knew almost nothing concrete about Guam. Until friends told me on the radio, I didn't know the indigenous people were called Chamorros.

As we sailed out the Puluwat Pass on May 30 bound for Guam, I thought about the Puluwatese sailors and navigators who today still sail the same route we were setting out on. It was a perfect sailing wind, 10 to 12 knots. Puffy clouds floated across an azure sky. Coming around the west side of the atoll, we struck a slight swell, caused by refraction. Tom and Jan, also sailing for Guam, left two hours after we did and within a few hours hove into view. The first part of the night was uneventful, but around midnight we began experiencing alternating periods of calms and squalls. This is the weather sailors most detest as it means constant adjustment of sails. To make things even more unnerving, *Ambler* was not carrying a light because Tom wanted to save on power. For our own peace of mind, once an hour we turned on the radar to check their position. At one point they were within three quarters of a mile, which is a little too cozy for me. I think it was this night that we passed over Grand Feather Banks. Because of the shallowness, the water's action became more turbulent. And suddenly a horrible, putrid, fishy smell enveloped us. It was gagging. We spoke with the folks on *Ambler* who said they also smelled it. We thought it might be a dead whale, but, of course, this mystery remained unsolved. I have since wondered if some enigmatic lines in a Chuukese navigation chant are describing the Grand Feather Banks:

Olap [the navigator] sees

Giant fish Malakule
whipping a whirlpool into such fury
that it sucks every passing thing
to the sea's bottom
flings salt at the sun
moans

And then in the chant the giant fish Melakule give directions to
Olap:
"Heed my advice:
North is your route
north without deviation
north though your mouth dries up
and crazy fears infect you
north until spotted porpoise, Uruha
rises up before you
to check your credentials
and whale Purusa
guards a school of sacred skipjack
This is where all the sea routes cross, Olap
Mark it well."

Some researchers have said they felt such descriptions of sea life set
to memory by Chuukese navigators were fanciful, but actually abundant
sea life does live around these banks and would be another navigational
indicator for the native navigator. Incidentally, these instructions were
used recently by a Puluwatese navigator making the same 450-mile
trip as we from Puluwat to Guam. He made this trip to show these sea
marks to a nine-year-old boy learning navigation.

Winds were light in the early morning on May 31. By nine, though,
they filled in and we were pushing along at 4.5 knots. But weather at sea
often changes abruptly and without warning. By 11:00, a squall packing
35 to 40 knots hit and brought a tropical downpour. We had to drop the
main and roll up the genny to keep from heeling excessively. The squall
hung around, lashing us for about an hour. Afterwards, we could no
longer see *Ambler*, not even on the radar screen. Later, when we talked
to them on the radio, they said they had been on the periphery of the

squall and sailed at 8 knots. No wonder they had vanished from our vision — even electronically. About four hours later, however, we were catching up. In lighter winds we made better time than they did.

June 2. The weather was perfect. With relatively smooth seas and a fair wind, we were zipping along at a nice clip. In fact, when we projected our arrival time on Guam, based on our present rate of progress, we knew we needed to slow down or we would be arriving in the middle of the night.

In the gray dawn, Cocos Island at the south end of Guam bulged on the horizon. Gradually, as we came closer, we could see the breakers on the reef and behind these the jagged mountains of Guam. We still had about 17 miles to go to reach Apra Harbor. By 11:00, still moving along nicely on a moderate breeze, we sailed into the harbor. On the previous day, our friend Dave had said on the radio that he would meet us as we came into the harbor and lead us to the Marianas Yacht Club where we could take a mooring and then proceed to complete our formalities with Customs and Immigration. Dave had been talking to us on his handheld VHF. Soon he appeared, plowing across the harbor chop in a Boston Whaler. How good to see him! It had been about two years since we had said goodbye when he and Mary left Australia. With Dave was a friend. They led us to a mooring in front of the yacht club. It was next to *Quickstep*, friends we had last seen in Vanuatu.

Both Joy and I were hired that summer and began our jobs in the fall session. Originally, I was teaching Freshman Composition at the University of Guam, but soon that expanded to include literature, composition, writing and women and gender studies. I had cashed in my seafaring adventures for the academic world, eventually gaining tenure and promotion. Eleven years later, I felt it was time to retire and return to the States after almost a 20-year absence. What an exciting time it was. Living and working on Guam brought me into close contact with students and faculty from many cultures: local Chamorros, out islanders, Asians, South American, East Indians. In the eleven years I taught there, I witnessed multiple ways colonialism continues to take its toll on individuals and their culture, and how even the educational system facilitates this maneuver. When I began teaching, the university offered only one course on Pacific literature with readings limited to oral literature that has been written down by whites and literature by white colonial writers about the Pacific. Yet, since the 1960s, indigenous South Pacific writers have been publishing poetry, short stories, novels and plays, and more recently, literary criticism of their own indigenous literature. A decade or so later, indigenous North Pacific writers also began publishing fiction and poetry. What, I wondered, was taught in the primary and secondary schools in Guam? As I soon learned, the curriculum mostly ignored Pacific literature. Instead, the schools teach American writers with a few Europeans thrown in for good measure. As for history and geography, the situation is no better. Students in Guam and Micronesia learn about the American Civil War, the World Wars, but very little about their own subjugation under Spanish, Japanese, German and American rulers, and until recently, nothing about the indigenous culture before the Europeans arrived. Students in Guam may be able to name the capital cities in America, but they, like other Americans, don't know the location of Fiji, Vanuatu, the Solomon Islands or other Pacific islands or the distances of these places from Guam. Until very recently, they didn't know that their ancestors could navigate around the islands and made long ocean voyages in seaworthy canoes. In essence, their birthright, their culture and its significance have systematically been denied them. These are some of the insidious ways "colonization of the mind" is promoted.

Over the years that I remained at the university, I developed and taught two courses on indigenous literature. The reward was seeing students come alive and thrive when they learned they had their own growing body of literature, some of it in native languages and most in English so it would be available to a larger number of readers than a local language would afford. As editor of *Storyboard: A Journal of Pacific Imagery*, published by the University of Guam, I was able to encourage young indigenous writers to submit their poetry and fiction for consideration in the journal. Some of these students have gone on to do graduate work in Pacific Studies. It's only a matter of time before these cultural treasures will be given to youth at the primary and secondary level. To the small island of Guam, such information will bring pride and identity to many, enriching their lives as they come to know their own history and culture so long obscured by colonial influence.

I never cease being amazed to think about the paths of such diverse individuals that have intersected on this thirty-mile long island that has been an American territory since 1898. Guam, U.S.A. In many ways, though, this name is misleading. Although the veneer is American and the residents are American citizens, underneath other identities still claim the heart of these individuals.

On Guam I became more acutely aware of the fateful impact of Europeans on Pacific Island cultures. In many respects, Guam epitomizes the "successful" transformation of a traditional island culture to a Western one — everything from its gridlock traffic on Marine Drive at rush hour to its zealous consumerism played out daily in shopping centers and abundantly stocked stores. To all appearances, it could be Main Street, U.S.A., but beneath the surface it is not Main Street or mainstream U.S.A. The Chamorros have their own history, their own customs, traditions and language. Identity is a complex issue for people who have been colonized. Injustices, inequities, abuses, and discrimination have shaped their cultural past and present. For example, as recently as 1970, Chamorros were forbidden to speak their language in public places. If children spoke it at school, they were punished. Such treatment by outsiders —Americans — leaves an indelible mark, a stigma that doesn't vanish easily. Fortunately, over the years some things have improved. Chamorro language is taught in the schools today, as is English. Everyone must study Chamorro, for a limited time. But even so, the native tongue appears to be losing ground. Most young people up to about thirty or forty years old, do not speak Chamorro. Many Chamorros see this disappearance of their culture, traditions and language as a terrible loss that they want to stem. Some local elders and scholars attempt to recover and reconstruct their past, their precolonial identity. To do so is difficult. So little is known about what it was like when Magellan landed on Guam on March 6, 1521. Though his ships only stayed three days, his arrival put Guam and the Northern Marianas on the map. These islands, lying in the route of the Spanish ships transiting from Mexico to the Philippines, from that time became important provisioning stops for the Spanish galleon trade. And by virtue of its geographical location, Guam and its neighbors were destined to become a vulnerable place during World War II. Unlike Guam, the rest of the Pacific islands had about a 200-year reprieve before they experienced European intrusion and colonization. Guam, however, has sustained four centuries of outside cultural assault from three different cultures: Spanish, American and Japanese.

Even though Guam is a U.S. territory, most Americans don't have any idea of its location or know any of the particulars about this island and her native people. Certainly few Americans know the history or even what is happening here in the present. Because the impact of Europeans has been occurring for four centuries, I believe it is necessary to reveal the contours of this history in some detail. Briefly, here is what happened.

From 1521 until 1565, four fleets of Spanish galleons called in at Guam and the Northern Marianas, also inhabited by Chamorros. The latter islands, stretching north of Guam some 500 miles, were first discovered by Europeans in 1522. The *Trinidad,* one of the ships in Magellan's expedition, had left Tidore, one of the Spice Islands, after making repairs. In search of a return route to Mexico, Captain Gonzalo Gómez de Espinosa encountered a storm when he reached latitude 42° N. Suffering severe damage from the storm, the Spaniards limped south to 20° N. where they anchored near present-day Maug, one of the Northern Marianas. Three crewmen jumped ship here, but only one, Gonzalo Alvavez de Vigo, escaped death at the hands of the Chamorros. Gonzalo was later picked up by the Spaniards in 1526.

In all of these voyages, the Spanish had been attempting to lay claim to some of the Spice Islands, the Moluccas, but the Portuguese were already well established there and fought to keep the Spanish out. According to Robert F. Rogers in *Destiny's Landfall: A History of Guam*, as early as 1628, the Portuguese dominated the Moluccan spice trade and held prisoners from all three initial Spanish expeditions into the Pacific.

When King Philip II of Spain saw the futility of trying to capture some of the spice trade in the Moluccas, he shifted his focus to the Philippines, mistakenly thinking they would find cloves there. Thus in 1559, Philip II ordered the colonization of the Philippines. It took five years to build ships in Mexico that would carry the colonizers to the Philippines. In November 1564, four square-riggers set sail from north of Acapulco under the command of Miguel López de Legazpi. Three of the ships reached Guam on January 21, 1565, and Legazpi ceremonially claimed the Marianas, including Guam, in the name of Philip II of Spain. In reality, though, Spain focused for the next century on the Philippines, not on Guam or the Marianas.

Except for a few superficial accounts, Spanish explorers revealed little about the life of the Chamorros. The earliest account of Chamorro customs comes from Friar Juan Pobra de Zamora who by chance happened to land on Guam in 1602. To that time, at least, the islanders had not been drastically changed by European contact. Even so, most of the myths and legends, which generally provide valuable information about a society, were lost or changed after the Spanish conquest.

Anthropological data provides useful information to convey something about the natural environment as it was when Magellan arrived in 1521. Micronesia itself was a region of tremendous biological and cultural diversity. The Chamorros, a unilingual society, used shell and stone tools. The inhabitants, of strong physique, were larger than Europeans. Apparently they enjoyed good health and lived long lives. The only diseases mentioned by the early Spaniards were edema and a high incidence of yaws, an infectious skin disease.

Two outstanding technological developments of pre-contact Chamorros were their sophisticated outrigger canoes and their use of stone pillars called *latte*. The outriggers, *proa*, were fast and graceful. Apparently they were the fastest of this kind of craft, hence the moniker, "flying *proas.*" Another type of craft used for interisland trade, *sakman*, resembled those still used by the Chuukese today for occasional open ocean voyaging. The *latte* stones are thought to be foundations for the houses of high-ranking Chamorro families and for communal buildings.

Ranging in size from three to sixteen feet in height, these upright rounded pillars were carved out of limestone or basalt and topped off with a capstone called a *tasa* and shaped like an upside down mushroom. These pillars were paired, and most buildings had eight or ten pairs. High pitched thatched roofs covered wood beams and wood floors made from either *daok* or *ifil*. Lashings made of coconut rope secured the buildings to the foundation. *Latte* stones were unique to the Chamorros and occur only on islands inhabited by them. Both the *latte* stone and the flying *proa* ceased being constructed after the Spanish conquest. The reasons for the demise of these two technologies is complex and not completed understood. What is clear is that the near extinction of the Chamorro people and the total subjugation of the survivors were significant factors. In a sense, the Spanish wielded a double-edged sword, one political and the other religious. Seldom were the two powers in agreement. Spanish rulers cared nothing about the island people or their culture. Guam and Rota were simply convenient stops on the galleon trade route passing yearly from Mexico to the Philippines and back. On the other hand, the priests, whose object was to save souls — who may sometimes have shown human kindness when dealing with Chamorros — never once doubted their moral correctness in forcing these people to convert to Christianity. The Chamorros, as is true of other Pacific Islanders, strongly resisted being converted. No doubt their resistance was eventually worn down by the large numbers of people who died from contracting European diseases to which the locals had no immunity and from ongoing physical conflicts with the Spanish military.

Ironically, during the first 200 years the Spanish were attempting to subjugate the Chamorros, the latter actually had more mobility than the former. If, for example, the Spanish waged an all out attack on a Chamorro village, the Chamorros fled; the entire village escaped by *proa* to another island. Usually the Spanish themselves had no means of pursuing them. To end this situation, the Spanish authorities eventually moved the greatly depleted population to two islands — Guam and Rota — and forbade interisland trips or sailing past the reef. This enforced confinement of these seafarers doomed the flying *proa*, and by the 1780s it was obsolete.

Had it not been for an earthquake that shook Mexico City in 1667, Guam might never have been missionized. Although the Spanish Jesuit, Father Diego Luis de San Vitores, fervently sought to persuade the Spanish king to let him establish a mission on Guam, the king was reluctant to take on this financial commitment because it promised no financial rewards for Spain. San Vitores, who was in the Philippines, began to approach King Philip IV to send him to Guam. Eventually, after protracted attempts to convince the king and using all his court connections, San Vitores succeeded. On June 24, 1655, Philip agreed to the establishment of a mission. But only a few months later, in September, the king died before the arrangements had been made. Governor-General Salcedo in Manila, though irritated that San Vitores had gone over his head, carried out the decree and ordered a galleon to be built and named *San Diego* in honor of himself and San Vitores. When construction of the galleon was completed, San Vitores sailed from the Philippines to Acapulco. Upon his arrival, he hurried to Mexico City to request money for the mission in Guam. The Marqués de Mancera and of the Audiencia of Mexico, refused funds on the grounds that none existed for this purpose, and that he had not received instructions to provide money to San Vitores. But during one of these sessions, when San Vitores was pleading with the viceroy and his wife, an earthquake struck. It was perceived as a divine sign and San Vitores was therefore granted the money for his mission.

To honor Philip's widow, Queen Mariana of Austria, San Vitores changed the names of the islands from Islas de las Ladrones (islands of the thieves, so-called by the Spanish) to the Marianas in 1668. (To this day Chamorros still suffer and agonize over this early labeling of them as thieves.) In many respects, San Vitores was an amazing man. He made it a point to learn the Chamorro language before he arrived on Guam and thus he preached his first sermon on Guam completely in Chamorro. Nevertheless, despite his linguistic acumen, San Vitores' plan of conversion did not progress smoothly. Initially, the padre's efforts at conversion were doomed to failure because the Spanish did not understand anything about Chamorro culture and because the Chamorros preferred their own traditional ways to the foreign ones foisted upon them.

Chamorro society was divided into the nobles — *chamorri* — and commoners — *manachang*. At first Chief Quipuha and his noble clan in Agaña considered baptism prestigious. Consequently, they wanted it reserved for themselves only, but San Vitores insisted that everyone be accorded baptism as part of their conversion.

In his zealous efforts to rid the Chamorros of their pagan ways, San Vitores had all the ancestor skulls and carved idols destroyed. This act was probably about the most provocative thing he could have done.

Like many early Pacific and Asian cultures, the Chamorros worshipped their ancestors. Skulls of one's ancestors were the most prized part of the ancestor; often they were kept in private homes. Still another problem arose in this tedious and offensive process of conversion. Rumor began to circulate that the baptismal water was poisonous. Credence for this rumor was based on the fact that some infants died soon after baptism. Of course, it was the Christian belief that a child or infant near death should be baptized in order to save its soul.

Only six weeks after San Vitores and his Jesuits arrived, many Chamorros became openly hostile, wounding several priests and killing a Spanish soldier. Despite these conflicts, San Vitores remained blind to the reasons for antagonism and unremittingly pursued his religious agenda with unmitigated zeal. In February 1669, Chief Quipuha, who had been a strong supporter of San Vitores, died. San Vitores insisted that Quipuha be buried in the Agaña church, but Quipuha's family wanted his burial to be in accord with their traditions. They wanted him interred under one of the big houses where his spirit could protect the living members of his family. Cultural conflicts, centered on such key issues as these, led to increasing violence on both sides.

Ultimately, San Vitores' overzealous passion to convert Chamorros led to his own violent death at the hands of the natives. Two Chamorros, Mata'pang and Hirao, became enraged when San Vitores, against Mata'pang's desire, baptized his newborn girl child. As San Vitores left the house after the baptism, the Chamorros threw lances at him and then slashed the priest's head with a machete. Thus, only four years after founding the mission on Guam, San Vitores was martyred.

It is estimated that there were 12,000 Chamorros on Guam when San Vitores arrived in 1668, but just over 20 years later the population had shrunk to a mere 2,000. To be sure, many had fled to other islands. Even so, many had succumbed to various diseases, and quite a few died between 1671 and 1685 as a result of continuous fighting with Spanish soldiers. Impossible to measure, but surely another significant number of people suffered from demoralization created by social changes, which caused psychological distress, culminating in death or even suicide.

An informal census taken in 1708 found the total population of the Marianas was only 5,532 people. An epidemic of diphtheria and typhus the following year reduced the population further to about 5,000. The eighteenth century did not bring improvements in either the treatment or the conditions of the Chamorros. They endured forced labor as well as other forms of exploitation by the Spanish. The first official Spanish census in 1742 showed only 1,576 pureblooded Chamorros remained. Rota had only 248 Chamorros who were required to cultivate rice for Guam. To "revitalize" the population, volunteer Filipino families were resettled in the Marianas. Additionally, many Spanish soldiers took Chamorro wives.

Despite the hardships and violence that had shattered so much of the structure and pattern of the Chamorro way of life, other aspects endured tenaciously. As the nineteenth century began, the native people still clung to their language, and the matriarchs controlled family life. Halfway into the century, Governor Felipe de las Corte reported that 600 pureblooded Chamorros still survived, contrary to earlier speculation by Otto August von Kotzebue — commander of the Russian Navy vessel that came to Guam — who had assumed in 1817 that the Chamorros would soon be extinct. Members of the French expedition that came to Guam in 1819, commented that compared with other Pacific Islanders they had visited, the Chamorros were living in great poverty. Nonetheless, they also observed that the Chamorros loved singing and continued much of their traditional folkways even though their customs were mixed with those of the Spanish and the Filipinos. Louis de Freycinet, the leader of the French expedition, noted that Guam's economy was stagnating. Their meager source of income derived primarily from sales of provisions, entertainment and prostitution to whalers who stopped at Apra Harbor. Repeatedly, just as it seemed the population was increasing, some form of disaster struck. In 1856, it was a smallpox epidemic that was brought in by the American schooner *Edward L. Frost* which arrived from Manila and released passengers after only a three day quarantine, despite the fact that one passenger had died of smallpox at sea. By November 5, 535 people on Guam had died — 60 percent of the population.

Toward the end of the nineteenth century, Guam's schools were so poor that the students wrote with sticks on banana leaves. Almost 90 percent of the island people were partially or entirely illiterate. But one positive development was that the Chamorros were allowed to elect local officials instead of Spanish nationals. Basically, though, at this period in their history, it was religion that cemented the population together rather than politics.

Rogers has enumerated the main themes that evolved during Guam's Spanish rule. First are the close ties between Guam and the Philippines whose people have infused the native inhabitants with a new gene pool, customs and vitality. The second theme concerns Guam's geopolitical role whereby imperialist powers used Guam as a link to Asia. The third theme is Christianity, which came to be an "abiding spiritual heritage of the peoples of the Marianas." A fourth theme is governmental inadequacy. The government, usually "top heavy" and "under financed," did not protect the interests of Spain or the Chamorros. The fifth theme, developed under a colonial military government, rendered the Chamorros impotent in the political and economic development of their island.

Perhaps the most valuable theme, however, is the Chamorros' ability to survive and, even in the face of acculturation, still maintain their Chamorro identity through their language and their family ties. Such a strong identity surfaced in the 1970s when the Chamorros were first allowed by the U.S. to elect a Chamorro governor and begin thinking about self-determination. This desire for self-determination, which became a hotly contested issue in the final decade of the twentieth century, continues to the present time.

The way the U.S. gained possession of Guam and the manner in which the country acted toward its new territory adds yet another checkered chapter to the history of this small island. Somehow America determined that Spain was running Cuba incorrectly, and we sent U.S. support to Cuban rebels. The American battleship, *Maine*, part of this support, was blown up while on a visit to Havana on February 15, 1898. We still don't know to this day who was responsible for the destruction of the ship, but it was blamed on the Spanish. Like a player setting up his chessboard, President William McKinley sent a naval squadron to Hong Kong, poised to go to Manila should war break out with Spain. When all the players were in place, the U.S. Congress declared war on Spain on April 25, 1898, and the U.S. naval squadron immediately steamed to Manila in order to block the Spanish warships in that port. The naval part of the battle was an instant success, but the U.S. had failed to provide ground troops, so Manila could not be taken from the Spanish troops.

In an attempt to rectify this gross oversight, Captain Henry Glass of the U.S. Marines was ordered to sail the USS *Charleston* with troops from San Francisco to Manila via Honolulu where the U.S. had claimed exclusive use of Pearl Harbor since 1887. On June 4, four ships left for Honolulu. Glass opened his sealed orders underway to learn that he was ordered to take the Port of Guam and to imprison the governor and other officials and armed forces, a task he was expected to accomplish in one or two days and then proceed to the Philippines.

His entrance into Apra Harbor, Guam, on June 20, verged on pure buffoonery. Glass fired on Fort Santa Cruz, which unbeknownst to him had been abandoned for years. There were no responding shots. Spanish officials and civilians, unaware that the U.S. and Spain were at war, gathered at the harbor for the customary health and customs inspection. They perceived the firing of weapons as a mere welcome salute! Needless to say this "capture" was effortless and without bloodshed. On the following day, Glass sent two naval officers ashore to make the capture official by taking all Spanish military officers prisoner. Later in the day, Glass and a select party went ashore to make things official by raising Old Glory on June 21, 1898. To add the right tone, the formalities were concluded with a twenty-one-gun salute and the ships' bands playing "The Star Spangled Banner."

Following this unopposed victory, the Spanish troops and Chamorro militiamen were disarmed. The Chamorros were released, but the Spanish officers and troops were taken aboard the American fleet. The next day, anxious to get to Manila, Glass and his entire convoy sailed away from Guam. Not one American was left on Guam to oversee the administration of the U.S.'s newly acquired territory.

Lasting less than four months, the Spanish-American War ended with Spain agreeing to relinquish Cuba, to cede Puerto Rico and Guam to the United States and to let the U.S. occupy the city, bay and harbor at Manila. At the Paris peace settlement, the U.S. offered Spain $20 million for Guam and all the Philippines. Spain agreed. During discussions between the U.S. and Spain over the transfer of these lands, the Chamorros were never consulted or given an opportunity to voice their concerns or desires. Let me interject here that the Spanish never consulted with the local inhabitants either. They never paid the Chamorros for their land; they simply took it. Both Spain and the U.S. acted as if this was a normal, moral and legal thing to do — to take possession of other people's land. The United States did not commit itself to assist the people of Guam to achieve self-government or to improve their political, social or economic well being. The only rights given to the indigenous people were those decided by the U.S. Congress. Probably most of these congressmen did not even know the location of Guam or anything of her people and their centuries of abuse at the hands of Europeans.

Finally on August 7, 1899, Captain Richard Phillips Leary arrived on Guam as the first American governor. From the beginning, it was clear that the U.S. Navy controlled the island. One of Leary's first acts was to declare the separation of church and state, and he abolished the clergy's authority. Leary even prohibited celebrations for patron saints and the tolling of church bells in the morning and evening. The well-ingrained American prejudice toward Catholicism was transplanted to Guam. Still another grievous wrong happened at this time. Because the Spanish had lost the northern Marianas also and Germany had acquired them, there was now the artificial separation of the Chamorro people into two different countries.

The Chamorros responded to this heavy-handed control by attempting to effect change in a peaceful manner. In December 1901, thirty-two island leaders requested Washington to study ways to create a civilian government of Guam. Many such Chamorro requests were periodically made and consistently rejected until 1950. It is not as if the Chamorro people were enemies of the United States, but by maintaining military rule, the U.S. acted as if they were.

A change instituted by Governor William E. Sewell, a Navy commander in 1903, had a severe effect on Chamorros. In that year, he applied a property tax that exceeded the ability of many to pay since most Chamorros had very little cash and few opportunities to earn money. Gradually, the naval government acquired more and more property when landowners could not pay their taxes. The cultural impact on the Chamorros as a result of losing their land was especially detrimental because land ownership was an important traditional means of denoting class differences among them and was an integral means of self-identification. Even more basic, without land many would lose their ability to grow food and be rendered dependent.

One of the most demeaning acts was the official institution of racial segregation established in 1907. The Naval Station "opposed marriages between marines and natives except in specially meritorious cases..." (whatever those were). Already there were a number of marriages between Americans and Chamorros, many of whose families are prominent on the island today.

In 1922, Governor Adelbert Althouse patterned the Guam public school system on the California system. An inflexible, proscribed curriculum, which did not relate to the island community, denoted which textbooks could be used and allowed no deviation by teachers or principals. The use of Chamorro at school was punished, and Chamorro-English dictionaries were collected and burned.

In 1926, the Guam Congress composed of Chamorros appointed by the governor, asked Washington for full U. S. citizenship. The bill was submitted to Congress but failed because the Navy opposed it. But the issue was only momentarily laid to rest. Commander Willis W. Bradley, Jr., who became governor in 1929, recommended U.S. citizenship be granted. Showing confidence it would be accepted, Bradley issued a proclamation for Guam citizenship and established procedures for the naturalization of Guamanians, as they were now called. But once again citizenship was refused. Bradley also recommended a Guam Bill of Rights, but Washington failed to respond. At this point, Bradley simply took matters into his own hands and proclaimed the Guam Bill of Rights on December 4, 1930. Bradley, a man of action and commitment, proposed many other progressive programs that eventually led to the navy threatening to remove him. The governor responded that he would fight for Guam even if it meant the end of his naval career. The navy backed down momentarily, but in April 1931 it was learned he would be recalled.

Whereas the average term of the Spanish governors had lasted about three and a half years, the average length of American governorship was but one year and five months, a period too short to permit these men to become acquainted with Chamorros and their customs. This factor in itself inhibited the development of a solid relationship between the two peoples, which no doubt would have benefited the Chamorros and perhaps even aided them in achieving the self-governing they so desired.

In learning about Guam's history, I also learned some surprising things about the United States as colonizers in the Pacific, as well as information about World War II that I had not known. No doubt many Americans have grown up with the idea that the attack on Pearl Harbor (and Guam) was a surprise to our government. Long after the war, I heard that the U.S. had had many signals of the imminent attack, but the government leaders chose to ignore them. What I didn't know was that as early as 1904, the U.S. Navy was formulating war plans with Japan, even though there were no rumblings of war at that time. They referred to these plans as "War Plan Orange" with Japan being orange and the U.S. blue. These plans were highly secret and from time to time would be updated as the geopolitical situation in the Pacific continued to change. During World War I, Japan quickly captured the islands of German Micronesia, leaving little Guam surrounded by Japanese possessions. Despite a U.A. Army-Navy Board assessment in 1914 that in case of war Guam would need 8,500 marines to defend it, Congress had only authorized enough funds to increase troops by 200 men. This response reflects the continuing attitude of neglect the U.S. exercised toward the Territory of Guam. Whereas it was not a critical issue during World War I, the lack of preparedness to defend the island when Japan invaded in World War II left the Chamorros and the few Americans on Guam totally unprotected. Consequently, they suffered considerably when the Japanese invaded Guam. In 1938, a report made by Rear Admiral Arthur J. Hepburn recommended for Plan Orange that Guam be provided a major air and submarine base. The base cost would require $200 million dollars. In fact, the Navy graded Guam as category F, meaning it was a U.S. territory that could not be defended. On February 14, 1941, President Roosevelt declared Guam to be off limits to foreign and domestic U.S. sea and air carriers without permission of the U.S. Navy.

The previous year a 1940 census showed a total population on Guam of 23,067 people. Only 778 of this total were military personnel and their dependents. The increase in population under the U.S. was credited to improved health care. Even so, life for the ordinary Chamorro was not greatly improved. Among the shortcomings were: subsistence economy; no commerce, as the port remained closed; segregation between Chamorros and Americans; dependency by the majority of the population on government support of some kind. Furthermore, the limited infrastructure catered to naval rather than civilian needs. Perhaps the worst aspect of the American presence was that just before World War II the military had taken over one third of the Chamorros' land. The island government was under the absolute control of the governor, and the Chamorros still had no right to protection by grand jury, no trial by jury or appeal to federal courts off island. Moreover, the governor appointed all judges and attorneys.

U.S. expenditures for education dropped from $16.09 per pupil in 1934 to $14.10 by 1941 on island. Teachers were paid $.80 per day while laborers in Navy jobs got $1.00. The Spanish had introduced the Chamorros to new ways of self-expression and spiritual growth, while Americans perpetuated population increase and physical development but hindered and, even in some cases, suppressed, their native creativity.

The U.S. Congress is the ultimate culprit in the prevailing social, educational and economic limitations placed on Guam. According to the U.S. Constitution, the U.S. Congress is responsible for developing democratic government in all U.S. territories, but because of sheer neglect and racial discrimination, Guam was run under colonial authority. Furthermore, repeated appeals by the native inhabitants for civil liberties were denied, thus continuing military colonialism on the island.

Just a few minutes after Guam received the news that Pearl Harbor was under Japanese attack, Japan bombed Guam. That was in the morning, December 8, 1941. They struck again in the afternoon, hitting Agaña, the capital. Around 8:30 the next morning, they bombed again and strafed villages all over the island. The U.S. fighting force numbered about 100 officers and men. But underarmed and undermanned, U.S. forces were no deterrent to the Japanese. By 2 a. m. on Wednesday, December 10, Japanese troops were landing on Guam.

All of the American prisoners were shipped to Japan on January 10, 1942. As Japanese prisoners, Chamorros were often subjected to beatings and even torture, and sometimes an entire family would be put to death for the actions of one of its members. From the beginning of the Japanese occupation, Chamorros were forced into fulfilling agricultural quotas, often barely having enough food for themselves. Many Chamorro women were forced to become "comfort women" for the Japanese military. This subject remained taboo on Guam until the early years of the twenty-first century, so that unlike women of other nationalities who have demanded reparations and apologies from the Japanese, the Chamorro women remained silent.

When the U.S. began its counterattack a little over two years later in February 1944, the Japanese tightened their reins on the Chamorros, who had not been granted U.S. citizenship (which did not come until 1950). Toward the end of their occupation, they became more and more brutal and irrational in their treatment of the indigenous peoples. At various times toward the end, when the Japanese realized the Americans were coming to recapture Guam, they rounded up groups of Chamorros and took them into the jungle or to caves and raped the women before killing men, women and children. On May 6, 1944, the Americans began bombing Saipan and Guam. They bombed and strafed everyone —Japanese, Koreans, Okinawans and Chamorros. Just over a month later, on June 15, the U.S. attack began in earnest. The U.S. invaded the Marianas and 46 Navy fighters and 96 dive bombers hit Guam. This action was followed the next day by a three-hour gunfire bombardment from two U.S. battleships. The final preparation for the invasion of Guam started on July 8 and continued for 13 days. It was a joint ship and air attack by day and night. The U. S. invaded on July 21. By then American troops outnumbered Japanese three to one, and a fleet of 11 battleships, 24 aircraft carriers and 390 other ships waited off Guam. The assault waged and won by the U.S., finally concluded on July 30. Over 3,500 Japanese men died in combat on just two nights alone — July 25 and 26. By August 11, the U.S. servicemen killed in action or having died of wounds in Guam, numbered 1,747. The number of Chamorros killed and wounded has never been determined. The number witnessed from beginning to end of the Japanese occupation were 320 dead, 258 injured. No doubt the actual numbers were considerably higher.

Among some of the more bizarre episodes of the battle of Guam was the slowness with which Japanese fighters surrendered even after the end of the war had been declared. For the next three decades, 114 stragglers kept turning up on the island. The last was Sergeant Shoichi Yokoi who held out for 26 and one-half years, until January 1972!

All of this expense and effort to reoccupy Guam was not merely enacted to liberate the island because it was a territory. The intent was primarily to secure military objectives. The seizure of Saipan first cut off Japanese reinforcements from Tinian and Guam. Liberation from the Japanese once again established naval authority and control of Guam. The native inhabitants, however, were soon to be plunged into a new manner of living. Until the conclusion of the war, the military provided free food to all Chamorros. Many were housed in refugee camps waiting to be relocated because about 80 percent of the prewar dwellings had been destroyed. By mid-1945, still almost 5,000 Chamorros were homeless. Many were unable to return to their own land as it had been acquired by the military for its own purposes. Although the navy government encouraged agricultural development, most locals, soon to be called Guamanians, sought jobs with the military and civilian contractors. Because of the heavy demand for laborers, for the first time Chamorro women went to work outside the home for a salary. Only a few native people still farmed or fished as a livelihood.

At the conclusion of the war, the U.S. had changed its view about the strategic importance of Guam and the Marianas. These islands were now regarded as mandatory for national security. Subsidizing the Guamanians for the use of their island was not terribly costly then, considering the benefits to the U.S. government.

Perhaps some of the undefined negative images that I had of Guam prior to coming derive from the postwar images that were circulated by journalists and American military who came to the island. Naturally, the war had caused enormous damage and mounds of battlefield debris lay strewn everywhere. The reputation of Guam as a junkyard lingered years afterward. To be sure, the U.S. government had been none too quick to tidy up and dispose of the trash because it was so costly to do so.

Postwar changes on island were dramatic although most changes evolved over the next four decades rather than happening immediately. Even though the United Nations in 1945 had mandated that the United States assume a trustee relationship with Guam, thereby assisting them to achieve economic independence, the United States did not direct its course toward this end. Guam went back into the hands of the U.S. Navy, and, despite the Guamanians persistent plea for civil liberties and self-government, the U.S. Congress did not comply with their wishes. As in previous years under American rule, Congress awarded grossly inadequate funding for rehabilitation and postwar construction. For example, the Navy had estimated rehabilitation construction of new villages and a general hospital would cost $20 million. However, Congress only appropriated $6 million.

During the last half of the 1940s, the pressure on the Navy and the United States government to liberalize Guam's government and grant U.S. citizenship continued to mount. The first step towards a slacking of U.S. control came when President Harry Truman signed the Executive Order on September 7, 1949, which transferred the administration of Guam from the U.S. Navy to the Department of the Interior, to be effective July 1, 1950. The next act in the step toward liberalization would be the acceptance of the Organic Act. At long last, Truman signed the Guam Organic Act on August 1, 1950. Among other things, this Act made Guamanians U.S. citizens, established civilian government and would provide the basic law of the island until the Guamanians approved their own constitution.

Gradually, as Guam attained more economic freedom to develop businesses, Governor Manuel Guerrero established a tourist commission in 1963, and by 1965, 5,000 tourists had come to Guam. Thus began construction of Guam's first luxury hotel, the Guam Hilton. A decade earlier, in June 1952, the Territorial College of Guam, a two-year institution, had opened its doors to students. It was the first institution of higher learning in Micronesia. By 1961, the college had become a four-year undergraduate institution. On August 12, 1968, the institution gained university status.

As Guamanians acquired more autonomy, they also moved further away from Chamorro culture. By the late 1960s, English began to replace Chamorro in a majority of island homes. By then various Protestant faiths had established themselves, eroding the previous solidarity of Catholicism. Likewise, in the mid-1970s, the island's extended family structure was becoming modified by American practices. Where formerly newly married couples would have settled with parents, now they moved into single-family dwellings. No longer were new homes built of wood with tin roofs. Housing projects were of concrete so as to be typhoon-proof. Simultaneously, in one decade, the tourist industry had expanded considerably. A total of 1,270 hotel rooms in 1973 could not accommodate the more than a quarter of a million tourists who poured into Guam, mostly from Japan. As a result of economic growth, per capita income for Guamanians soared to over $2.000 in 1970 and went to over $3,000 by 1976. Although by mainland standards this income seems low, for the island, it meant a large leap in monetary income.

But all was not smooth sailing. In an arrogant manner, the Navy made a unilateral decision to build an ammo wharf at Sella Bay, a peaceful piece of coast situated on the west coast between Agat and Umatac. Strong local opposition was guided by Senators Paul J. Bordallo and Frank G. Lujan. Bordallo and his brother, Ricky, who later became governor, were defenders of Chamorro rights. Not only that, Ricky owned quite a bit of land at Sella. Siding with them was a new local group, the Guam Environmental Council. They attempted to persuade the Department of Interior to make Sella Bay into a seashore park. As the issue heated up, Governor Camacho signed a land swap agreement with the Rear Admiral Paul E. Pugh. Paul Bordallo and thirteen other Democrats sued Governor Camacho. After losing the suit, they appealed to the Ninth Circuit Court of Appeals and won. However, the naval officials in Washington decided to push the Sella ammo project through despite the court's ruling. In the meantime, Rear Admiral Pugh was replaced by Rear Admiral G. Steve Morrison who had the wisdom to avert this pending political disaster. He proposed and persuaded the concerned parties to select an alternative site on Orote Peninsula, which was already Navy property.

A spin-off from this heated confrontation was the emergence of Chamorro-rights advocacy whose main concern was the amount of land the military possessed. The land issue went back to the time the United States first acquired Guam and has been a perennial thorn in the side of Chamorros, as it still is today.

In the 1970s, many changes were brewing in the Pacific. The Micronesian islands that had been designated at the end of World War II as the Trust Territory of the Pacific Islands (TTPI) now negotiated with Washington for changes. They became four entities: The Marshalls,

Palau, the Northern Marianas and a group of four — Kosrae, Pohnpei, Truk (Chuuk) and Yap. These later places would become the Federated States of Micronesia (FSM). All except the Northern Marianas wanted a free association with the United States. The people of the Northern Marianas wanted unification with Guam, to form a new U.S. Territory of the Marianas. Chamorros on Guam, however, did not want this reunification, as evidenced when 58 percent of those who voted on the issue voted against it. Some simply could not forget or forgive the brutality they had received from some of the Rotanese and Saipanese Chamorros on Guam during the Second World War. Additionally, some people feared that the Northern Marianas would be a financial drain on Guam.

No doubt Chamorros perceived it as not only a surprise, but a slight when they learned Washington would extend more local autonomy and money to the Northern Marianas than to Guam. Whereas it had taken Guam almost 50 years to attain the Organic Act and citizenship, it took the Northern Marianas less than three years to become a commonwealth and gain citizenship. Not content to let their attempts at self-determination slide into the cracks, the Thirteenth Guam Legislature created a second political status commission in 1975. Over the next three decades, Guamanian citizens and politicians have continued to debate what kind of relationship they want their island to have with the United States. On numerous occasions, voters were asked to choose their preferred option from several, such as statehood, commonwealth, or status quo. In 1980, Guam Senator Tony Palomo conducted a study of the feasibility of various political status options available to the island. Part of the study was an opinion poll, which determined that the majority of islanders wanted closer ties with the United States. Commonwealth status seemed the most logical goal. Over the next decade, much time, money and effort were expended in an effort to achieve commonwealth status. Too often the program, on the brink of success, was derailed by political infighting between Guam's Democrats and Republicans. In part, too, the problem came down to certain factions and individuals unwilling to negotiate terms with the United States. Wanting complete autonomy without responsibility to the U.S. was not a position that would promote a change to commonwealth status.

This "in limbo" position is detrimental to Guam in several ways. Many problems, particularly in education, stem from the excessive power the Organic Act gives to the governor and the budgetary control placed in the hands of the legislature. Such politicizing results in instability and lack of continuity in various government agencies. Many of Guam's leaders realize the need to institute changes and there has been no lack of ingenuity. In 1982, Governor Ricky Bordallo thought of a strategy to reunify the Chamorro people on Guam and the Marianas, which eventually would permit the two entities to apply for statehood. Bordallo, an astute politician, voiced his plans to only a few close advisers, knowing it would not then be acceptable to most Guamanians. His plan, however, never came to fruition. In the late 1980s Bordallo was indicted on 17 criminal counts. After court appeals in December 1989, he was resentenced to serve four years on his conviction. On the last day of January, he was scheduled to fly to California and report to a federal minimum-security facility to begin serving his term. On this day, he stood by the bronze statue of Chief Quipuha, draped a Guam flag over his shoulders, then fired a bullet into his temple.

The Chamorros' desire for self-determination has become even more acute since 1986. Those who identify themselves as Chamorro want control over immigration and authority to determine which federal laws apply to the island. This same group wants to protect the indigenous people and culture from being overwhelmed by outsiders. Since the 1940s, the indigenous peoples have been declining in the percentage of the total population. This situation began becoming more pronounced in 1986 when citizens of the Federated States of Micronesia (FSM) and the Republics of the Marshalls and Palau attained the status of U.S. nationals, which allows them to travel without visas to U.S. areas, which of course includes Guam. From this time, Micronesians have been flooding into Guam. This influx of Micronesians has strained local programs in the areas of education, public health, welfare and criminal justice. While the U.S. has promised to provide ample funding for the added expense of Micronesian immigrants, it has never fully covered its obligation.

An overarching problem is the need for planning in general. Many of Guam's changes and development have occurred haphazardly, without any notion of outcome or impact. Both the government and private sector have become too dependent on tourism as the primary source of income (except for federal money). Every time tourism dips, everyone gets the jitters and starts talking about what can be done to get the tourist industry back on track, continuing to expand. The Asian financial crisis of the 1990s seriously affected Guam's economy. Such dependence on tourism is risky for several reasons, and therefore, development of other types of businesses should be a top priority. Beyond a certain point, expanding tourism becomes impractical and certainly undesirable. No one seems to raise the issue of just where these limits should be set or how. At present, tourism outstrips Guam's infrastructure. During the dry season each year, water rationing is necessary. With over a million tourists each year, not only is the island short of fresh water, things are further complicated by frequent power outages and sewage problems. Roads are over crowded and parking insufficient in many areas. More luxury hotels will only take away the best land on the beach, causing further environmental degradation and reef damage. Above all, on this small island where certain habitats and species are rare or endangered, environmental concerns need to be factored into the equation to set limits for the development of tourism.

The lure of the trade winds and the promise of exotic cultures compelled me to begin my voyage of adventure and discovery. This venture, however, differed in significant ways from my expectations. Some of what I had anticipated — natural beauty of lush islands and friendly people — were there in abundance. But, there was much that disturbed me: the devastation of colonialism and its enduring impact. Sailing into this world changed my views of the world because what I saw made me probe deeper for answers. As so often happens, the outward journey is but a metaphor for the inward journey, and it is the latter which transforms the human spirit. Such experiences — person to person, culture to culture — have taught me things no book or course of study could convey. It is the human contact that matters most. For this reason, I often wonder what the Internet bodes for humanity. Is the world being reduced to a kind of monoculture? As everyone tunes into virtual reality, what happens to reality? The dwindling diversity of the natural world seems paralleled by the dwindling of cultural diversity. Are these positive changes? It is hard to think that diminishing of forms (species) in the natural world and in the human community could be positive because with the loss of diversity comes the loss of opportunity. Does this not mean fewer paths for the human spirit to venture forth upon? Colonialism and imperialism have reinforced and institutionalized racism, sexism, and classism. But the ultimate outcome of these Western imposed paradigms and prototypes is human alienation from each other and from our rootedness in the natural world. We have much to learn from Pacific Islanders — many of whom still feel their connection with the earth and the sea.

Pacific Ocean Sailing Route

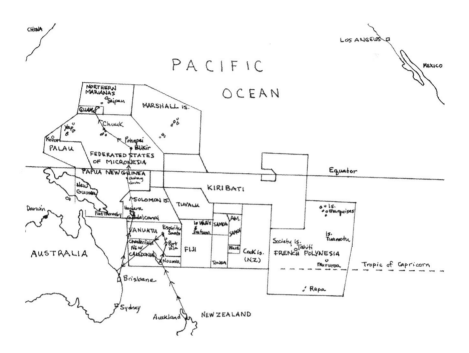

NEW CALEDONIA

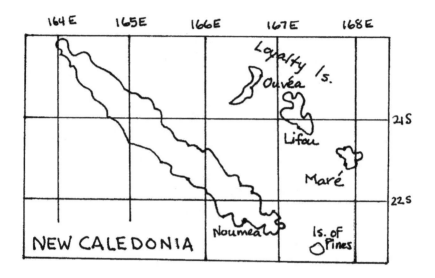

VANUATU

Solomon Islands

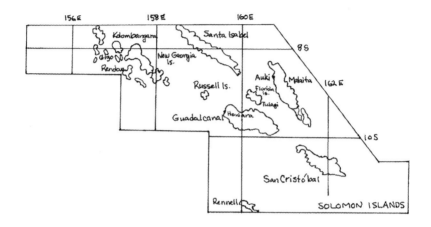

ONTONG JAVA

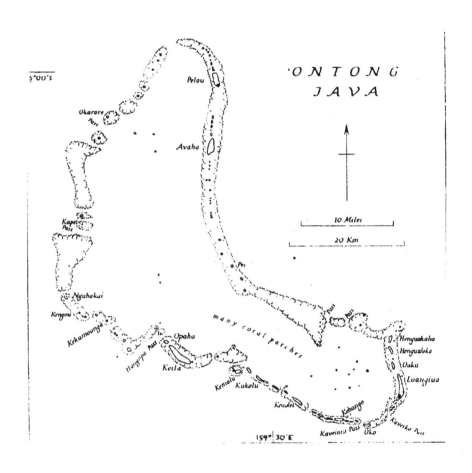

FEDERATED STATES OF MICRONESIA

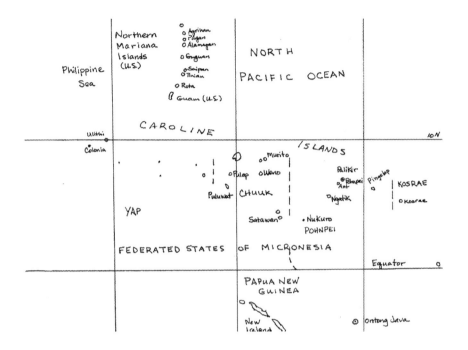

GUAM

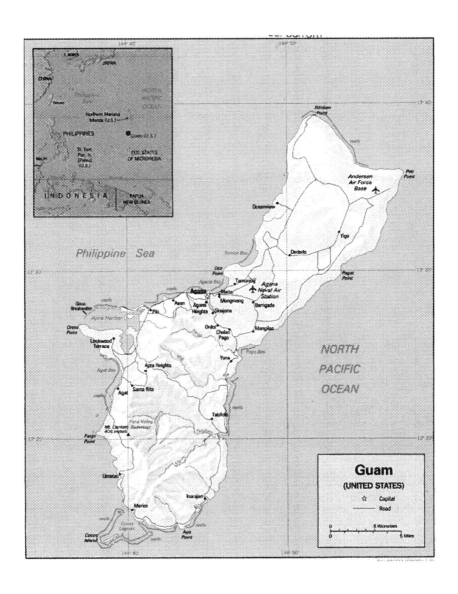